ERIC SLOANE'S
SKETCHES OF AMERICA PAST

ERIC SLOANE'S SKETCHES OF AMERICA PAST

Written and Illustrated by
Eric Sloane

PROMONTORY PRESS

Originally published in three volumes as *Diary of an Early American Boy, A Museum of Early American Tools*, and *A Reverence for Wood*.

Copyright © 1962, 1964, 1965 by Wilfred Funk, Inc.

Published in 1986 by
Promontory Press
166 Fifth Avenue
New York, New York 10010

By arrangement with Dodd, Mead & Co.

Library of Congress Catalog Card Number: 86-61269

ISBN: 0-88394-065-5

Printed in The United States of America

CONTENTS

DIARY

of an

EARLY AMERICAN BOY

Noah Blake 1805

ERIC SLOANE

To my young niece Pam
whose enthusiasm about
the diary gave me the
incentive for doing this book

The DIARY of NOAH BLAKE . 1805 .

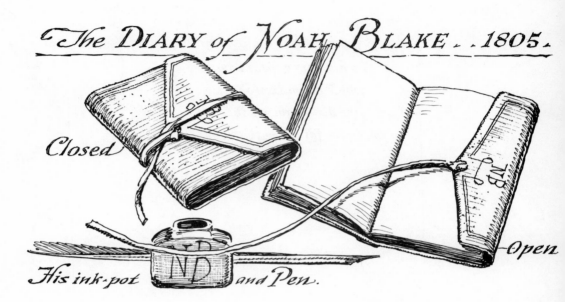

Closed

Open

His ink-pot and Pen.

Author's Note

One time a young boy visited a museum of early American things. There were ladies' bustles and men's wigs and other obsolete things. There were tremendous planes and broadaxes that appeared much too heavy for actual use. There were whole aisles of kitchen equipment and farm tools that no one would care to use now. To the boy, it all looked very much like a neatly arranged and well-cared-for junk yard. He wasn't quite sure what was meant by the title "Americana": all he could think of was, "How dreary life must have been in those days and how unhappy the people must have been, and how glad I am that I live today instead of then."

I am sure that whoever collected and arranged those things did so to excite admiration for the old days; he would have been very displeased with the boy's reaction. Yet I cannot blame the boy, for just as in so many museums of early Americana, the chief attraction of the pieces was made to be *just old age*.

Even now (for I was the little boy), I can feel no reverence for old age. Respect is not due older people for their age and wrinkles or gray hair; respect is due them simply for the things they have learned and for their extra years of experience.

The old-time craftsmen would have been the very first to have junked crude or obsolete things, so why should we seek them and collect them for display as examples of early American life? Indeed, there are ugly things in all ages which should be discarded and forgotten. Only the good things of either the past or the present are worthy of collection.

The good things of the past were not so often *articles* as they were the *manner in which people lived* or the *things that the people thought*. This, of course, is still true; the fine TV sets and modern kitchen equipment we prize now will be junk within a matter of years; the lasting examples of our time will turn out to be the *ways that we live* or the *things that we think*.

For a long while I have collected early American wooden tools—those things that pioneer people fashioned at home. It seems that they put so much of themselves into these implements that just being with them is like being with the people who created them. Closing your hand around a worn wooden hammer handle is very much like reaching back into the years and feeling the very hand that wore it smooth.

And so it is my special pleasure to behold the lines of hand-made things and to see the patina of seasoned wood and to feel a patriotic pride in the good workmanship there.

My collection is not a collection of implements as much as it is a collection of works of art. Many of the pieces would actually win merit in any gallery of sculpture, for when a man creates something he has become a designer, often an artist.

When I show my collection to young people, I am very careful to avoid saying, "See how old these things are." Instead I say, "See how carefully and beautifully people created things in those days. How aware these people were of the kinds of materials they worked with. How aware they were of the time in which they lived; everything is dated and signed. How richly awake they must have been to every moment of each day!"

This book is based upon a diary written in 1805. It was a small wood-backed, leather-bound volume that I found in an ancient house; with it I found a hand-made stone inkwell initialed N.B. I have taken a writer's liberty to imagine a great deal, but I have tried thereby to recreate seasons of activities as they might have been during 1805.

Before reading this book I ask you first to study the sketches on the following pages where I have tried to create the scene of Noah Blake's countryside both before and after he was born. Do compare these two sketches, so that you may better follow the activities at the Blake Homestead during the year of the diary.

If you get the slightest portion of the immense pleasure I got while researching this material, my book will have been worth the while.

Eric Sloane

Weather Hill
Cornwall Bridge
Connecticut

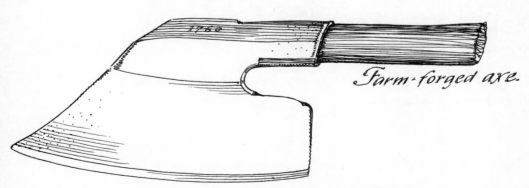

Farm-forged axe.

...*"would win top honor in any Gallery of Sculpture."*

Here, in the condition in which they were found, are Noah Blake's diary, inkwell, and almanac. . . .

The log at the wood pile, the axe supported by it;

The sylvan hut, the vine over the doorway, the space
cleared for a garden,

The irregular tapping of rain down on the leaves,
after the storm is lulled,

. . . The sentiment of the huge timbers of old fashion'd
houses and barns.

WALT WHITMAN

Chapter I

That March dawn in the year 1805 seemed like any other dawn. Yet to Noah there was something different. Clearer and more crimson than a sunset, the morning sun blazed out of the east and struck the four small panes of his window as if they were its prime target. Glass was hard enough to come by in pioneer days, but these panes had special meaning. Made in faraway London, they had been Noah's tenth birthday gift from his mother and father five years ago. Before Noah's tenth birthday the window had been covered with one pine slab that swung outward on leather hinges along the top. This made it possible to leave the window open all during warm weather except for the stormiest days; the rain fell away from the opening, running off the pine slab as if it were an awning. In the winter the slab was closed upon a room that would have been totally dark except for the light of a candle.

The four glass panes of Noah's window were unlike present-day glass.

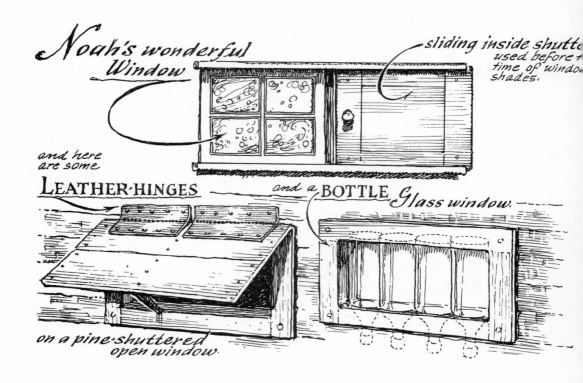

Noah's wonderful Window

sliding inside shutter used before the time of window shades.

and here are some LEATHER·HINGES *and a* BOTTLE *Glass window.*

on a pine·shuttered open window.

Being hand-made, they were full of irregular ripples and bubbles that changed the appearance of everything viewed through them. The moon was a special treat, assuming almost every shape but its own whenever you moved the slightest bit. In even a slight breeze the straightest trees wiggled and swayed as if they were blowing in a big storm.

There was only one other glass window in the house, and that window had six panes in it. Those six panes and Noah's four made up the set of ten pieces of glass which was once the allowable limit in a house, without a tax charge. Some people saved the glass tax by using oiled paper for their windowpanes, but that didn't let much light through; others made their windows of rows of bottles cemented into the windowframes, though all too little light filtered through the greenish glass of the old bottles. The double thickness of rounded bottle glass, however, was good protection against arrows and even gunshot. Of course you couldn't open a bottle-glass window.

Glass-paned windows were actually so rare in the early country

4

houses that people often carried their windows with them from house to house whenever they moved. You often rented a house "without benefit of glass!" Few of us today could imagine how a simple glass window could bring such unending joy to a child.

Curtains were almost unknown in the back country houses, but every window had its shutter. Some shutters closed at night from the outside, but Noah's shutter simply slid back and forth from the inside, a solid wooden slab.

Noah's view of his window each morning was usually from his special "doorway" in the folds of his big patchwork quilt. Father and Mother wore nightcaps like everyone else of that time, but since early childhood Noah had enjoyed making a "blanket tent" over his head and, like the cow in the barn, making his own breath and body heat keep the tent warm.

At the foot of the bed where tomorrow's clothing was folded and packed beside a stone bed-warmer during winter, there was still a glow of warmth from last night's heat. But the piece of hot soapstone wrapped in a towel had about done its work for the night, and the coldness of forest dawn had begun to penetrate. The hearth of the fireplace in the big room (that space reserved by Noah's parents for morning dressing) was losing its heat fast.

Except during winter weather, this was the moment when Noah usually grabbed his clothing from its place beneath the covers, tucked it all under his nightshirt, and bounded across the road into the barn "before the coldness could catch up with him." Into the barn he would go and make Bessie the cow or Daniel the ox rise up and move away from their soft beds of hay. Then, standing in the warmed flat spot, he would go about the business of dressing for the day.

But today was a special sort of day. It was the twenty-fifth of March, not only Noah's birthday, but also the first day of the early American farming-man's Spring. The almanac calendar simply read, "Monday, the twenty-fifth," but to many farmers who kept the old European customs, it was New Year Day; so farm accounts and farm diaries were often started at that time. This day was to be marked by Noah's first entry in his new diary.

5

The sunlight came through the windowpanes and fell upon the diary; it was bound in calf and wrapped once around with a leather thong just like father's ledger book. Its pages were crisp and freshly made at the new paper mill in town. Alongside it was a little stone well of butternut ink that Noah had made himself and put there last night, ready for this special morning. Reaching out from his warm tent of blankets, Noah dipped a crow quill into the ink and held it poised for a moment, thinking. Then he wrote in a clear hand at the top of the first page:

NOAH BLAKE, *my book*

March the twenty-fifth, Year of Our Lord 1805
Given to me by my Father Izaak Blake and my Mother
Rachel upon the fifteenth year of my Life.

In keeping with the custom for drying ink, he sprinkled the wet writing with sand. After admiring the freshly sanded page with its first written message, Noah blew away the sand and closed the book. The first day's entry would go on the next page and that would be added at bedtime by candlelight. Feeling beneath the covers for his clothing, he exploded out of his warm "tent" and headed for his springtime dressing room in the barn.

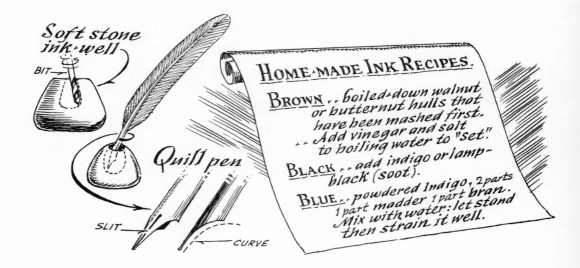

Soft stone ink well

BIT

Quill pen

SLIT

CURVE

HOME-MADE INK RECIPES.

BROWN .. boiled-down walnut or butternut hulls that have been mashed first. .. Add vinegar and salt to boiling water to "set".

BLACK .. add indigo or lamp-black (soot).

BLUE .. powdered Indigo, 2 parts 1 part madder 1 part bran. Mix with water: let stand then strain it well.

6

Chapter 2

25 : A cold and windy day. Neighbor Adams with son Robert stopp'd by. We drank mead * and mint tea. No work done this day. Father is going to the woodlot behind the barn tomorrow for floor timbers. I shall assist him.

26 : A light snow fell which Father believes will be the last of the winter. We fell'd a fine oak and rolled it upon rails for Spring seasoning. Mother is joyous at the thought of a good wood floor.

One might wonder why a floor should be planned for a house already existing. Like the earliest country houses, which were built hurriedly, the Blake house still had a plain dirt floor. The earth was pounded hard and swept smooth each day. Housewives sometimes made designs on their dirt floors to amuse their families; Rachel Blake often did this.

---

* *Recipes for the three types of mead may be found on page 144 of* THE SEASONS OF AMERICA PAST *by Eric Sloane.*

7

The DIRT FLOOR *swept and ready for Visitors,*

*with a floral
design scratched
on the packed surface*

*the
keeping room*

"Get the floor ready for visitors," Izaak would say, and the procedure which followed would amuse anyone of today. Rachel would sweep the hard-packed floor and then with a stick she would scratch designs upon it in the manner of a decorative carpet. The Blake's "dirt carpet" changed in design according to the occasion: at Christmas there was a holly design and on a birthday there might be a birthday greeting scratched on the floor near the hearth. The whole idea was unending fun, yet even Noah looked forward to the more civilized pleasure of a hard, dry oak-plank flooring instead of earth.

> *27 : Father was wrong about the weather, for it snowed again today. We kept within the house, sharping and making ready tools for the year's farming.*

Just as boys are taught the proper handling of firearms today, the early American child soon learned how to handle an axe and keep it ready for use. It was as important to know how not to handle an axe, and the first lesson was to lay your blade to the wall or sink it well into a soft log for safety's sake.

8

The axe was the pioneer's most important tool; a man could walk into the forest with nothing but his axe, yet fashion snares to catch game, fell trees, and fit them into a cabin. He could even clear brush for growing a garden and by holding an axe blade in his palm, he could use the sharp blade in the manner of a knife and whittle with it.

In very cold weather Izaak would heat his blade before using it to make it less brittle; when he was through using it for the day he rubbed it carefully with fat. Axe handles often cracked or broke, but there was always a new one charring and seasoning close to the hearth.

Noah's axe had no flat head or "poll" like the axe of today. The axe handle was long and straight; the curved handle that we know so well now didn't appear for another fifty years.

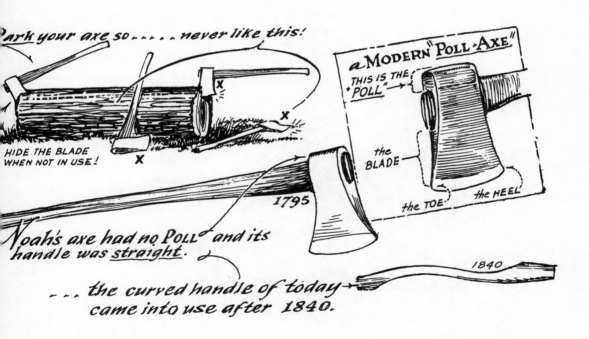

'ark your axe so ..... never like this!

HIDE THE BLADE WHEN NOT IN USE!

a MODERN "POLL · AXE"

THIS IS THE "POLL"

the BLADE

the TOE   the HEEL

1795

Noah's axe had no POLL and its handle was straight.

... the curved handle of today came into use after 1840.

1840

28 : *Snow stopp'd during the night but it is very cold. My window glass is frosty and my ink froze.*

29 : *I moved bed into the Loft for warmth. It is good to be with Mother and Father but I do miss my good window.*

30 : Worked in the forge barn. The Loft proved too warm so I moved back into my room.

31 : A fine Sunday. The roads were bad and we could not get to Meeting. Had Service to our Lord at home.

Before Noah moved into the wing which was once his borning room, he had slept on a loft at one end of the big keeping-room. Sleeping lofts were made by placing planks on the cross beams of a cabin to form a sort of balcony overhead. A ladder gave access to the loft, and in the early days when a pioneer would leave the door of his windowless cabin open for ventilation, he would pull the ladder up after him for protection against Indians and wild animals.

Sleeping-loft ladders were always a challenge to wood craftsmen because there are so many ways to make a ladder. Some ladders folded into one fat round pole; others were heavy and permanent—the forerunners of built-in staircases. Some were just pegs driven into the wall.

A few years after a cabin had been built, when there was more time

HEAT

LOFT-- WARMEST SPOT IN THE CABIN

FIREPLACE

a LOFT LADDER

an old-time SLEEPING·LOFT

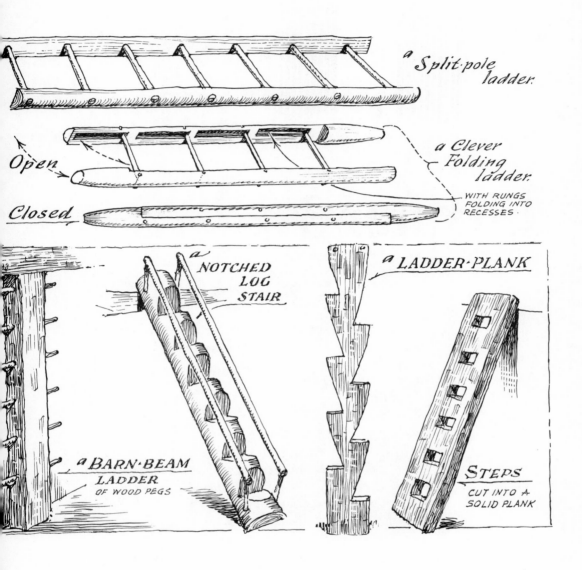

a Split-pole ladder.

Open

Closed

a Clever Folding ladder.

WITH RUNGS FOLDING INTO RECESSES.

a NOTCHED LOG STAIR

a LADDER·PLANK

a BARN·BEAM LADDER OF WOOD PEGS

STEPS CUT INTO A SOLID PLANK

for remodeling and refining it, the crossbeams were often covered and made into a flat ceiling. Then the place where the sleeping loft had been became part of an attic room, and the old-time loft bed became a thing of the past. But country boys still found great pleasure in ladders and lofts and the game of pulling the ladder up to protect themselves against imaginary bears or Indians who might come in the open door of the room below.

11

Chapter 3

*1 : Robert Adams came by in his Father's sleigh to take me
to the Adams place. I shall help them for the week with
maple sugaring.*

2 : Worked at the Adams place.

3 : do. (ditto)

4 : do.

5 : do.

6 : do.

*7 : Palm Sunday. Went to Meeting with the Adams and re-
turned home with Mother and Father. I earned a tub of
sweetening for my week's work. It is good to be home
again.*

Noah's "tub of sweetening" was a wooden sugar-bucket of thick
maple syrup which was his pay for the help he had given to the Adams
family. No pay could be more appreciated, for sweets and sweetening
were rare things in the pantry closet of 1805. At that time there was no
such thing in all America as candy as we know it now, for the word was

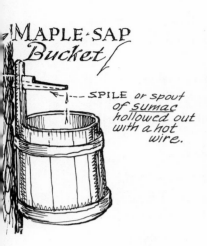

MAPLE·SAP Bucket

SPILE or spout of sumac hollowed out with a hot wire.

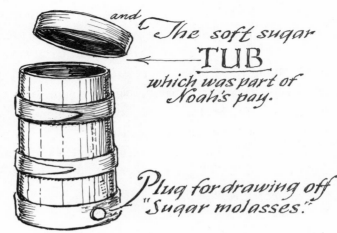

and The soft sugar TUB which was part of Noah's pay.

Plug for drawing off "Sugar molasses."

either a verb meaning "to sweeten" or it referred to broken pieces of sugar.

"We have *candy* for dessert today," Rachel Blake would say, and she would place on the dinner table a bowl of hard loaf sugar, with either a "sugar-hammer" or a pair of "sugar scissors" to cut it with.

"The wooden tub was part of my salary," Noah said. "So I'll not have to return it. I'd like to give that to you, Mother."

"And who," asked Rachel Blake, "Did you meet at the sugaring?"

"There were a great many people," replied Noah. "Some I've never seen before. Mrs. Adams tended the stirring and boiling along with a new girl named Sarah Trowbridge. The boys and men collected buckets and sledded the sap back to the sugar house."

Rachel noted a peculiar interest in Noah's voice. "A new girl, did you say?"

"Yes," Noah answered with some attempt to bring attention back to the sugar-bucket, "just a new girl from the south to help Mrs. Adams with the sugaring and farm chores."

> 8 : *The snow has gone and seasonable weather for Spring business has arrived. I finished the winter's lot of nail-making and put the forge to rights.*

In the little forge barn half-way down to the bridge (see the 1790 diagram below), Izaak had earned most of the money needed around the homestead. Not that any early American had great need for cash, as most things were traded; but a good farmer always had a cash crop or some paying trade other than farming. Izaak was a nail-maker. He had taught Noah the art of making hand-wrought nails by letting him pump the bellows of the forge as a little fellow; now and then he actually hammered or broke the iron nail rods.

"Some day," said Izaak, "we will have a water mill right about here, and there will be a big mill-wheel to take your place pumping the bellows. By then you'll be an expert yourself." As a matter of fact, Noah was already an expert.

By the time he reached his fifteenth birthday he could make upward of nine hundred nails a day, and he seldom went over the professional four strokes of the hammer to flatten out the heads.

"As soon as we have the new bridge done so we can haul it over," Izaak told Noah, "we shall get the new water wheel and begin building the

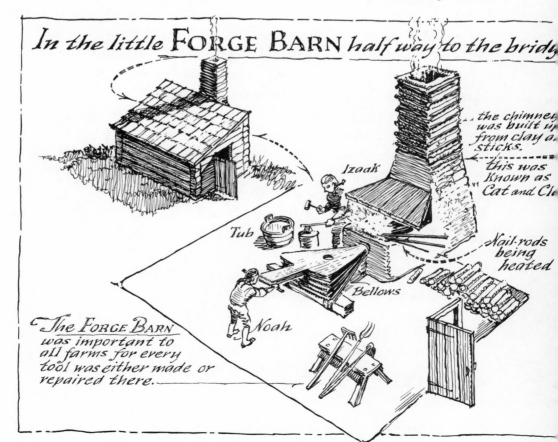

In the little FORGE BARN half way to the bridg

the chimney was built up from clay and sticks.

this was known as Cat and Clo

Izaak

Nail-rods being heated

Tub

Bellows

Noah

The FORGE BARN was important to all farms for every tool was either made or repaired there.

mill." Mr. Beach, the carpenter and joiner, had been working on the Blake mill-wheel for almost a year and had promised to have it done by this spring.

Actually, the new bridge and a new mill would be twin projects, because as soon as the mill was ready people would want to come by wagon to buy ironware and nails, and there would have to be a bridge strong enough for the heaviest wagons. Many an American town grew up in just this way, around a lone mill that had its own bridge. That is why you will find so many towns named after some mill, such as the many Miltons (Mill Town), Millvilles, Milbrooks, and so on.

The reader might be interested in knowing just how wrought-iron nails were made and what Noah had to learn about the trade. So this two-page spread of drawings will give you a "nut-shell" lesson in early American nail-making.

9 : Flooding all but washed our bridge away. Father says the new bridge beams are seasoned and ready. When the wa-

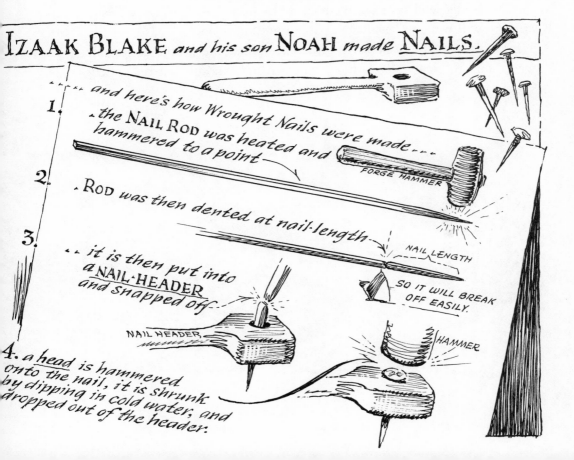

IZAAK BLAKE *and his son* NOAH *made* NAILS.

... *and here's how Wrought Nails were made* ...

1. *the* NAIL ROD *was heated and hammered to a point* —

FORGE HAMMER

2. *ROD was then dented at nail-length* -

NAIL LENGTH

SO IT WILL BREAK OFF EASILY.

3. *... it is then put into a* NAIL-HEADER *and snapped off* -

NAIL HEADER

HAMMER

4. *a head is hammered onto the nail, it is shrunk by dipping in cold water, and dropped out of the header.*

15

ters subside, he shall begin to erect it. We are shaping up the abutments.

10 : Worked on the bridge abutments. Daniel helped with the bigger stones.

11 : do.

12 : Good Friday. It rained all day. Brook went up.

13 : Bluebirds arrived. We finished the abutments without help of Mr. Adams and his son Robert who came by to assist. River lower.

14 : Easter Sunday. A fine Service. Saw Sarah Trowbridge the new girl at the Adams. She is very pretty.

The little bridge across Red Man Brook was nothing more than two very long tree trunks with planks set atop to walk across. It had lasted ten years, but in the meantime Izaak had prepared a set of truss beams ready for erection as a new bridge as soon as Noah was old enough and strong enough to help.

"The bridge will be a big memory in the boy's life," Izaak had said, "and he will want to have taken part in putting it up."

Like most masonry of early American times, the bridge abutments were built in "dry wall" fashion, which merely meant that no cement

IZAAK BLAKE *and his son build the Abutments.*
where the New Bridge *will go.*

A STONE BEING MOVED

DANIEL THE OX

Sliding a stone
WITH A FULCRUM (1.)
AND LEVER (2.)

RED MAN BROOK

OLD TRAIL

Planks to slide *stones a*

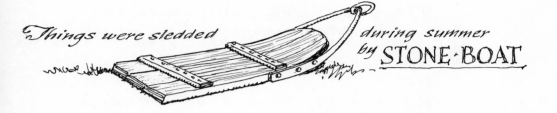

was used. The old-timers had a knack of fitting stones together so cleverly that no binding at all was necessary. This art of "dry-masonry" used to be so well known that you could just look at a wall or a foundation and recognize it as the work of a particular builder.

All the stones for the Blake bridge were fitted together by Izaak, but the actual moving of the heaviest stones was accomplished with a lever-pole fulcrum (see the drawing) which was operated by Daniel the ox. You might wonder how the pioneers moved some of the great stones that you see in old walls and foundations; the secret was simply in their ability to *slide* things. A two-ton slab of rock that could not be lifted or carted by wagon, could be slid to location with ease just by waiting for winter and *sliding* the stone over ice. Almost no heavy farm loads were hauled on wheels; that was put off till winter when the loads could be slid across the countryside on sled runners. For each wagon the old-time farmer had, he had about four sleds. Even smaller stones were thrown on a flat wooden slab known as a "stone-boat" and slid across the grass during summer, with much less effort than it would take to lift them onto a wagon and cart them on wheels.

Mr. Adams and his son came by to help with the final stone work, but found that they were more in the way than anything else.

"The way Noah handles that lever for you," said Adams, "I guess you'll not be needing us. But when it's time to raise the bridge timbers, we'll be on hand."

> *15 : Father used Daniel this morning to set the bridge beams in place for homing the joints. I tried my hand at spring plowing in the afternoon, with Daniel.*

17

16 : More plowing. Father still setting up the trusses. He says the joints have swollen with the rains and need new chiselling.

17 : do. Weather fine.

18 : do.

19 : Finished plowing. Father has the bridge trusses ready for raising. Tomorrow I shall go to the Adams and ask them to come upon Saturday the next.

20 : Spent the day at the Adams. They shall certainly assist with the bridge next Saturday. Sarah Trowbridge did the cooking and she is most excellent.

21 : First Sunday past Easter. The Meeting House was very cold. I visited with Sarah after the Service.

"Setting the timbers in place" and "driving the joints home" were well-known procedures in the days when men built their own barns. The complete skeleton of any building was laid out upon the ground and fastened together loosely with wooden nails (called tree-nails or "trunnels") before raising the sections up and fastening them together.

The drawing shows how Izaak Blake had put together two complete kingpost trusses, ready to be erected into the final bridge. The beams were pounded into place on the ground with a very heavy hammer called a "commander" or "beetle," and then the wooden pins were inserted and hammered into place. Nowadays we assume that people once used wooden pins because it was too hard to make nails or spikes. But metal nails would have either rusted away or split the wood, so wood against wood made a much better fastening. It breathed with weather changes and finally welded itself together into the best possible union. Even today you may find oak trunnels fastening together two barn beams that are solid and firm after two centuries, while a spike would have rusted away long ago and rotted the wood next to it.

It seemed that Noah had taken a great liking to Sarah Trowbridge; although he had had little time for visiting, the two-hour-long church service afforded him plenty of time for admiring her and seeing her in her best dress. You might wonder why his diary mentions that "the

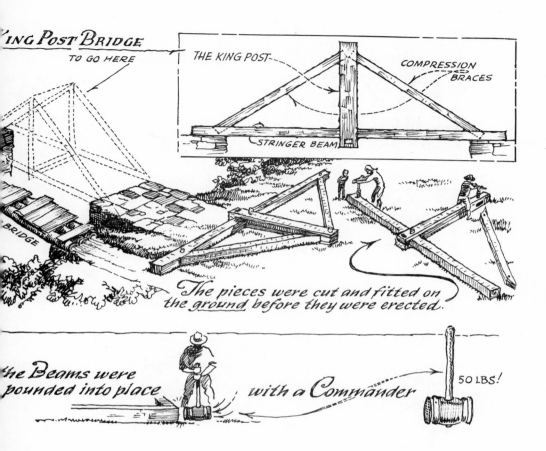

KING POST BRIDGE

TO GO HERE

THE KING POST

COMPRESSION BRACES

STRINGER BEAM

BRIDGE

The pieces were cut and fitted on the ground before they were erected.

The Beams were pounded into place   *with a Commander*   50 LBS!

Meeting House was very cold," until we remember that even in the early 1800's it was still considered improper to put a stove in a place of worship. People came to church in great fur coats and lap robes; the preacher himself often stood on a tin of hot coals and wore heavy fur mittens while he conducted services.

The long drive to church during winter was made comfortable by a small charcoal stove under the lap robes, and when you entered church you carried your stove with you!

22 : *Day spent in forge barn fashioning trunnels for bridge. Did forty.*

23 : *Rain and wind. Worked in the garden sowing pease (peas) and beans.*

19

a **Tin foot-stove** under the blanket

Charcoal fired heater

a **FOOT WARMER** *for a Sleigh.*

for Coal

... and one to hold hot water

about 180.

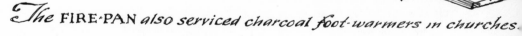

EMBERS *were carried from room-to-room, or house-to-house to start fireplace fires, in a metal* **FIRE-PAN**

The **FIRE-PAN** *also serviced charcoal foot-warmers in churches.*

24 : *Rain stopped and brook is down. Prepared the beams and we put them in place for Saturday's work.*

25 : *Mr. Thoms came by with a new rope from his walk. I have seldom seen so long and white a rope.*

26 : *Rain again. Too wet to work in the garden but we thinn'd brush, and we pruned in the woodlot with hooks.*

27 : *The Adams arrived with six townspeople at sunrise. We*

set the stringers and put the kingposts in place. We have made a fine bridge. Father put a brush atop the posts and we all sang and drank. Sarah brought a cake. One man fell into the brook but he was not hurt. We knocked down the old bridge, which made me feel a little sad.

28 : *Without yet a floor in the new bridge, we could not yet proceed over it to Sunday Meeting so held Service at home.*

Mr. Thoms's "walk" was the place where he made his rope. Rope-walks were sometimes a quarter of a mile long; they were usually at the edge of town where traffic would not interfere with the business of rope-winding. In the early days, for example, New York's main street, Broadway, ended as a rope-walk which extended uptown for about two thousand feet and into a meadow.

The rope-spinner had a large bundle of fiber gathered loosely around his waist; he pulled out strands from this and wove them into cords, walking backward along the rope-walk as he worked. Another man wound the twisted cords into rope.

It was once the custom for rope-makers to rent rope for special purposes, so we might presume that Mr. Thoms rented Izaak the rope for raising his bridge. A backwoods farmer seldom had any use for such great lengths of rope. Moreover, the expense made good rope a rare thing around the farmyard.

On the twenty-sixth day of April, Noah's diary said that they pruned trees "with hooks," and that statement harks back to an ancient phrase which most of us still use, to get anything *"by hook or by crook."* As dead tree limbs harbor insects and disease, the old-timers were careful to remove as much deadwood from a stand of trees as they could, and people used to walk through the forest with a hooked stick much like a shepherd's staff; the hook was used to pull dead branches from trees.

Very early house leases forbade the tenant to cut trees for firewood, although he was always allowed "as much wood as could be taken by *hook* or *crook*." How long this legal phrase has lived, although few of us realize whence it came!

Another ancient custom is seen in Izaak's "putting a brush on top"

21

of the new structure. Even nowadays you will see workmen put a small tree or bush on the top of a new roof when it has been completed. That ceremony always calls for a round of drinks for the builders, and although we don't seem to know why we do it, we say it is "just to give

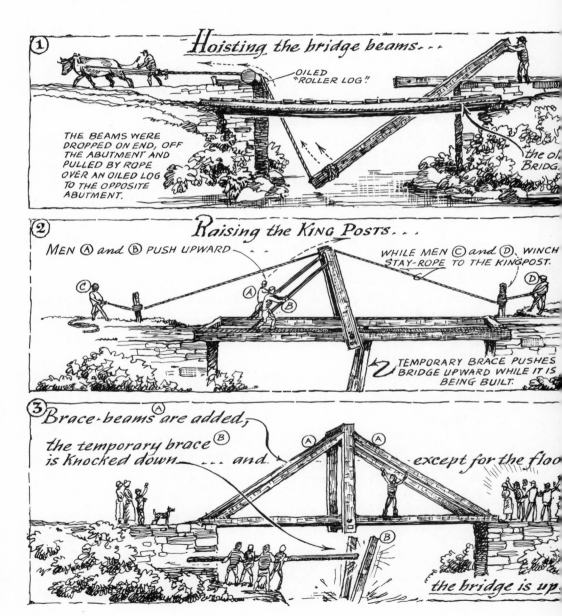

① *Hoisting the bridge beams...*

OILED "ROLLER LOG"

THE BEAMS WERE DROPPED ON END, OFF THE ABUTMENT AND PULLED BY ROPE OVER AN OILED LOG TO THE OPPOSITE ABUTMENT.

the ol... BRIDG...

② *Raising the King Posts...*

MEN Ⓐ and Ⓑ PUSH UPWARD

WHILE MEN Ⓒ and Ⓓ WINCH STAY-ROPE TO THE KINGPOST.

TEMPORARY BRACE PUSHES BRIDGE UPWARD WHILE IT IS BEING BUILT.

③ *Brace-beams* Ⓐ *are added;* *the temporary brace* Ⓑ *is Knocked down... and* Ⓐ Ⓐ *... except for the floo...*

Ⓑ

the bridge is up

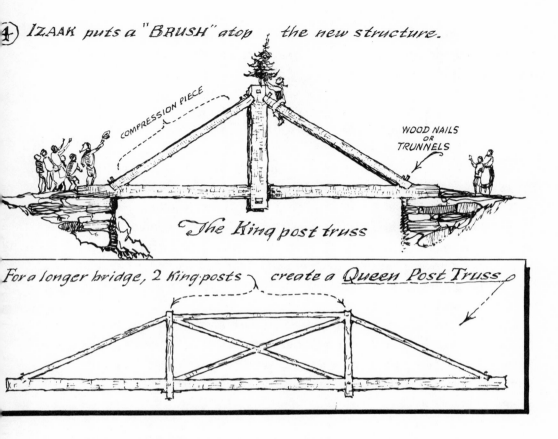

4) IZAAK puts a "BRUSH" atop the new structure.

COMPRESSION PIECE

WOOD NAILS
OR
TRUNNELS

The King post truss

For a longer bridge, 2 King posts create a <u>Queen Post Truss</u>

the house luck." That tree tacked atop a new building goes all the way back to Druid lore when men worshipped trees!

Whether the "raising" was of a home or a church or a bridge, people used to come from all around to help. The women brought food and drink while the men just brought their strong backs. Children used to make up rhymes to recite or songs to sing at the raisings, and a house often got its name through one of these impromptu house-raising songs.

Often the house-raising song was sewed into a sampler by some enterprising young girl and presented to the owner at the house-warming when the owners moved in. For example, there is on record a house in Rochester, New Hampshire which was so celebrated in verse:

> "*Flower of the Plain* is the name of this frame,
> We've had exceeding good luck in raising the Same."

23

Sarah brought with her a rhyme for the occasion, and though she had not sewed it into a sampler, she had made several copies of it and everyone sang:

"On Red Man Brook we've raised a frame
And *Noah Blake Bridge* will be its name."

If you look at the drawing of the bridge-raising, you can see how the timbers were put in place and raised into a permanent truss, first with the help of Daniel the ox, and then with the help of the Adams family and other neighbors. You may also see how the slanted beams tend to push against each other as "compression pieces" and lift the kingpost. The kingpost truss was the simplest of bridge trusses, followed by the "queenpost truss" which was simply two kingposts put together for a longer span.

Just about the time that Noah and his father built their bridge, many Americans were designing different kinds of trusses, getting their designs patented, and selling their plans at a dollar a foot to bridge builders. Some of America's first fortunes were earned by these enterprising designers.

29 : A sloppy day. Started splitting boards for bridge floor.
30 : Still working on the bridge floor. Father splits while I saw.

the SPLIT·AXE *for splitting logs* (ALSO CALLED HOLZAXT)

wedgelike head for hitting

1800

Chapter 4

> *1 : The First of May! We have nearly finished the bridge floor but we must abandon this work for the garden. Father is planting corn.*
>
> *2 : A sour chilly day. Stayed indoors.*
>
> *3 : We finished the bridge floor in time for the Adams to be first across it. They brought with them a paper with news about the Great Permanent Bridge in Philadelphia. Sarah did not come with them. Yesterday was the Birth Day of new pigs at the Adams.*
>
> *4 : A splendid day. Went to the Adams to see the pigs. Sarah looked very well.*

We certainly might wonder if Noah went to the Adamses to see the new pigs or to see Sarah. He didn't remark about the pigs, but Sarah seemed to "look very well!"

One of the satisfactions of working with wood is the ability to split it expertly. If you season (dry) wood properly and place a wedge in the right place, you can split shingles or rails or boards from it with a single good blow; such a cut might take hours if tried with a saw!

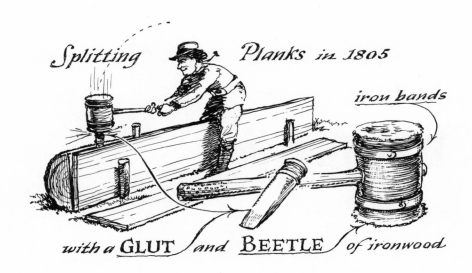

Splitting   Planks in 1805

iron bands

with a GLUT *and* BEETLE *of ironwood*

"Here," said Izaak, "is a saw for cutting across the ends of the boards. You do that while I split the logs into planks."

Axes were too valuable ever to be used as hammers—even now a good woodsman will never hammer a wedge with the head of an axe when there is a sledge hammer to do the job. Izaak's hammer was made of hardwood. Even his wedges were made of hardwood; they were known as "gluts."

"Do we nail the boards down soon?" asked Noah.

"No," said his father. "The trick is just to lay them down loosely so they won't warp. Then you place a roadway going the opposite way across the top. Nails would only split boards and rust the cracks into rot. Loose boards weather best."

"I know," said Noah, "that a good carpenter doesn't use nails unless he has to. I just forgot."

"If we **can do it**," said Izaak, with some pride in his voice, "we will finish this bridge without the use of iron at all. Not even one nail will be used!"

Just as the last floor board was laid down, a shout sounded from on top of the trail and Mr. Adams came into view, his son Robert close behind him.

"It is beautiful," they called out. "May we be the first visitors across?"

"Welcome!" said Izaak. "This will call for a celebration! We shall let you cross even before the cross boards are done with, and then we shall all go to the house for hot tea."

Rachel had seen them coming, and tea was ready by the time they arrived. At the house, Mr. Adams brought out a copy of the latest Philadelphia newspaper which he said would be of the greatest interest to Izaak. The newspaper was a single folded sheet (all newspapers and even letters were single sheets of paper, because you paid full postage for each sheet no matter how small or large) and the name of the paper was *The Pennsylvania Packet and General Advertiser.*

"Look here," said Mr. Adams, "and you may read the latest news about the new Permanent Bridge over the Schuylkill. They are going to cover it over like a house! They say that any bridge with a cover on it will last twice as long as one without a cover. Mark my words, every wooden bridge in America will be adding a roof and sides before long! What about covering yours?"

Izaak read through the account silently and seriously; during the quiet, everyone pondered the new idea and they had a mind's eye picture of how the new bridge would look "with a house around it."

"I think it's a good idea," said Izaak. "We can put the roof on it first, then we can add siding before the winter comes. I guess if those Philadelphia builders can have a covered bridge, we can have one, too."

"Wow!" howled Noah. "What an idea! We can get out of the rain in it. Maybe we can even have windows in it."

"I suppose you'll want curtains too," added Rachel with a chuckle.

Today, covered bridges are treated as a curiosity so antique that many of us believe that they began during the Revolutionary War or even before that. Yet until the Schuylkill Bridge added its covering, there

27

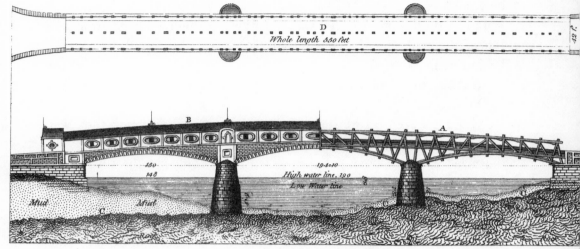

Architectural Plan and Elevation of the Schuylkill P. Bridge.

D

Whole length 550 feet

150
148

High water line. 190
Low Water line

Mud
Mud

A *The Frame before Covering.*
B *The Cover.*
C *Surface of the Rock at the Bottom.*
D *Platform.*

were no covered bridges at all in America. The idea took over so quickly, however, it seemed that almost overnight all of our wooden bridges became covered and the famous "early American covered bridge" was born. The stories we may hear of how "George Washington crossed over this or that covered bridge," are of course, untrue.

The Blake covered bridge could have been the second one in America, as the Schuylkill Bridge put on its roof during the year 1805. By that time Washington had died; so an American covered bridge was never even viewed by our first president. But, as this book is being written, there are still over fifteen hundred of these bridges left.

5 : *First Sunday to pass across new bridge to Meeting.*
6 : *Father and I layed the cross-planks upon the bridge. He says it will take a month before they become dry and lay right. It will be my chore to turn them over when they warp or bend.*
7 : *Some of my pease are up! But spring is backward.*

*8 : Helped Father with stump-pulling to enlarge the corn-
field. Started plowing this evening.*
9 : Plowed all the day. High winds from the west.
*10 : Took the day off and went into the woods looking for
hoop wood. Found muskrat den. Will set snares soon.*

Both stump-pulling and finding "hoop wood" were spring chores of
early times. After the ground had heaved and settled when winter was
done, roots were looser and the big tree stumps were then easier to pull
out. The tough roots were almost impossible to burn, so farmers used
to push them into a fence formation that wasn't very pretty to look at,
but lasted for many more years than an ordinary fence. Even now in
Canada and on some remote farms, you will find good root-fences almost a century old!

Noah helped his father with the stumps for a while, but with the
help of Daniel the ox, Izaak found he could do the job alone, so Noah
disappeared into the woods for an afternoon jaunt. He came back laden
with an armful of newly cut poles.

"What," exclaimed Izaak, "are you going to do with all of those?"

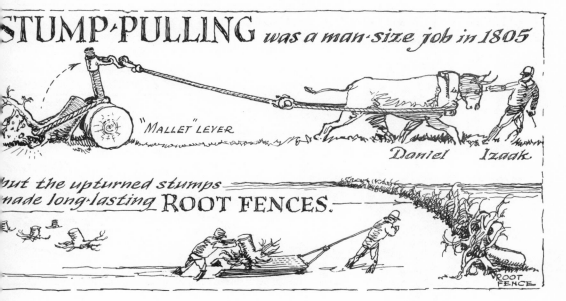

STUMP·PULLING *was a man-size job in 1805*

"MALLET" LEVER

Daniel Izaak

*ut the upturned stumps
made long-lasting* ROOT FENCES.

ROOT FENCE

"I guess you haven't heard about the new cooper in the village," replied Noah. "He told Robert and me that he could use all the good hoop wood that we can supply him with. Robert and I shall keep a

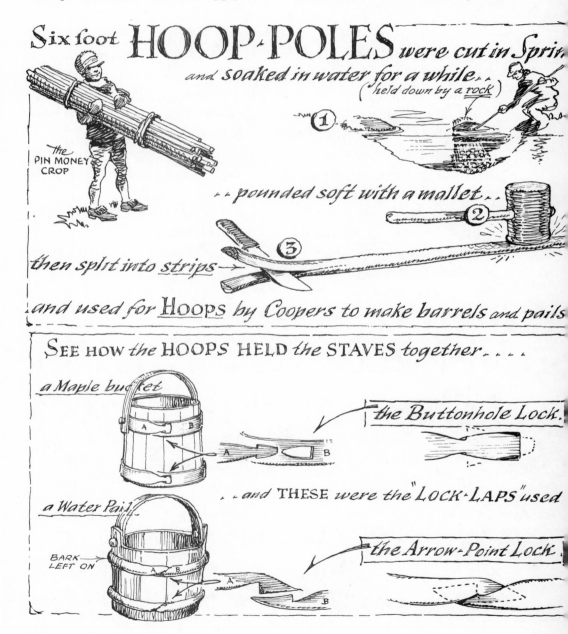

Six foot HOOP·POLES were cut in Spring

and soaked in water for a while..
(held down by a rock)

①

the
PIN MONEY
CROP

..pounded soft with a mallet...

②

then split into strips →

③

..and used for Hoops by Coopers to make barrels and pails

SEE HOW the HOOPS HELD the STAVES together....

a Maple bucket

the Buttonhole Lock.

A B

A   B

..and THESE were the "LOCK·LAPS" used

a Water Pail

the Arrow·Point Lock.

BARK
LEFT ON

A B

A

B

supply soaking in a bank over in Indian Brook meadow. Then whenever we go to the village and need a bit of spending money, we shall pick up a bundle of hoop wood and sell it to Mr. Minor. He's the new cooper."

In May, when black ash and hickory are alive with new sap, six-foot poles were cut from the saplings in the swamplands. After a good soaking, the poles were pounded soft and "rived" or cut into strips for making barrel hoops. You just pounded the softened wood strip around a barrel and when it dried, you had a hoop that was as hard as iron and even outlasted metal.

> *11 : Rain. Split shingle wood for a roof on the new bridge.*
> *12 : Sunday. Sarah walked home from Meeting with me to admire the new bridge. I walked back with her.*
> *13 : A sour day. Worked indoors again splitting wood.*
> *14 : Rain again. Brook ran high but the new bridge is much higher than flood level.*
> *15 : Saw flock of bluebirds. There are blossoms on the pea vine in the garden. Warm day.*
> *16 : do.*

During the spring rains, farmers found time for doing indoor chores such as repairing equipment or splitting firewood under cover. Noah seems to have found lots of time for splitting shingles and firewood during this rainy spring week.

Few of us today would think of wood splitting as anything but a tedious chore, but when one learns to do it well, there is a certain joy involved. Striking your axe in an exact spot, watching a log divide miraculously into segments and squares with single blows, or even learning to stack a simple pile of wood correctly, gives pleasure to the art of woodsmanship.

Noah's diary doesn't mention what tool he used to split shingles with, but we know it must have been a "frow." This was a heavy knife blade attached to a handle and struck on the top with a "maul" or heavy club. If you take any two- or three-foot pine or cedar log and let it dry for a year, it needs only a frow to divide it nicely into a dozen or so fine shingles.

31

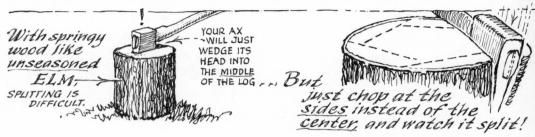

With springy wood like unseasoned **ELM,** SPLITTING IS DIFFICULT.

YOUR AX WILL JUST WEDGE ITS HEAD INTO THE MIDDLE OF THE LOG...

But just chop at the sides *instead of the* center, *and watch it split!*

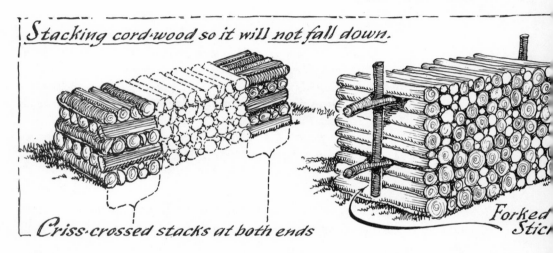

Stacking cord-wood so it will not fall down.

Criss-crossed stacks at both ends

Forked Stick

If you will notice in the large drawing of the Blake Place in 1790, the house had a bark roof. Bark roofs were easier to make in a hurry, and as shingle material had to be dried for a year or more before splitting, we might assume that proper wood shingles were added to the Blake place a year or so later.

Riving shingles used to be known as "grandfather's favorite pastime" for it was a man's chore that could be done while sitting down.

> *17 : Father and I took Daniel and the wagon to Mr. Beach's to collect our mill-wheel. It is beautiful. It weighs over two tons!*
>
> *18 : We rolled the mill-wheel over the new bridge, which did not sag an inch!*

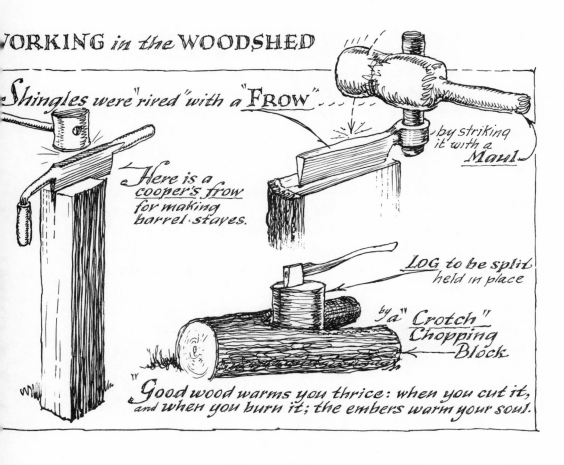

WORKING in the WOODSHED

Shingles were "rived" with a "FROW"

...by striking it with a _Maul_

Here is a cooper's _frow_ for making barrel·staves.

LOG to be split held in place

"by a" _Crotch_ Chopping ·Block·

Good wood warms you thrice: when you cut it, and when you burn it; the embers warm your soul.

19 : Rog. Sunday. After meeting, we all walked our boundaries. Met the Adams doing the same.

"Rog. Sunday" as Noah put it in his diary, meant Rogation Sunday, which was the day when farmers looked to their land and crops and prayed for a bountiful harvest. On this day, the clergyman and his flock walked through the village and out into the fields to bless the planted ground.

In the evening on Rogation Sunday, farmers and their families walked the boundaries of their property; it was both inventory and time for giving thanks for their land. At points along the way, some boy of the family group was "bumped" against a marker tree or a boundary stone, or he was ducked into whatever pond or stream marked the boundary.

33

It was all in good fun, and the bumping or ducking was accompanied by a small gift to the boy. In this way, he well remembered the boundaries of the land which he would some day fall heir to.

The Adams family met with the Blakes as both families were walking the boundaries of their land. Noah spotted the Adamses first, probably because he was so eager to see Sarah.

"Hi there!" he yelled. "Over here are some markers—I guess we are right on the line!"

"We've bumped Robert on two trees already," called out Mr. Adams. "Have you been bumped yet, Noah?"

Noah felt he was too old for such childish customs, but just to join in the fun, and perhaps to delight Sarah, he allowed himself to be bumped against a pile of marker stones. And it was Sarah who rewarded him with a package of sweet cookies.

After Rogationtide walk and before the sun had set, the Adams family went back with the Blakes to view the new mill-wheel.

"What a fine wheel!" exclaimed Mr. Adams. "It should give you extraordinary power."

"Yes," said Izaak, "It is an *overshot wheel* and they say that they are most efficient. With it we can keep the water power locked up in the mill-pond till we want to use it. Even when the stream ceases to flow, we can still have water for the mill. The first thing I shall attach to the wheel will be a bellows for the forge. Then perhaps a drop-hammer and a wood saw or maybe a device for grinding linseed oil."

"And what about a *gristmill?*" asked Rachel. "I am tired of buying meal from town or grinding it in my ancient quern."

"Yes," said Izaak, "your quern shall go to Indian Tom who has so often admired it. And I shall put in a small gristmill just for you!"

Everyone looked at the big wheel as it sat resting on the far end of the new bridge, and they imagined the wonderful things it would some day do. But to Izaak, who had to do most of the work, the stone foundations and the mill house with its final machinery, seemed a long way off.

But things were beginning to shape up. There was the new bridge for hauling materials across, there was a fine new water wheel ready to go

The QUERN was a simple hand-mill.

Grain was poured through a hole in the upper millstone. . . .

A

LOWER (STATIONARY) STONE

...ground against a lower stone, and thrown outward to fall as meal

Rachel swings the "Quern stick to turn the upper mill stone

to work, there was the pond and there was the sluice box ready to lead water from the pond to the wheel.

As with all back-country places, the Blake homesite was near a spring of running water; a well had been made only after the house had been completed. By the year of Noah's diary, the old stream used both for washing and drinking water (marked "watering place" on the 1790 drawing) had been diverted into a pond and a real well had been dug. If you look at the second ("after 1805") drawing you will see the well and wellsweep at the upper right corner.

"We'll build the sweep," Izaak had said, "even before we have finished the well. And you'll probably want to know why. Well, the reason is simple. It will be an easy way to lift out the earth as I dig it away; that will be your job, Noah."

And so a crotched tree was found and a big spruce sweep was pinioned into the crotch; another spruce pole hung from the sweep tip, and a bucket was hung from that. The butt end of the pole was so heavy that it lifted the bucket up, even with water or earth in it. And it was always easier to pull that sweep *down* by your own natural weight than

35

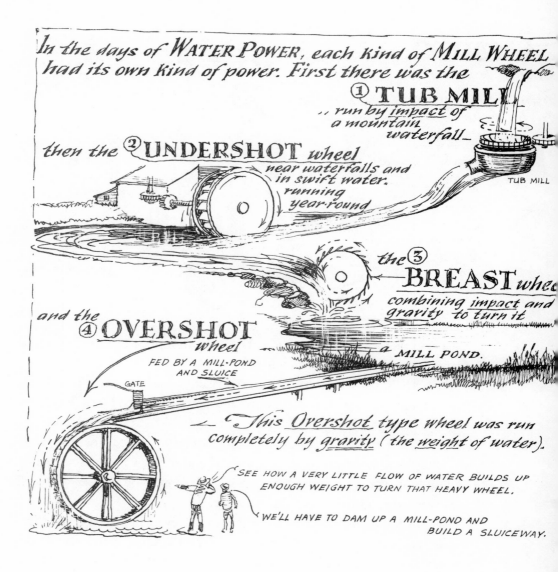

In the days of *WATER POWER*, each kind of *MILL WHEEL* had its own kind of power. First there was the

① *TUB MILL*

.. run by *impact* of a mountain waterfall—

TUB MILL

then the ② *UNDERSHOT* wheel near waterfalls and in swift water. running year-round

the ③ *BREAST* wheel combining *impact and gravity* to turn it

a *MILL POND.*

and the ④ *OVERSHOT* wheel

FED BY A MILL-POND AND *SLUICE*

GATE

This Overshot type wheel was run completely by gravity (the weight of water).

SEE HOW A VERY LITTLE FLOW OF WATER BUILDS UP ENOUGH WEIGHT TO TURN THAT HEAVY WHEEL.

WE'LL HAVE TO DAM UP A MILL-POND AND BUILD A SLUICEWAY.

it would be to pull the loaded bucket up, using your strength instead of your weight.

With the well finished, a pond became the new project. We might presume that building a pond took a year or two, but nature takes over quickly and within a short time after any pond is designed, you will find frogs and fish and weeds and water-snakes, all appearing miraculously and as if the pond had always been there.

36

Of course, the object of the pond was to eventually feed the mill-to-be and during off hours and rainy days, Izaak and Noah had worked on building the wooden sluice which would carry the pond water down to the mill and then by the water's weight, turn the wheel. It was the sluice box that first gave American designers the idea for the canal, for on some of the farms, men made wooden canal-like boxes with water in them and by floating long narrow boats in these "sluices," heavy loads could be carried easily from the barn to the road, from a mine to the smelter, or from the forest to the sawmill. By the 1800's, and just before the locomotive came into being, America had really become canal-minded and everything went from town to town by canal-boat. Even today we still say that we "ship" things from town to town although

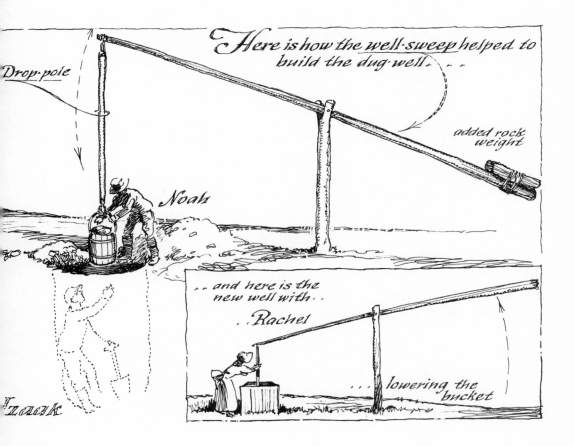

Drop-pole

Here is how the well-sweep helped to build the dug-well...

added rock weight

Noah

... and here is the new well with..

..Rachel

... lowering the bucket

Izaak

Even farmers had their private little canals, for hauling heavy loads,
a sluice filled with water, a cargo-boat floating in it.

now it really goes by railroad or truck. And even now, if you look carefully, you will see evidence along many highways that there was once
a canal. Most of our railroads were built along the tow-path of old
canals where the mules once walked to pull canal boats: the actual
canal (long since dry) will still be seen running along one side of the
railroad tracks and still acting as a good drainage for rain water.

> *20 : Showers.*
> *21 : do.*
> *22 : do.*
> *23 : Father and Mr. Beach started on the mill (foundation).*
> *24 : I helped at the mill site. Began a plumping mill for Mother.*

"Mother," said Noah, "I've a surprise for you! Come down to the
mill bank and see what I have begun. I know that Father promised
to attach a grain mill to his water wheel for you, but I think I've beat
him to it! I am making you a real plumping mill."

Rachel was eager to see Noah's invention; even as she neared the
bank where her husband and Mr. Beach were hard at work with the
dry-wall foundations, she could hear the steady sound of plumping.
When she reached the bank, she saw it.

"It may be slow," explained Noah, "but it will work on and on all
by itself. I guess it might pound out a full measure of meal in about half
an hour. Father says when he gets his water wheel in place, I can use
just the spray from it to make my mill work."

Using merely the overflow and leakage from the sluice, Noah's mill had a little box that filled with water every now and then. When it filled, the added weight lifted a big hammer-like object at the other end. And as soon as this went up, the box emptied itself so the hammer lost balance and fell down into a hollowed mortar log with a resounding thud.

"It works fine," called out Izaak from the other bank. "I guess we have a pretty clever son. Takes after his father, all right!" he added with a chuckle.

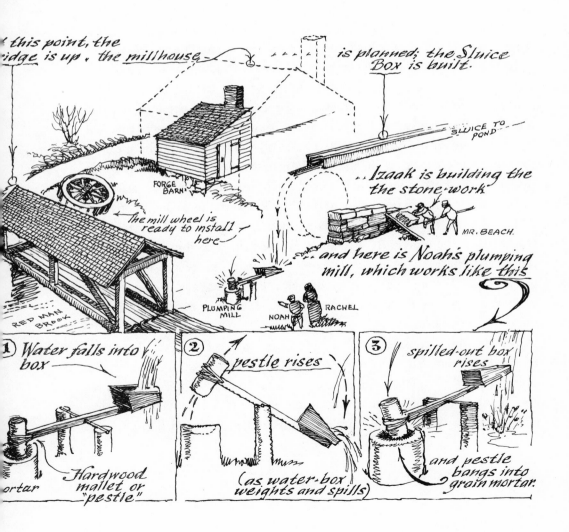

this point, the ridge is up, the millhouse — is planned; the Sluice Box is built.

SLUICE TO POND

Izaak is building the the stone-work

MR. BEACH.

FORGE BARN

the mill wheel is ready to install here

... and here is Noah's plumping mill, which works like this

PLUMPING MILL

NOAH   RACHEL

RED MAN BROOK

① Water falls into box

Hardwood mallet or "pestle"

ortar

② pestle rises

(as water-box weights and spills)

③ spilled-out box rises

and pestle bangs into grain mortar.

39

"Izaak Blake, you can go right back to your mill-building," replied Rachel, with a twinkle in her eye. "You can saw wood, or grind linseed, or pump a bellows, or mix snuff with your old mill for all I care! Noah and I have our own mill! If you are real good and polite to us, we might just let you have some of our good cornmeal!"

Rachel knew how her husband had wanted for a long while to build himself a mill for sawing wood and to do other mechanical jobs. After all, she really didn't mind grinding the small amount of meal needed for a family of three, but still she must have been proud of her son's new invention.

"When I get it in place," said Noah, "I'll carve my initials and the date into it. And your initials too, Mother, for it shall be your mill."

In modern times when everything a person needs may be bought in a store, there are very few hand-made things left. So we are robbed of that rare and wonderful satisfaction that comes with personal accomplishment. In Noah's time, nearly every single thing a person touched was the result of his own efforts. The cloth of his clothing, the meal on the table, the chair he sat in, and the floor he walked upon, all were made by the user. This is why those people had an extraordinary awareness of life. They knew wood intimately; they knew the ingredients of food and medicines and inks and paints because *they* grew it and ground it and mixed it themselves. It was this awareness of everything about them that made the early American people so full of inner satisfaction, so grateful for life and all that went with it. Nowadays modern conveniences allow us to be forgetful, and we easily become less aware of the wonders of life.

We are apt to ponder why almost everything of the old days was initialed and dated. It was simply because almost everything was made by the one who initialed it; the date was added because everyone was so completely aware of the times in which he lived. Any boy would certainly put his name and the date on a mill he had designed himself, and Noah was no exception.

25 : Father and Mr. Beach at sawing.

26 : Rained all day. Set the saws with Father and later went fishing.

27 : I took Mr. Beach's place at the saw. He hurt his eye and is ill.

We might argue as to what kind of a saw Izaak and Mr. Beach used and what they were sawing, but it is most likely they were smooth-sawing timbers for the wheel and gear housing—that place where the water wheel would turn a wooden gear on the big axle. This gear would then mesh with a larger gear and become the machine for doing whatever work Izaak wanted it to do. In those days, big square beams were either broadaxed from round logs or they were sawed into a square shape with a pit-saw. Either the log being sawed was propped up so one of the sawyers could get under it, or the log was shoved across a pit in the ground with one man in the pit. In either case, the man on top had the more desirable job, for the man beneath was showered with sawdust at every stroke of the pit-saw. Perhaps Mr. Beach "hurt his eye" by getting sawdust into it which would indicate that he was "box-man" (or the man below) while Izaak worked from above as the "tiller-man."

All the first sawmills were "up-and-down sawmills" and the saw was like the framed pit-saw shown in the drawing; the frame slid up and down just as a window sash does in its framing. In fact, the saw was held in a "sash" and it slid up and down in a "frame," and with little doubt our modern wooden window was designed from the old up-and-down sawmill's sash and frame.

On the page opposite the pit-saw drawing, you will see how later on, the framed hand saw became mechanized. For a smaller saw, the workman's foot pushed the blade down and then it sprang back by itself by means of a springy sapling. An apprentice (helper-student) sometimes did this work for him. For rougher and heavier sawing, an apprentice turned a big wheel, or a horse entered the picture by working some kind of a treadmill, which in turn slid a saw back and forth, as the drawing shows.

28 : Fruit trees are in full blossom. Plowed today.

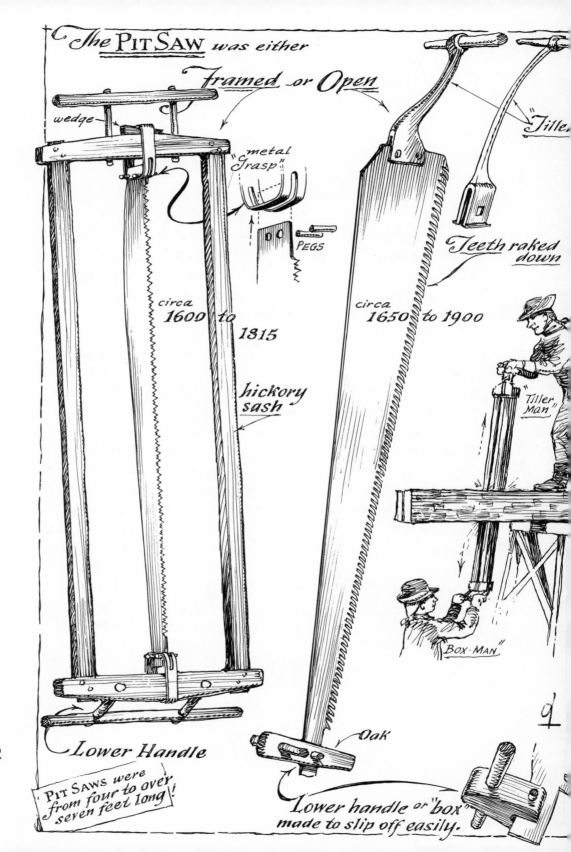

The PIT SAW was either

Framed or Open

wedge

"Tiller"

metal "Grasp"

PEGS

Teeth raked down

circa 1600 to 1815

circa 1650 to 1900

hickory sash

Tiller Man

Box-Man

Oak

42

Lower Handle

PIT SAWS were from four to over seven feet long!

Lower handle or "box" made to slip off easily.

29 : *Plowed.*
30 : *Rain set in again. Father is working under cover at the mill.*
31 : *Finished plowing. Signs of a few days of dry weather.*

"Signs of a few days of dry weather" can be good news to any farmer who has been walking about in mud for a whole week. These weather "signs" were what the old-time farmer looked for in the sky, the di-

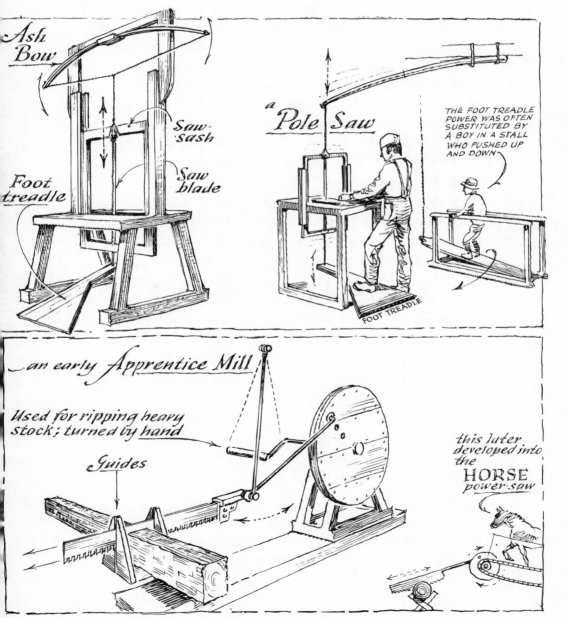

Ash Bow

Saw sash

Foot treadle

Saw blade

a "Pole Saw"

THE FOOT TREADLE POWER WAS OFTEN SUBSTITUTED BY A BOY IN A STALL WHO PUSHED UP AND DOWN

FOOT TREADLE

an early Apprentice Mill

Used for ripping heavy stock; turned by hand

Guides

this later developed into the HORSE power saw

rection of the wind, and the disposition of his cattle. Today we go about our business regardless of rain or shine, but not so long ago what we did the next day depended entirely upon the weather. When roads were made of dirt, even the slightest rain often made carriage traffic out of the question. A round trip to town at five miles an hour might take all day, and part of the trip might even have to be made at night on dark roads, so people chose a time of month when the moon stayed fullest and the skies were clearest. Your almanac was your timetable.

People now look upon almanacs as silly superstitious writings that dealt with the moon in a mystic way and predicted what the weather would be, using witchcraft methods. Nothing could be more incorrect. Just as modern scientists use information about last year's storms and seasons, and feed that information to electronic calculator machines, so did the old-time farmer keep daily weather accounts of the past and add them up year after year. Farm diaries and almanacs were the books which kept such records.

Want to take your cattle on a three-day trip to the market? Just open your almanac and see when the moon is fullest to make your night travel possible. Did your clock stop and do you want to set it again? Just open your almanac and find out the minute of sunrise or sunset today. Want to start on a boat trip to deliver your grain? Consult your almanac and find out what hour tomorrow's tide will be highest.

And so it went; in the days when there were no telephones or even neighbors close by, your almanac was far from being a scrap-book of superstitions—it was an absolute necessity.

Noah's "signs of dry weather" might have been some of those listed in his almanacs and which you might want to remember:

Heavy dew at night means a fair dry day tomorrow.
Halo around sun or moon means a lengthy slow rain within eight hours.
Smoke refusing to rise signifies oncoming storm.
Increased odors of swamps, ditches, cellars, warns of rain.
Rolls of dark clouds under cobwebby sky warns of high wind.
Bats and swallows fly near the ground before a rain.

Chapter 5

1 : First day of June! Earliest sunrise this month.
2 : Whitsunday. Worked on garden which is entirely up.
Was real hoe-boy.

Here you might wonder, for knowing how religious the early American was, and remembering how even stagecoaches stopped running on the Sabbath, doesn't it seem odd that Noah "worked on the garden" during Sunday? The answer is likely that he worked *after sundown*, for at that time the Sabbath began on Saturday at sundown and ended on Sunday at sundown. In fact, the old "Saturday night bath" started from the adage about cleanliness being akin to Godliness. So we might assume that Noah worked in the garden as Sunday night drew on.

It is interesting to note here how farmers used to work in what we now call darkness. Many present-day scientists insist that the early countryman had extraordinary eyesight, keener than the average eyesight of

45

today. Farmers frequently did their haying at night, using the moon or the stars for illumination, and taking advantage of the coolness of summer night. At any rate, it seems remarkable that so much work did get done with so few mechanical conveniences and without the use of outdoor lanterns. Many farms had no lanterns and those that did used them more for carrying a flame from place to place than for actual illumination.

The most common farm lantern was the metal one, punched with many holes. Glass lanterns are most rare. The drawing also shows a simple tin measuring can with holes punched through it for carrying a candle.

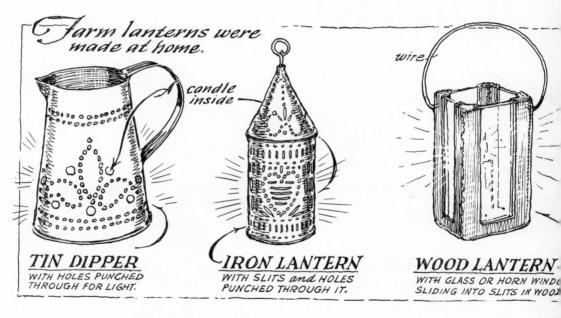

Farm lanterns were made at home.

candle inside —

wire

TIN DIPPER
WITH HOLES PUNCHED
THROUGH FOR LIGHT.

IRON LANTERN
WITH SLITS *and* HOLES
PUNCHED THROUGH IT.

WOOD LANTERN
WITH GLASS OR HORN WINDO
SLIDING INTO SLITS IN WOO

a Hoe Boy

balanced on the end of the table, — *by a weight*

46

Below the lantern drawings you may see the author's explanation of what Noah might have meant when he wrote in his diary, ". . . was real hoe-boy." A popular toy of the early 1800's was a balancing figure that sat on the end of a table and moved up and down for a great while. First it was a man riding a horse; but then there was a very popular song called "The Hoe Boy," and the toy took on the form of the boy with a hoe, who once started, went up and down with his little hoe. Several hoe-boy toys have been found in New England.

3 : Helped Father build rope hoist to move the water wheel.
4 : Father and Mr. Adams worked at putting the water wheel in place. Sarah did not come.
5 : Tried the wheel: it is quite true and has great force. Father will begin fashioning the cog wheel.
6 : Cut grass until rain started. First hay of the year.
7 : Mowed.
8 : do.
9 : Sunday. Saw Sarah and she promised to visit me at mowing.
10 : Rain. Sarah did not come. Will use half the hay for bedding and half for the pit.

It almost takes a detective to decide what Noah might have meant by using half the hay "for the pit." This must have been the early version of the modern farm silo, for believe it or not, the first silos were pits in the ground! The word silo cannot be found in the early American dictionary; it comes from the French, meaning a hole or pit. And in the beginning of our farm life, people stored cattle food in the ground instead of in those towering round buildings we are now so familiar with.

As you travel across the countryside, you might notice how most of the old farm silos are leaning. The reason for this is that, unlike old barns that have big beam framework, the silo has no such skeleton—it is all skin and suffers from poor design. If the early farmers had designed them, they would probably have big beams and they would not lean. Noticing such things makes a detective of the historian and tells us how architecture changes from time to time.

47

SILO.. the building that is all skin and wants to lean.
.. Noah's storage silo was a hole in the ground

← Corn and Hay

11 : I am to do all the farm work. Father shall work full time on the mill.

12 : Mr. Beach is fitting the mill machinery while Father frames the mill house. I have never been so tired from farm chores!

For a young boy to have taken over the farm chores in mid-June certainly must have been a tiresome bit of work. But in those days people did not farm to raise saleable crops; they farmed for their own table and for their own livestock.

Noah and his father seldom saw each other except at mealtime, each one working so hard at his own chores; Rachel managed to hear the progress report then.

"Goodness!" remarked Rachel to her husband, "I don't see why your mill house must be so much better built than our own home. Why those timbers you are using for framing are big enough to support a herd of elephants!"

"When the mill begins to operate," said Izaak, "you'll think there *is* a herd of elephants within the mill. I guess you've never been in a mill house."

Rachel hadn't, or she would have known how a water wheel will make the whole mill structure shudder and weave with its tremendous power. Just as a modern man might enjoy the power and noise of a sports automobile, or any mechanical device, the old-time miller derived great satisfaction from the enormous energy that turned the wheel and operated many tons of massive gears. It is the sort of job a man becomes wedded to.

The drawing of house framing might appear technical and boring to the reader at first, but when you inspect it closely and see how the whole house frame went up without even one nail, each piece locking into another and holding itself fast, one can only marvel at the early craftsmanship. Nowadays people build merely to get the house up and to live in it or to sell it. Once people created buildings for themselves and their children's children. They enjoyed looking at the beams that made a castle of a farmhouse, withstanding the ages; and they derived the greatest pleasure from perfection of craftsmanship.

Looking at the old-time workmanship, the modern builder will always remark, "You couldn't afford to do that today," or "They had all the time in the world then." Both statements are so untrue! We are richer now than ever. And as for having more time in the old days, the lack of mechanical time-savers made the early American's work day about three times as long as our present day.

> *13 : Robert Adams came by; said his family are coming Saturday to see the new mill house. It is all framed. Sarah will be here on Saturday!*
> *14 : Finished plowing and planting too; helped Father make tidy around the mill.*
> *15 : All the Adams arrived. Sarah and I took lunch upstream to see the beavers and Sarah cut her foot in wading. I carried her all the way back.*
> *16 : Sunday. Sarah not at Meeting. Her foot bled.*

Here we might wonder if the cut on Sarah's foot reopened and so bled again, or if a doctor had "bled" her. For even in 1805 (and indeed much later) the custom of bleeding was resorted to in almost every serious ailment. George Washington, whose death had occurred only six years before in 1799, probably died from his doctor's "remedy" of bleeding rather than from his ailment, which was only a sore throat!

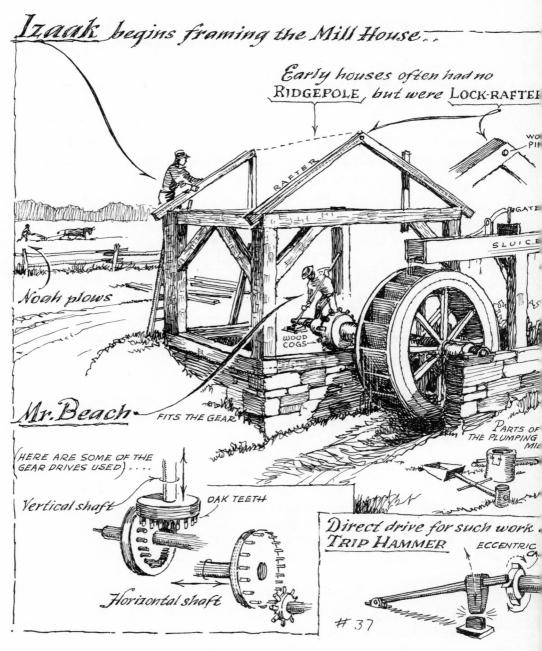

Izaak begins framing the Mill House...

Early houses often had no RIDGEPOLE, but were LOCK-RAFTER

WO[O]
PI[N]

RAFTER

GATE

SLUICE

Noah plows

WOOD COGS

Mr. Beach FITS THE GEAR

PARTS OF THE PLUMPING MIL[L]

(HERE ARE SOME OF THE GEAR DRIVES USED) ....

Vertical shaft

OAK TEETH

Horizontal shaft

Direct drive for such work. TRIP HAMMER

ECCENTRIC CA[M]

#37

50

17 : *Alarm of frost last night but no thing was harm'd. In spite of the coolness, I saw several humming birds and humble-bees in the garden.*

Here again the author was puzzled by the wording in Noah's diary.

Did Noah mean *bumblebees?* Oddly enough, however, we find that none of the early dictionaries have any mention of *bumblebee*, but they all do list *humblebee!* The early Quakers were called "the humble people" because they refused to fight or kill; the humblebee was so called because it was thought that it, too, did not fight or sting. How the name finally became bumblebee is strange, except that it certainly does look more "bumble" than "humble."

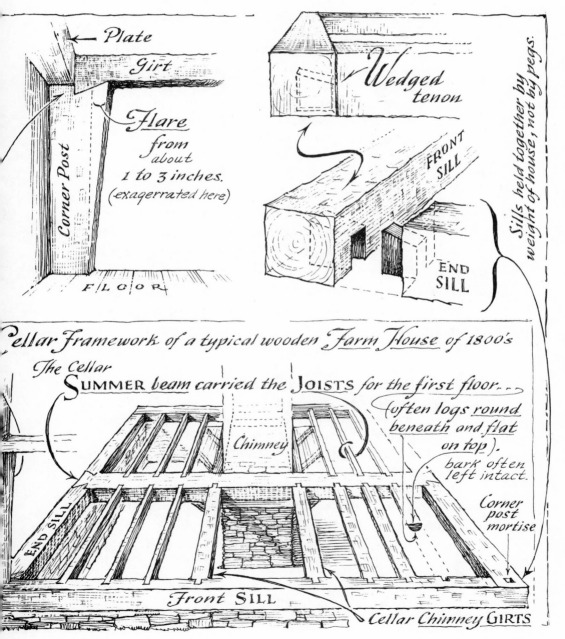

Plate

Girt

Flare from about 1 to 3 inches. (exagerrated here)

Corner Post

FLOOR

Wedged tenon

FRONT SILL

END SILL

Sills held together by weight of house, not by pegs.

Cellar Framework of a typical wooden Farm House of 1800's

The Cellar SUMMER *beam carried the* JOISTS *for the first floor...*

(often logs <u>round</u> beneath and <u>flat</u> on top).

bark often left intact.

Chimney

Corner post mortise

END SILL

Front SILL

Cellar Chimney GIRTS

51

18 : Father still working at the mill. Mr. Beach stayed with us.

19 : The mill wheel has been set and there will be several diversions (evidentally this meant several machines harnessed to the same power). Father and Mr. Beach making use of the longest days of the year. Cogs will work both a hammer and the bellows, so some of my forge work shall be eliminated. It is all very wonderful.

20 : Rain stopped all work at the mill. I worked at farming.

21 : do.

22 : Went to see Sarah this night, bringing some wild honeysuckle. She was much better and might go to Meeting tomorrow.

23 : Sarah was at Meeting. She wore a sprig of my honeysuckle, which had become very brown'd. The weather is warm and the days have become beautiful.

Certainly the days are beautiful when your best girl remembers to wear a bit of your bouquet to her!

But Noah's mind must have also been filled with the wonders of his father's new mill machinery. The magic of water power did so many things that before were drudgery, that adding some new device was as thrilling as our buying a new TV or washing machine for our home today. Some millers, so the records say, even attached a cord to the big wheel to rock the baby's cradle or to turn a spit in the fireplace and revolve the roast.

24 : Worked in the garden today and pruned in the orchard. Found many of the apple and pear trees with insects.

25 : Cleaned the chimneys at the forge barn and in the house and sooted about the trees. First dish of pease from the garden!

26 : Father and I sledded the oaks from the woodlot and put them down near the mill.

"It won't be long now, son," said Izaak, "before we can saw these oak logs into flooring for the house. And with our own saw!"

"You mean you will have the machinery set up before winter?" asked Noah.

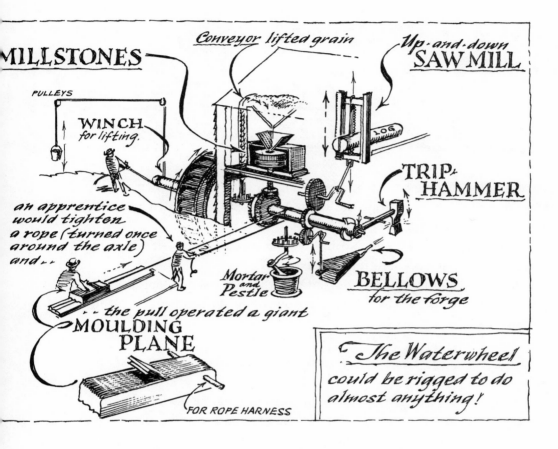

MILLSTONES

PULLEYS

WINCH
for lifting.

Conveyor lifted grain

Up·and·down
SAW MILL

*an apprentice
would tighten
a rope (turned once
around the axle)
and -·*

TRIP·
HAMMER

Mortar
and
Pestle

-· the pull operated a giant
MOULDING
PLANE

FOR ROPE HARNESS

BELLOWS
for the forge

*The Waterwheel
could be rigged to do
almost anything!*

"Mr. Beach is in town working on the saw-frame this very minute. But there's a lot of timber work to be cut and placed before we can set up the sawmill."

The thought of their own sawmill, and logs being cut into fine new planks, made Noah's work easier as he jacked the oaks up a skid and onto the sled. Sleds were used as much in summer as they were in winter at that time, for wheels were all but useless in heavy hauling across the old unimproved trails. And Daniel, who was used to pulling a sled, knew just how to push his great weight against the sled first, to jounce it loose from the earth, and then begin the slow pull across the grass and soft mud.

But Daniel was different today. He seemed slow and more attentive to Noah than he did to his work at logging. He nosed about Noah's

53

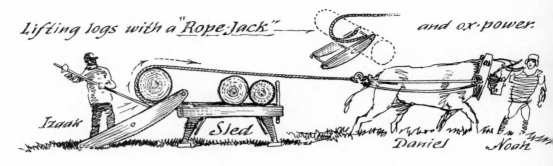

Lifting logs with a "Rope-Jack"——— and ox-power.

Izaak *Sled* *Daniel* *Noah*

clothes as if looking for salt and he swung his head up and down quickly in the manner that he always did when Noah came to the barn first thing in the morning.

"Come on Daniel," said Noah, "It's not morning now—it's time for work! Put your back into it and heave ho!"

Izaak was guiding the logs up and into the sled, using a long bar, but he couldn't help noticing there was something different about Daniel today.

27 : Thursday. This has been a poor day. Daniel is dead.

When Noah had gone to the barn that morning, he noticed Bessie at the door. It had always been Daniel who came to greet him first. Bessie had called with her usual low moo the instant she saw Noah coming, but there was no sign of Daniel.

When Noah reached the barn he saw Daniel lying in the hay. His eyes were open, but they were not focused on anything. It was clear that Daniel was dead.

Noah went inside and sat on the big body, which was still warm and soft. He must have been there for some time, and he must have remembered all the work and good times that he had lived through with Daniel. The big animal had become a part of the household, for he had helped to build it. He had helped to build the new bridge, even to pull the first logs for the old bridge. All the clearing and plowing was his work.

After a long while Noah felt the body beneath him growing stiff and cold. He rose slowly and opened the door to let Bessie out. But for the first time, the old cow stood still and refused to leave the barn. Noah

54

walked toward the house as if he were dragging all the weight that Daniel had pulled over those fields. It would be difficult to break the news.

> *28 : We buried Daniel. Father says we shall have a horse.*
> *29 : Mother layed out her flower garden today. I finished sooting the orchard trees.*
> *30 : Sunday. I told Sarah about Daniel. We shall plant a fine tree over his grave.*

Along with the old diary, there were several papers folded and inserted within the leather cover; one was a recipe "to destroy Insects on Fruit trees." It read:

> Take 2 shovelsfull of soot, one of Quick Lime; mixed together; take some of this and put it windward of the tree, and sprinkle some water upon it, when a great quantity of Gas will be evolved, which ascending into the Tree will destroy Insects, without injury to the Plant, as it rather helps Vegetable life.

The reader might enjoy the fine use and rhythm of language in this simple direction which was probably written by a plain farmer. Without knowing who did the writing, but knowing that this is probably what Noah followed when he "sooted the orchard trees," we herewith reproduce the actual writing:

55

Chapter 6

1 : July. The Adams and we are going to spend the Independence Day in the village to see the holyday fun. Father hopes to buy a horse on that day.

"Holyday" was first thought by the author to be a misspelling by Noah, but on searching through dictionaries of Noah's time, there was no word *holiday*; there was *holyday* instead, meaning exactly what our holiday now means.

2 : Thunder shower before sunrise. I dug new potatoes.
3 : More rain. It cleared tonight, and tomorrow should be clear for our going to town.
4 : Never heard so many bells and cannon shots. Several wagonloads were on their way as we walked to the village. Last year poor Daniel drove us in. Mr. Adams was reading the Declaration of Independence when we arrived

and Mr. Grimes said a long prayer. Sarah looked very pretty. Father bought a horse and a waggon! We shall collect them on Saturday.

"Here," cried the auctioneer, "is as fine a beast as any man would want! And with her goes an almost new wagon! Surely I can get one higher bid—who will raise it another five dollars?"

Just then someone in the crowd with a little cannon lit the fuse and held his ears. Bang! The cannon exploded only a few feet behind Izaak, and his two hands went over his head as if he were shot.

"Thank you, Izaak Blake!" said the auctioneer. "There's a man who knows what he wants. One hand was enough but he put up two! Sold to Mr. Blake!"

Izaak almost protested. In fact he had already begun—but he did admire the horse, and the old farm wagon that Daniel had pulled for so long had already rotted in many places. He walked to the auction table to pay.

"Well," said Izaak later on, "we have a new horse and he came to us by fate and because of a toy cannon. I don't know what they called him before, but I have a name for him now. It shall be *Bang*."

5 : We began making ready for Bang. Father says a horse will jump over such fences as ours so we began making them higher.

Noah and his father worked all the day carrying stone to heighten the stone fences.

"I sure miss Daniel," said Izaak as he struggled with a wheelbarrow of stones. "He could have slid this load and another ton as if it were nothing. But when I was a boy, we didn't have wheelbarrows! We had only handbarrows; some of them had long handles, and we slid the load behind us just as an Indian does with a travois."

"Mother will have a hard time climbing over the fence if we make it so high," observed Noah. "Shouldn't we make a little ladder for her—or one of those things called a *stile?*"

57

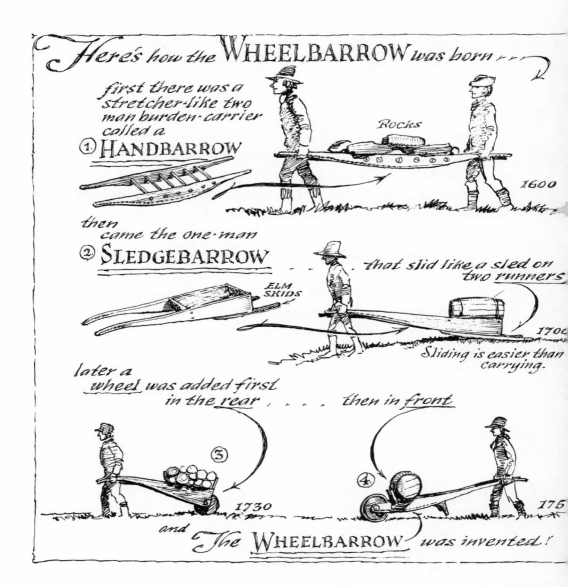

Here's how the **WHEELBARROW** was born ---

first there was a
stretcher-like two
man burden-carrier
called a
① **HANDBARROW**

Rocks

1600

then
came the one-man
② **SLEDGEBARROW**

ELM
SKIDS

that slid like a sled on
two runners

1700

Sliding is easier than
carrying.

later a
wheel was added first
in the rear . . . . then in front

③

1730

④

175

and The **WHEELBARROW** was invented!

"Perhaps we can put a grike here and there," replied Izaak. "These are slits in a fence where a person can pass over, but a farm animal would be too timid to squeeze through. I do admit grikes are more for men and boys than they are for ladies with flowing skirts, so perhaps we shall build a stile for Mother."

In 1805 wire was not yet used in fence work (barbed wire was in-

58

vented in 1873), but wood was so plentiful in America that two or three men could split rails and build a fence with them at close to a mile per week. Between the stone walls made just from land clearing and the stump fences resulting from the same work, there wasn't much more fence work to be done at the Blake place, except to heighten a wall here and there or to add a rail on top of the lower stumps. So before the day was over, there was good enclosure for Bang—high enough to keep the average horse from jumping over.

It is interesting to the student of early times to note that fence rails were cut (by law in some places) at a length of eleven feet. This was exactly one sixth of that old measuring device, the *chain*, which was a linked measure sixty-six feet long used by surveyors instead of the foot and inch calculation that we use now. By merely walking around your

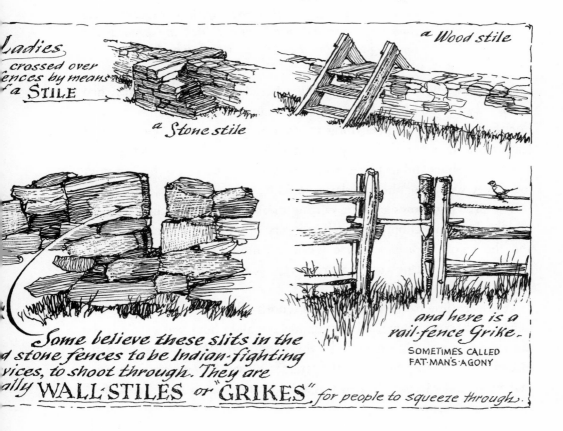

Ladies crossed over fences by means of a STILE

a Stone stile

a Wood stile

Some believe these slits in the stone fences to be Indian-fighting devices, to shoot through. They are really WALL-STILES or "GRIKES", for people to squeeze through.

and here is a rail-fence Grike. SOMETIMES CALLED FAT·MAN'S·AGONY

fence line and counting the fence rails, you could accurately tell the size of your land. Or by removing a rail, you could use that as a giant ruler for measuring out more land. Lay out two rails and you would have the legal width of a roadway where Noah lived. Yes, in those days there were many good reasons for custom, and the people enjoyed tradition because they knew the reason for it.

> 6 : *A most exciting Saturday. We went to the village to collect Bang and the waggon. Bang is faster on the road than Daniel; we arrived home in less than ten minutes. Bessie would have none of Bang and she kicked her stall through. We shall leave Bang at pasture until the two animals become better friends.*
> 7 : *Went to Meeting in the new waggon. It is great enjoyment to drive a horse.*
> 8 : *Brilliant warm day. Father and Mr. Beach squared new timbers for the mill machinery. I tried my hand at the squaring axe while Father and Mr. Beach chizelled.*

Any man who was expert at using a broadaxe (a squaring axe), had usually learned the hard way and had the marks on his legs to show it. For the broadaxe wasn't a thing to cut down trees with, but a sort of giant plane that chipped away at round logs to make them square. Its handle was short and its blades were razor sharp; you had to be "on your toes every second or the broadaxe would."

The drawing shows an adze, cutting measured notches while a broadaxe did the actual chopping away, but very often there was no adze used and the whole process was axe work. So most of the "antique adzed beams" that we see nowadays were never even touched by an adze; they were broadaxed instead.

When it came to the mortices and tenons (the interlocking units that joined timbers together), a combination axe and chisel was used (as the drawing shows). Almost none of these tools are left, as they were replaced in the early 1800's by the straight chisel, but we might assume that Izaak and Mr. Beach used this sort of thing when they "chizelled" as the diary relates.

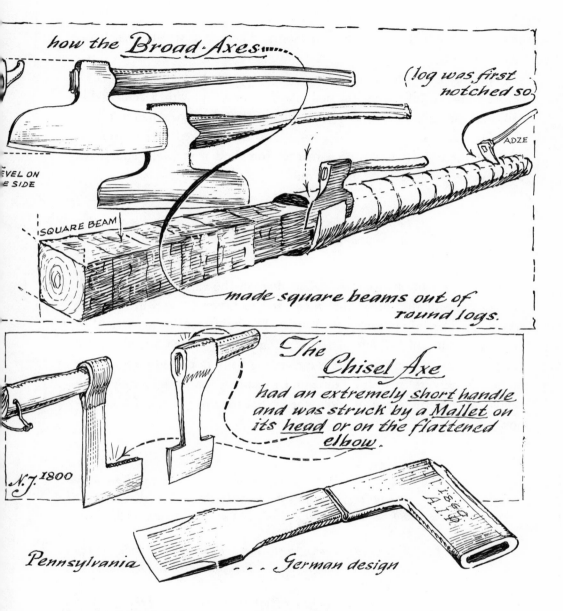

how the *Broad·Axes*

(log was first notched so)

ADZE

EVEL ON
E SIDE

SQUARE BEAM

made square beams out of
round logs.

The
Chisel Axe
had an extremely short handle
and was struck by a Mallet on
its head or on the flattened
elbow.

N.J. 1800

Pennsylvania ··· German design

"Well," said Izaak, "your work at the bellows is now past history! We have finally made a cog in the water wheel axle that should lift up the bellows twice with every revolution. Pretty soon we can dismantle the old forge barn and set it up in the new mill house."

"That's one job I'll never miss," laughed Noah, "but I'm sure you'll find another job for me, just as tiresome. There will still be nail hammering to do."

"The way things look," said Izaak, "we may not be making nails at all before long. A fellow in Philadelphia has come up with a remarkable nail machine, and I've already seen what it can do. They had a keg of machine-made nails in the town store, and they looked pretty good to me. But there will always be a market for good iron tools, and that's what we're going to make in our mill!"

9 : Father says we shall make iron hoes and shovels and dogs in the new mill; there will be a cutter for bar iron.

Dogs? A lot of things were called dogs in the early days, but Izaak probably ·meant the things that men used to fasten a log with when it was squared or otherwise worked upon. It would seem to be natural to progress from nail-making to forging staple-dogs which are like large sized double nails, anyway. (It is interesting to note that although these timber dogs were in every household a century or so ago, they have become one of the rarest of tools; the author has only two in his collection.)

10 : Helped Mother with her sallet garden. Planted Rosemary and saffron and lettice and gilly-flowers. (Sallet was the old way of spelling salad, just as lettuce was spelled lettice.)

11 : The brook is low, so we took advantage and built up the stonework. Bang drew his first load of stone by sled, but it was difficult.

12 : Two Indians came by from the mountains on their way to the village. We fed them. They marvelled at our new bridge.

13 : Rain all the day.

14 : Sarah drove back with us from Meeting and had Sunday night dinner with us. Mr. Adams collected and took her home in the evening.

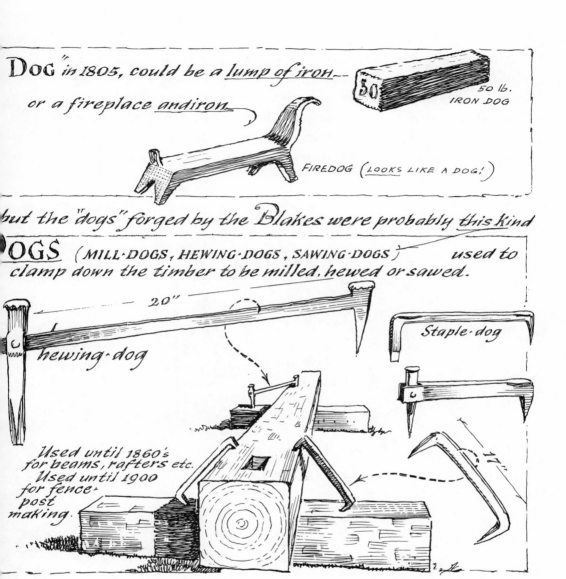

DOG" in 1805, could be a lump of iron—

or a fireplace andiron.

50 lb.
IRON DOG

FIREDOG (LOOKS LIKE A DOG!)

but the "dogs" forged by the Blakes were probably this kind

DOGS (MILL·DOGS, HEWING·DOGS, SAWING·DOGS) used to clamp down the timber to be milled, hewed or sawed.

20"

hewing·dog

Staple·dog

Used until 1860's for beams, rafters etc.
Used until 1900 for fence-post making.

17"

15 : Mr. Adams came by this morning to warn us of Indians. The same two that visited with us, followed them all the way home last night and would not reply when addressed. Perhaps they had been drinking. We shall draw our shutters at night.

16 : Good haying weather. Father and I worked in the field and we began building a rick.

63

Most people living today have never seen a real old-time haystack, or as they called it in the early days, a *rick*. Often hay ricks were square, but the usual kind was round and curving outward at the top like an inverted bell to ward off the downpour of rain. Ricks were not just piles of hay, but were built carefully with each sheaf folded neatly into place. They were constructed with all the finesse of an expert brickmason.

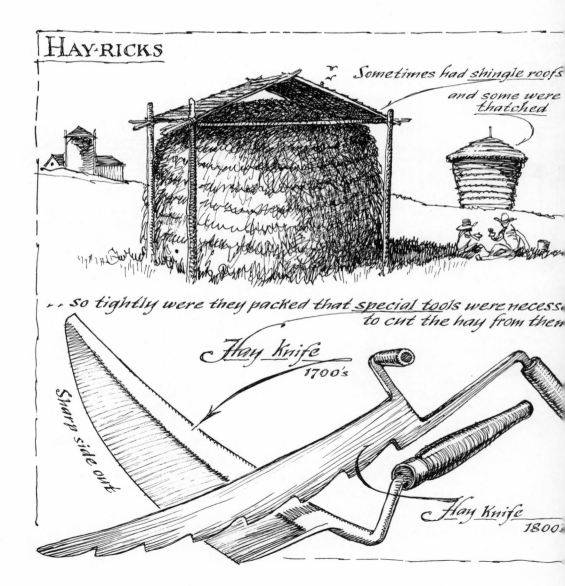

HAY·RICKS

Sometimes had shingle roofs
and some were *thatched*

.. so tightly were they packed that <u>special tools</u> were necess
to cut the hay from then

Hay Knife
1700's

Sharp side out

Hay Knife
1800

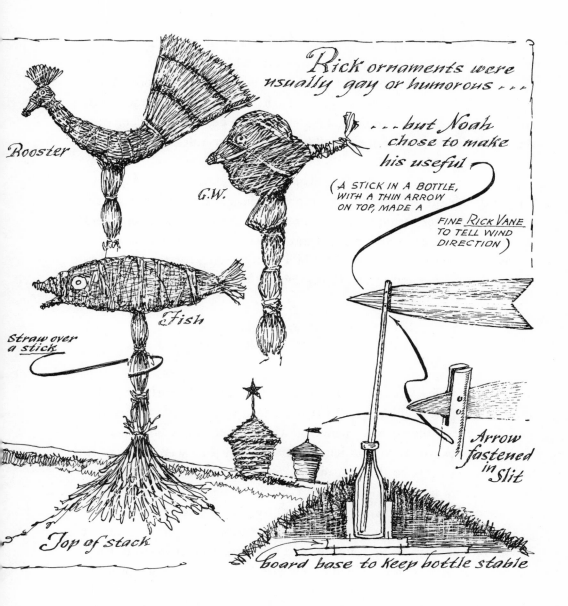

Rick ornaments were usually gay or humorous...

Rooster

G.W.

...but Noah chose to make his useful

(A STICK IN A BOTTLE, WITH A THIN ARROW ON TOP, MADE A FINE RICK VANE TO TELL WIND DIRECTION)

Fish

Straw over a stick

Arrow fastened in Slit

Top of stack

board base to keep bottle stable

Even the strongest winds seldom toppled a good rick. During hot weather it was the greatest pleasure to noon and lunch in its shade while the sweet smell of hay perfumed the air on the lee side.

In America it usually was the custom to place an adjustable shingle roof atop a hay rick, but those farmers who leaned toward the old European ways thatched the top and peaked it with a gay straw ornament.

65

Those who were expert at thatching would use their rainy days designing rick ornaments in the shapes of roosters, fish, a boat, or the head of some well-known statesman. Of course, the event of a "rick-crowning" always called for drinks and song, but during harvest festivals each farm tried to outdo the other in the same spirit that we decorate our doorways during Christmas; then the ricks all over the countryside looked like big fancy holiday cakes.

Noah had seen one rick-top ornament that he wanted to duplicate and he decided to start making it as soon as the stacking got under way. It was a *rick vane*, made with a bottle with a short stick in it that held an arrow that swung and pointed into the wind. It seemed about the simplest way that anyone could build a weathervane, for the slick glass made a permanent and workable bearing for the upright stick.

> *17 : Rick is under way. Mr. Adams is going to thatch the roof for us. Carried water to Mother's garden which is dry.*

Carrying water was always an important chore in the early days, for piping was almost unknown. As two buckets were as easy to carry as one, because of the counterbalance of weight, every household had one or more "neck yokes" or burden carriers. In fact they were made to fit each person's neck, so that a man's yoke was much different from that of a child or a woman, and in New York State, where they were made commercially, they had sizes from one to six, like shirts.

One favorite American burden carrier was made quickly from a square piece of canvas or waterproofed sailcloth, known in New England as a "summer cloth," which folded into a knapsack. Apples or grain could be carried in a summer cloth, but so could water or milk. The word summer had nothing to do with the season, but stemmed from the ancient word *sumpter* meaning *burden* or *burden-horse*. (The same applies to that main ceiling beam in the old houses known as a summer beam.)

Farmers in the north country still keep a square piece of waxed sailcloth in their wagons to carry water for their horses, for a bucket will

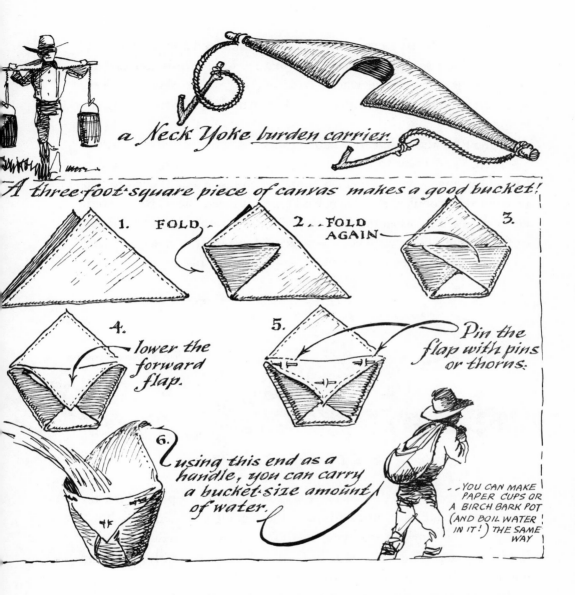

a Neck Yoke burden carrier.

A three-foot-square piece of canvas makes a good bucket!

1.

FOLD

2. ..FOLD AGAIN

3.

4. lower the forward flap.

5. Pin the flap with pins or thorns.

6. using this end as a handle, you can carry a bucket-size amount of water.

YOU CAN MAKE PAPER CUPS OR A BIRCH BARK POT (AND BOIL WATER IN IT!) THE SAME WAY

dry out and leak, but a canvas bucket will always hold water. The drawing shows how to fold a summer cloth; in place of pins a plain thorn from a thorn tree will do the job of fastening the material. Indians have been known to make such an arrangement of birchbark, which will not burn as long as there is liquid on the inside, and will boil water over an open fire!

67

"Now that we have a new wagon," said Izaak, "and a spirited horse to pull it, I don't see why we can't also have a little two-wheel cart for going to the village. The wheels from our old wagon should do very well for building this, and the other two wheels might make a handy logging cart."

"I'm all for the little cart," said Noah, "but what is a *logging cart?*"

"Well," said Izaak to his son, "now that we are looking forward to having our own sawmill, there will be logs to move about, even to haul in from the woodlot, and Daniel isn't here to sled them. Bang would never get used to a logging sled, so we'll have to use wheels. A logging cart is nothing but two wheels between a long shaft: the log is jacked up to the axle and it can then be slid from place to place."

a LOGGING CART

So as time went on, the old Blake wagon began to disappear. First the rear wheels were dismantled to make the logging cart and then Noah was given the work of removing the bolts for use in a new cart body. Bolts and nails were not things to be discarded in the early days, and houses were often burned just to get the nails from them.

The right woods would have to be found for the new cart, for the wrong wood in any vehicle was unforgivable. It was oak for the framework, elm for the sides and floor, ash for the spokes and shafts, pine for the seat, and hickory for the slats. Even a simple chair sometimes had as many as six kinds of wood, each kind working against the other in dry weather or damp, designed to stay tight and not to wear away or break. This is why an old wagon could sit outside year round in the weather and still exist, while a metal vehicle would rust and crumble. An automobile wheel left outside for twenty years would almost entirely disappear, yet you may see a two-hundred-year-old spinning wheel, sitting in the weather as they do outside many an antique shop, just about as good and useable as when it was made. It gives a thinking person food for thought, and to many of us a reverence for wood.

18 : We collected our first toll over the new bridge! A wagon crossed over, carrying a chapman and his wife.

"Father!" cried Noah, "There is a big wagon at our bridge!" Izaak came running and soon he and Noah were exchanging greetings with the driver, who had gotten down from a large covered wagon painted blue and filled with wares to sell. The sides were made like chests of boxes, each little door opening into a store of different articles, and each door with a title upon it.

The sides of the wagon were like chests of boxes...

"I see that you intend to roof over your bridge," said the man. "Good idea! A lot of people are planning to do that. I presume you ask a toll, but I see no sign."

"Well," said Izaak, "we just haven't come around to that yet. In fact, you are the first strangers to cross over. I shall be glad to give you free passing and our blessings."

NOAH·BLAKE·BRIDGE
Please walk your horse!

Foot passengers . . . . 1 cent
Horned cattle . . . . 3 do.
Horse, Jack or Mule . . . . 3 do.
4 wheel carriage . . . . 10 do.
Burden cart or waggon . . . . 6 do.
Sleds or sleighs . . . . 6 do.

Business with mill . . . nothing.
Sabbath day passage . . . do.

1805

PLEASE
RING

Probable toll list and toll house arrangement

"Not on your life!" cried the man. "That would be bad luck to your bridge. Accept the toll and keep it for luck."

"If you insist," said Izaak, "but we had in mind asking ten cents for all four-wheel carriages. You see, we hope a stagecoach might use this road soon. Customers to our mill, when we get it in operation, will not be charged any toll."

"It is my pleasure," said the man, as he turned toward his wife, up on the wagon seat, who had fished the money from her bag and was handing it to him. "In fact, this is such an event, I would like to present you with a small gift. Do give these nutmegs to your good wife, whom I see looking down from the house."

He reached into his coat and came up with a handful of nutmegs.

The diary referred to this man as "a chapman" because 1805 was before the days of the Yankee peddler, and traveling merchants were known as *chapmen* (or more often, *petty chapmen*). These men sold almost everything, but they became known for their nutmegs, which were a small item and easy to carry. Connecticut specialized in outfitting traveling peddlers, so since the wares were known to come from that state, most people thought of all peddlers as coming from there, too. It was the peddler and his practice of carrying nutmegs that eventually gave Connecticut the name of "The Nutmeg State."

"Thank you," said Izaak as he accepted the nutmegs, "My wife is just out of such seasoning. Now I wonder if you might have a supply of salt in your stores?"

"Indeed I have!" said the chapman. "And the very best it is. I have a shipment of sea salt from the Jersey shore at two dollars a quarter bushel."

"We've been using mined salt here," said Izaak, "but I'd like to try the sea salt. They say it is difficult to manufacture."

"It is a complicated procedure and it takes a week or two to get the salt from sea water, but the Jersey coast is already dotted with windmills that pump the water up into shallow vats. Some men just let the sun do the work, while others boil the water down over a fire. Every hundred pounds of sea water, they say, has three and a half pounds of salt in it."

"I think you shall sell some of your salt in the village," Izaak ventured, "for I am sure they have none of it at the store."

Later, as the chapman drove off in the direction of the village, the new bridge looked much more important to Izaak and Noah.

"What shall I do with this money?" asked Noah.

"Well, the bridge is called Noah Blake Bridge, and I think Noah Blake should keep the money. But you shall have to keep proper account books."

Keeping an account book in 1805 demanded an extraordinary mathematical knowledge because English money was still in use here and there, while the currency from one state seldom was worth the same in another state. Here the author offers the reader an original page folded into the Noah Blake diary; it was evidently written by Izaak for his son Noah. The exact date is not known, but it shows the immense difficulty of ascertaining what our money was worth. Notice, too, the last line, which lists the New England group of states, and that Maine and Vermont are not yet among them.

> *19 : Worked in the fields. The corn is much too dry.*
> *20 : Mrs. Adams and Sarah went berrying and visited us. They reported seeing a bear among the berry bushes, so I accompanied them home where they showed me how they make blackberry wine.*

An early nineteenth-century recipe for blackberry wine was found by the author of this book; it seems very simple to make. It had the amusing title: "a medicinal drink for summer affections," and it read as follows:

> To a gallon of smashed blackberries, add a quart of boiling water and let this stand for a full day. Strain through a coarse cloth and add three quarts of water with two pounds of good brown sugar. Mix and put in a jug or keg, closing only partially by leaving the cork loose. Leaving this in a cool place, it should be ready for drinking in October.

> *21 : A sour, foggy Sunday.*

22: Heavy downpour, but good for the crops.
23: Second day of rain. Father went to work under cover at the mill.
24: Clear day. Worked in the fields. Some of the corn has washed away.
25: Beginning of Dog Days. The Sun with Sirius now increases the heat.

A Table

Exhibiting the value of a Dollar in each of the United States and practical Theorems for exchanging the currency of either into that of any other

To exchange from / to	N. Engl States & Virginia	Pennsylvania Jer. Dela & Maryland	New York and N. Carolina	S. Carolina and Georgia
New England States and Virginia	Dollar 6/0	Add one 4th	Add one 3d.	Subtract ½ twice
Pennsylvania N Jersey Delaware and Maryland	Subtract one 5th	Dollars 7/6	Add one 15th	× 3 ½ & ÷ 5
New York and North Caroline	Subtract one 4th	Subtract one 16th	Dollar 8/0	To ½ add ⅙ of the ½
South Carolina and Georgia	Add two 7ths	Add ½ ⅐ that ½ & ½ that ⅐	× 28 Subt ⅐ Product	Dollar 4/8

*The New England States are New Hampshire Massachusets Rhode Island and Connecticut

Many people now believe that the "dog days" of summer has something to do with the way the heat affects a dog; some say it is when most dogs go mad. But in the early days, when people were more generally educated in the science of the stars and planets, everyone knew the true meaning of the dog days. It is when Sirius, the Dog Star, brightest of stars, rises in conjunction with the sun. Some readers might argue with the author in saying that people were better educated over a century ago than they may be now in this age of space flight. Yet it is true that almost every farmer knew the stars and the complete routes and time-tables of the sun and the moon. The 1805 almanac for example, gave one full page to "the coming six eclipses of the year." Although five of the eclipses were invisible in America (because of time of day or location), the complete program of the visible eclipse was printed, down to the hour and minute and second of the beginning, immersion, middle eclipse, and so on. (The duration, incidentally, was 2 hours, 37 minutes, and 5 seconds.)

It is not that such information is no longer known or that we have not progressed immensely in our knowledge; the pertinent fact is that the average person doesn't know such things because they are not necessary information. A child today might say, "Why would I want to know if there is an eclipse unless I may see it?" But Benjamin Franklin observed that "knowing only what is necessary, makes living dull and marks the regression of learning." Noah couldn't see it, for it occurred on the opposite side of the earth, yet he shows more interest than the average schoolboy of today, when he puts in his diary:

> *26 : Sun's eclipse at 25 minutes past one in the morning.*
> *27 : Father is plumbing a fine new door for the mill house.*

"Plumbing" did not mean what it would mean today; because *plumb* was the word for *lead*, and a plumber was a man who worked with lead. Because all the first metal pipes were made from folded lead, the water-pipe makers became known as lead men or "plumbers." Noah's father did his "plumbing" with a piece of lead on a string, to get his doorframe absolutely vertical. Nowadays, of course, a carpenter would use a spirit level which employs a bubble in a vial of spirits (alcohol). In Noah's time there was probably no builder's level other than a gravity level, such as is shown in the drawing. The square model with the weighted arrow was found in the same house where Noah's diary was found, and it is in the author's collection of early tools.

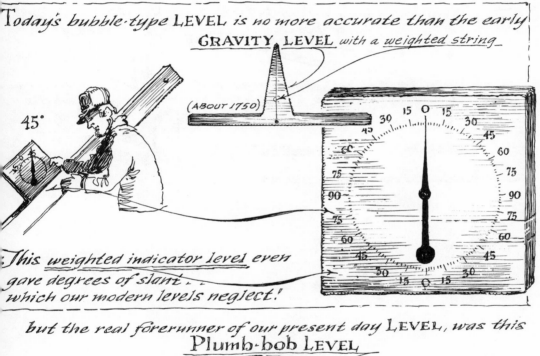

Today's bubble·type LEVEL is no more accurate than the early GRAVITY LEVEL with a weighted string

(ABOUT 1750)

45°

This weighted indicator level even gave degrees of slant... which our modern levels neglect!

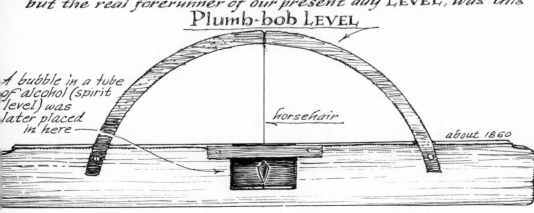

but the real forerunner of our present day LEVEL, was this Plumb·bob LEVEL

A bubble in a tube of alcohol (spirit level) was later placed in here

horsehair

about 1860

75

28 : *A hot Sunday. Robert and I shall take our poles into the village next Tuesday. Mr. Adams says he will thatch our rick for us. First melons of the year at Sunday dinner.*

29 : *The rick is ready for Mr. Adams to thatch.*

30 : *Took waggon load of poles to the village with Robert Adams and collected four dollars from Mr. Minor.*

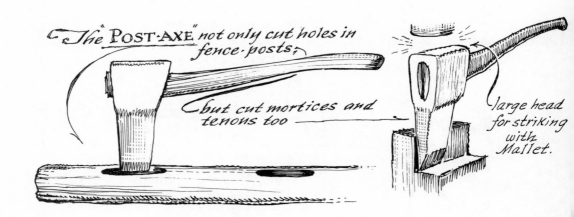

The "POST·AXE" not only cut holes in fence·posts,

but cut mortices and tenons too —

large head for striking with Mallet.

Chapter 7

1 : Lammis Day, the first day of August. Our rick was not ready in time but the Adams family joined us and Mr. Adams spent the day in thatching. While sitting at the harvest table at noon, we saw the same two Indians looking on and we gave them as much food as they could carry away. Robert brought a maze game with him but only Sarah could do it.

Here the author thought "maze" was a misspelling of *maize* which is an old name for common corn. As Lammis Day involved the blessing of the first corn crop, it seemed possible that the "maze game" mentioned in the diary was some sort of corn game. But no; it was found that "maze games" were puzzles marked on paper or carved into wood, copying some famous labyrinth. For an example, we present "Rosamond's Bower" (or the "Maze at Woodstock"). It is an ingenious puzzle

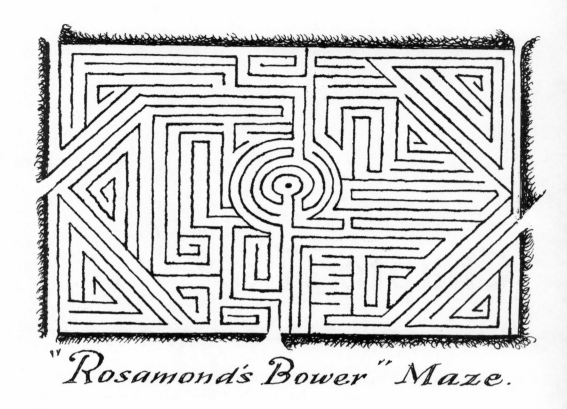

"*Rosamond's Bower*" *Maze*.

consisting of the problem of getting from one of the numerous outlets to the bower in the center without crossing any of the lines. Turf mazes were made during harvest festivals by turning up the sod into a maze design to keep the youngsters busy at play while the parents ate and drank at the tables. If making a turf maze was too difficult, or would spoil a good hayfield, sheaves of wheat were laid out in a giant maze at which even the adults might try their skill. The making of mazes became such a fad at one time in the late 16th century that the Puritans banned all maze games by law, in an attempt to suppress "those folyshe ceremonies."

2 : The two Indians returned this evening with gifts. They speak very little but they seem most friendly. They had dinner with us.

78

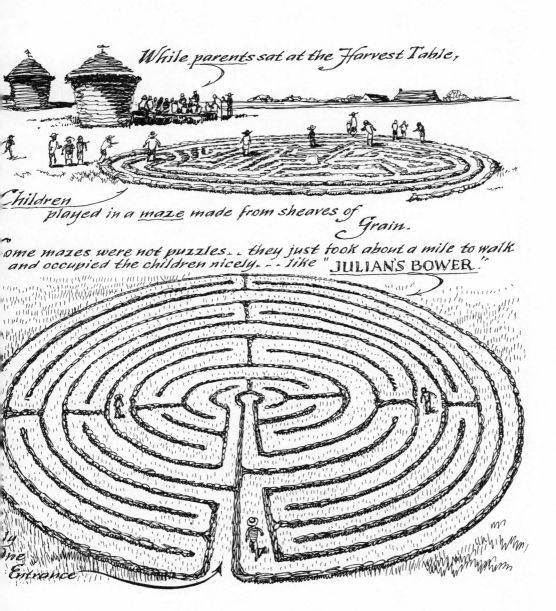

While parents sat at the Harvest Table,

Children played in a maze made from sheaves of Grain.

Some mazes were not puzzles... they just took about a mile to walk and occupied the children nicely... like "JULIAN'S BOWER."

Only one Entrance

Rachel saw them first, standing outside the window and peering inside.

"Quick Izaak," she whispered, "get your gun and close the shutters. There are Indians outside."

Izaak went to the window and recognized the Indians as those who had been to the harvest party yesterday.

TEMPORARY BARN

BARK ROOF OVER STONE FOUNDATION

FOREST being cut down

OLD·INDIAN·TRAIL

FORGE BARN

SITE for MILL

LOG·and·SLAT Bridge

RED MAN BROOK

80

CLAY and STICK CHIMNEY

TEMPORARY BARK ROOF

SOLID SHUTTER

BORNING ROOM

WATERING PLACE

The BLAKE place, —1790

This was the year when Noah was born... the year after Izaak Blake and his wife Rachel built their cabin near Red Man Brook. The bark roofs, the clay-and-stick chimney and the temporary lean-to barn were all replaced. Look at the next picture and see what changes occurred ⟶

81

STAND of UNCUT TIMBER

BARN

TOO[

CORNFIELD

STONE BOAT

SLED

a MILL

SLUICE

GATE

MILL WHEEL

COVERED BRIDGE

TOLL HOUSE

ROAD to Village

82

The **BLAKE HOUSE**

STONE FENCE

SHINGLE ROOF

WELL-SWEEP

NOAHS WINDOW

CELLAR

NOAH'S ROOM

MILL POND

...ED TO MILL-WHEEL

The **BLAKE** place some time after 1805 ..

With the help of Noah, Izaac Blake had created a workable homestead. The Indian Trail became a roadway .. the brook became a source of power to grind corn that grew where once a forest stood .. the shelter became home to an early American boy.

83

"They are only calling," he said quietly. "And they seem to have gifts."

Without as much as a nod, and as soon as the door was opened, the two Indian men entered with a noiseless step, placed things on the table, and then stepped aside. There was an ash hunting bow, and a dish of sweet-fern, and a string of coarse wooden beads. The older man went again to the table and lifted the bow and pointed to Noah.

"Thank you," said Noah with a deep but nervous bow. The Indian could understand no English, it seemed. He neither smiled nor acknowledged Noah's bow, but he lifted the beads up and placed them over Rachel's head and then upon her neck.

"How wonderful!" she exclaimed with genuine pleasure. "What a nice thing to do!"

Next the Indian pointed at the sweet-fern and then at Izaak, who seemed bewildered, not knowing what to say or do with it.

"Thank them!" said Rachel. "They use sweet-fern to make a tea with. They say in the village that it cures the ague. They probably saw you sneezing and blowing your nose yesterday!"

After many smiles and gestures of satisfaction from the Blakes, none of which were returned by the silent Indians, Rachel brought out some fresh milk and cornbread. She drew benches up to the table and she signaled for the men to sit down. They took their pieces of bread and cups of milk, however, and walked quickly outside as if they were departing.

"Oh, they are taking my cups," said Rachel as quietly as she could. But as she followed them outside, she saw them sit on the ground near the doorway and begin to eat.

"Indians don't use chairs," said Izaak, "and if we want to be gracious hosts we must sit on the ground with them."

So Rachel and Izaak and Noah spent a good part of the afternoon doing what they never dreamed they would ever be doing: sitting on the bare ground, eating and drinking with guests.

Noah laughed openly at the scene and everyone seemed to have a good time, yet the Indians, who appeared never to have learned to laugh or even smile, did nothing but eat. Suddenly the two Indians stood up and left, without the slightest sort of departing gesture.

"I guess we shall never have worry about them," said Izaak, "so you can go back to leaving your shutters open during the summer nights. I certainly will never understand their ways, but they do have gratitude in their hearts; to me that makes them gentlemen."

"Amen to that," said Rachel. "I am so glad that we were civil to them yesterday. I must tell the Adamses about this."

3 : Very warm. The harvest fly was two days late.

On Lammis Day (the beginning of harvest time) the *cicada* was supposed to make its first appearance, or at least start its buzzing song. The cicada is what we now incorrectly call a locust, and what in Noah's time was called the Great Harvest Fly (mostly because it looks like an oversize version of the common housefly). Nowadays when people hear the "locust" singing in the trees during summertime, they will say it is "a sign of hot weather." This is actually a harkback to the ancient Lammis Day ceremony and its sayings.

Even today we find New England "harvest tables" on the market, not knowing just why they are called that. The first harvest tables were

Today's "HARVEST TABLE"

was first a single plank <u>Lammis Table</u>

85

long narrow tables such as were reserved for Lammis Day gatherings. These gatherings resembled our present day Thanksgiving dinners in number and spirit. The tables were always made of one solid plank.

> 4 : *The hottest of days. It is good for those who have not yet finished their harvest, but there was prayer for rain at Meeting today. The grass has become parched. We have moved even our bread into the cellar so drying is the summer warmth.*

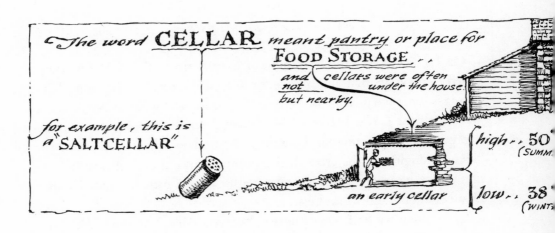

The cellar in Noah's time was not always under the house. It was more often off to one side. Usually it was on the north side of the house, and it was merely a room dug deep in the ground, with a dirt floor, for the storing of foods. *Cellar* was actually a mispronunciation of a French word *cella*, meaning *store-room*. The deepness of the underground store-room kept foods cool in summer yet warm enough to be above freezing in winter. The enclosed ice-box appeared and made the cella (or cellar) useless, and about that same time, the central furnace appeared. So the *cellar* has become the logical place for putting the heating system—a long way from what the word once implied!

> 5 : *A fine thunderstorm arrived at noon. Garden work.*
> 6 : *We have begun a corn cratch, and I have begun taking down the old forge barn.*

86

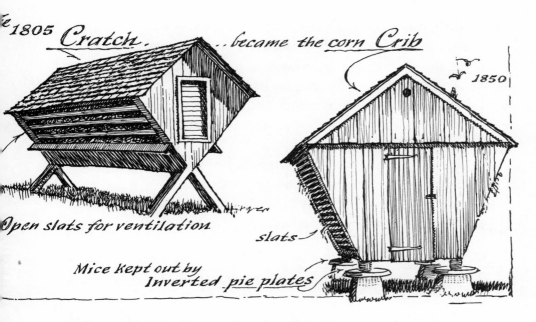

the 1805 *Cratch* ...became the corn *Crib*

1850

Open slats for ventilation

slats

Mice kept out by
Inverted pie plates

"The crop of corn will be so plentiful this year," said Izaak, "that we shall have no room for it in the loft. We shall make a good cratch to hold it."

"But can't we put the corn into the barn?" asked Noah.

"The purpose of a cratch," replied Izaak, "is to store the things in the open, yet keep it out of reach of mice or squirrels."

Cratch is an obsolete word, but what Izaak referred to was what we now call a *corn crib*. These open-slatted houses with outward slanting sides are for storing whole ears of corn and keeping them air-shrouded but dry. Since the mid 1800's these outbuildings have been built resting on large pie plates to keep mice from crawling up the foundation blocks, and the name corn *cratch* has changed to corn *crib*.

"We can use much of the forge barn material in building the cratch," Izaak told Noah, "and we must take care not to break the chimney bricks, for we shall have a stove in the mill this winter, and that will need a new chimney."

"A stove!" Noah thought out loud, "I've always hoped for a stove. The one the Adamses have in their place heats their kitchen so well during winter."

Stoves were scarce in back country villages, as almost every farm-

87

stead used fireplaces and brick ovens until the 1800's. Benjamin Franklin was perhaps the first to put a "fireplace into a box" which could be moved out into the room so that more heat might radiate from the same amount of fuel. In the 1790's the idea had been taken over so quickly and enthusiastically that many houses were built with a brick chimney starting up in the attic, and having numerous metal pipes leading from it to stoves in all the rooms.

The Adamses had been one of the first farm families to buy a stove, and Noah, as a boy of nine, had raced home to describe it.

"Oh, father!" he cried, "The Adamses have their fire locked up in a big black box, and it sits right in the middle of their room!"

The first American Heating Stove was fed from the Next ro[...]

the PENNSYLVANIA "FIVE PLATE"

Bedroom

Kitchen fireplace

HOT ASHES

7 : *The Forge barn is down. Only the chimney and forge remains. The bellows have been removed to the mill.*

8 : *Framed the corn cratch none too soon. Father has begun working in the corn fields.*

9 : *do.*

10 : *do.*

11 : *Sunday. Father's birthday. I presented him with a humorous toy. Mother baked a special pudding and Sarah joined us for dinner.*

88

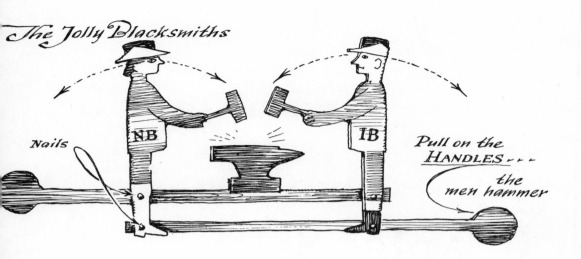

The Jolly Blacksmiths

Nails

NB IB

Pull on the HANDLES - - -

the men hammer

"Happy birthday father!" shouted Noah as he came to breakfast. "And here is a small gift for you that I have made by myself. When your mill is completed, it will remind you how we used to work at the anvil together. The one on the left is me and the handsome fellow on the right is you!"

"Thank you, son, and what a clever thing it is! I shall always keep it."

Izaak pulled the handles back and forth to see the two figures hammer on the anvil and he laughed aloud.

"It will always remind me that every time one of us works, so does the other—that we are a good team."

12 : *A great degree of heat with thunder. But no rain.*

13 : *Worked in the corn fields.*

14 : *do.*

15 : *Mr. Beach arrived with a saw frame and a fine four foot blade. Its teeth are nearly two inches long.*

16 : *Father and Mr. Beach worked in the mill. I helped.*

17 : *do.*

18 : *Father and I went to Meeting without Mother who is ill.*

Chapter 8

Here the diary is interrupted. A number of the center pages have been torn away and the next page begins on November sixth. Summer had passed and somewhere in the missing pages of the diary (on September 23rd to be exact), autumn had begun. The corn has now been cut and shocked, grain has been thrashed, all the hay is stacked, and the labors of summer are over. At this time of year all nature calls out from the wood-lots. Near the farm buildings the landscape becomes dotted with special apples like the Rambo, Maiden Blush, and Carolina Sweet. Off on the upper hillside, Rennets and Virginia Crabs and Cooper Russets show themselves on the thining orchard limbs. The insect chorus has reached its crescendo in the tall oatmeal-color grass that was green only yesterday.

The Blake mill now has been put together, and we find Izaak and Noah getting a shingle roof over it in time to protect the intricate wooden machinery from the late autumn rains.

The Full moon of November 6th 1805.

6 : Father and I have the mill roof all but shingled. It is fun working at night, but the weather is most cold.

"This moon is brighter than the harvest moon," said Isaak, "and that is because of the crisper, colder air. It is even brighter than last month's Hunter's Moon, I think."

"Why do they call it the Hunter's Moon?" asked Noah.

"I suppose because it occurs at the right time to light the forest during the good hunting season. Though gentle people like us, who seldom use the gun, usually refer to it as the Worker's Moon. That is because it is the best time to do outdoor farm work at night before the cold sets in."

"Well," said Noah, "the cold has certainly set in with this full moon. Isn't this our second heavy frost of the year?"

"That it is," replied Izaak as he pushed another packet of shingles toward his son and stopped to rub his hands together in the cold night air. "They say that Sham Summer (Indian Summer) begins right after the first frost, and that was during the last full moon. It looks like winter is nearing and 'most upon us."

Just then there was a call from the direction of the house, from Rachel.

"Time for a warm drink, men! Come down from that roof before you catch your deaths. It is near midnight!"

Over a cup of steaming sassafras tea and a plate of cornbread, Noah and Izaak felt the satisfaction of having done a good day's work.

"I can't see why you must work on a slanting roof at night," said Rachel. "Just because the almanac says it's the best time for shingling. It sounds silly and dangerous to me!"

"Oh come now!" said Izaak. "We are not as superstitious as all that. We just work best in the cold of the evening. And shingles left to dry out their first time in the heat of midday, are apt to curl. There are a lot of moonlore sayings full of common sense, and there are a lot full of hearsay and nonsense too."

"Well I think we should sort them out and not bring up a son on anything but knowledge and good sense."

Noah laughed, but he had no retort. He was comfortably tired, and the hearth was warming him to sleep. It had been a good day, and a good night.

When he went to his room and blew out the candle, the moon lit the room so well that he looked about for a second or so, seeking another candle to blow out. And when he drew the covers up to make a tent to build up body warmth, the moon danced a silly dance through the bubbles of his window pane.

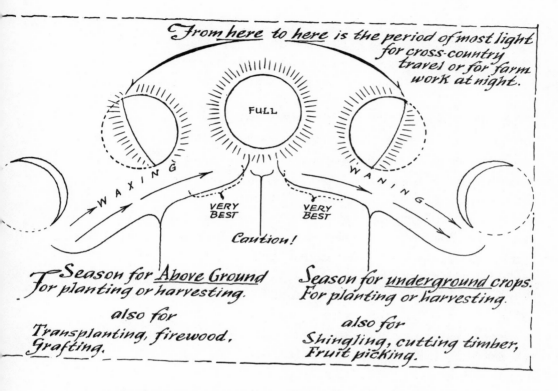

From _here_ to _here_ is the period of most light for cross-country travel or for farm work at night.

WAXING

FULL

WANING

VERY BEST

VERY BEST

Caution!

Season for _Above Ground_
For planting or harvesting.

also for

Transplanting, firewood.
Grafting.

Season for _underground crops._
For planting or harvesting.

also for

Shingling, cutting timber,
Fruit picking.

What a pleasure it is, he thought, to spice the world with things like moonlore and weatherlore. The moon is an exact timepiece that will never change, and the seasons will always be with us; yet not to be sure about tomorrow's weather is more of a joy than a worry; and to wonder about the moon is an unending pleasure of life. If ever man should find his way there and learn everything about the moon, would the loss be greater than the accomplishment? It was a profound thought to go to sleep on.

7 : _Finished the mill roof in time for a rain._
8 : _Windy and chilly weather. Closing in the open places with strips._
9 : _Spent the day closing in the mill._
10 : _Sunday. Robert Adams will come over tomorrow to help us with the apples._
11 : _Spent the day gathering apples. Robert stayed over._

12 : More work in the orchard.

13 : Gathered cyder apples. Will drive them to the village to-morrow and deliver Robert to his home. Shall dinner with the Adams and Sarah.

The Blake orchards were a scattering of trees rather than a set plot, for Izaak wanted first to grow trees of special fruits before he transplanted seedlings into a patterned orchard. The "cyder" apples were of a dwarf type known as *crab*; a crab apple in Noah's time was not like the crab apple of today, as the word crab merely meant it was a wild variety. The eating apples were known as Russet, Golden, Ribston, and Normandy. All the eating apples of 1805 were "pippins" because they were raised from a pip (apple seed), although now we think of a "pippin" as just one kind of apple.

It seems a pity nowadays that the American apple tree has lost much favor as a useful landscape tree. For a full century the early American worked at cultivating apple trees, and you can still see the evidences wherever the landscape has not been "developed" and "improved." Walking through any wooded area, you will come upon a few ancient apple trees, and they will always mark the place where a farmhouse once stood. If children in this country made the effort of starting orchards, even one tree to each child, what an interesting project it would be, and what a contribution it would be to the nation!

" Where a farmhouse once stood "

Robert Adams and Noah Blake first picked the eating apples. These were picked very carefully from the stem, using cotton gloves or without using the hands. The least pulling or squeezing, according to the

94

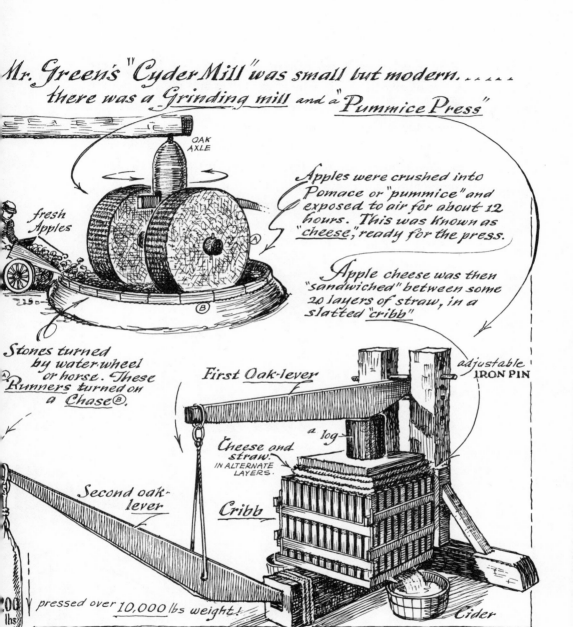

Mr. Green's "Cyder Mill" was small but modern......
there was a _Grinding mill_ and a "_Pummice Press_"

OAK
AXLE

fresh
Apples

Apples were crushed into Pomace or "pummice" and exposed to air for about 12 hours. This was known as "cheese," ready for the press.

Apple cheese was then "sandwiched" between some 20 layers of straw, in a slatted "cribb"

Stones turned by water-wheel or horse. These A _Runners_ turned on a _Chase_ B.

First Oak-lever

adjustable IRON PIN

a log

Cheese and straw. IN ALTERNATE LAYERS.

Second oak-lever

Cribb

pressed over 10,000 lbs weight!

00 lbs

Cider

old ways, rendered the apple unfit for whole winter storage. These apples were put stem up in a straw-packed box and taken into the cellar as soon as frost threatened them. There they were put on stone (very often native marble) shelves (wood shelves were never used). One apple was never allowed to touch another while in storage. When all the prime eating apples were taken care of, the apples for drying were picked. Then, last of all, the apples which had fallen and the few poorer apples still left on the tree. These were doomed to decay before long, so they were used for applesauce and for vinegar.

One may see why there was a law against cutting down apple trees in the earliest American days, for the one tree provided raw fruit, cider for drinking, apple sauce, dried fruit, and vinegar.

Early apple trees were trained to grow low, so pickers did not always use ladders. But in New England there was once a chair-ladder that

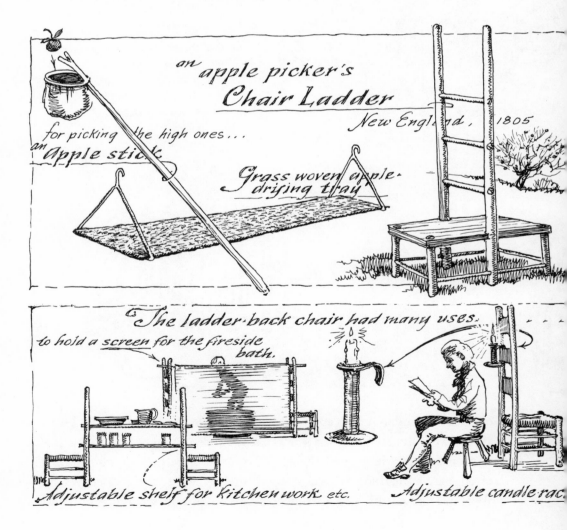

an apple picker's
Chair Ladder
New England, 1805

for picking the high ones...
an Apple stick

Grass woven apple-drying tray

The ladder-back chair had many uses.

to hold a screen for the fireside bath.

Adjustable shelf for kitchen work. etc.

Adjustable candle rac

could either be stood upon or climbed, and was light enough to carry about. These were rough farm devices, so there are very few left to be found; they were nothing like the well-made ladder-chair, which was a piece of indoor furniture. It has been said, however, that the ladder-chair might have been designed from the chair-ladder device. (The author, who collected ladder-chairs, was intrigued with the frequent burns he found on the backs of such chairs; not until he visited a back-woods home in New Hampshire and saw someone using a ladder-chair as an adjustable candle rack, did he solve the mystery. This also explains the reason for the projecting lip on many old candlesticks which hitherto was thought to be simply a handle for carrying it.)

> *14 : Bang drove a great load of apples to Mr. Green's cyder mill. Bang is lighter than Daniel and I fear we shall need a drag-shoe for the waggon. Had dinner at the Adams. Sarah had a letter from her home in Pennsylvania. Her parents wish her to return.*

The drag-shoe or ruggle is an obsolete piece of wagon hardware that few people know about today. It was hung in front of the rear wheels, and when, in going downhill, a heavy load threatened to roll forward and push the horse over, the iron shoe was slid under the wheel (one wheel or both rear wheels). Then the back part of the wagon became a sled, and the horse actually pulled the load downhill. This, of course, was before the addition of wheel-brakes to wagons.

The Drag Shoe — HAND LEVER — was released on going down a steep hill with a very heavy load. and the wheel ran right up onto the shoe.

15 : Stayed over at the Adams house, to work the same amount
of time that Robert worked helping me.
16 : Finished at the Adams and returned home.
18 : Sunday. Mother had begun apple-drying yesterday. I hope
Sarah does not go home.

It is interesting to note that Robert first helped the Blakes, and then Noah helped the Adamses. This was a custom practiced religiously in the early farm days; when there was a job that took more than one person, a group of people did the work, not for pay, but to get that same kind of job done for themselves later. In that way, there was no hiring of help. For example, when a harvest mowing job was ready, some eight men showed up at the designated farm and did the whole job in one day. Then each of the eight men was entitled to the same service on his own farm. Food and switchel (drinks) were the obligation of the farmer whose land was being worked. For a farmer to hire help to raise a barn or frame a house was unheard of. Cooperative labor was the answer.

Apple drying is a practice long forgotten. Yet you may take almost any fruit nowadays and dry it into slices that can be eaten raw or sugared. It is still a good way to make apples keep into the winter. You may often see hooks in the ceiling beams near the fireplaces of old houses; they were used for hanging a long tray of apple slices where the heat of the fire could effectively dry them out and seldom were the drying trays empty. These same hooks were the ones which held a tent of blankets around the fire to house the Saturday-night bather.

19 : A day of high winds. Father believes that many nuts have
fallen from the woodlot trees and he suggests that we
gather them before the squirrels do.
20 : Went to the woodlot with Bang, and wheeled in several
logs we had left to season for flooring. Father will try out
the new sawmill with them.
21 : Our first log was cut today. Father says he will save the
center piece for a harvest table. The noise was so loud

98

that Mr. Adams heard it and came over to see. Mother and Father are pleased with the saw, but Father says the wheel ratio must be changed. I asked Mr. Adams to send Robert over tomorrow for nutting.

22 : Robert and I spent the day nutting. We gathered four baskets of chestnuts and about half as many walnuts.

23 : Gathered almost twice the amount today as yesterday. Our hands are dyed dark brown from the nut juice.

24 : Sunday. Went to Meeting. Sarah was amused with my stained hands which will not clean. I told her that I hope she does not return home.

25 : Father cut several boards for the new floor but I had a great disappointment for I thought we would have the wood floor this year. Father says the boards must season for nearly one year! Mother is disappointed too, but she is accustomed to the dirt floor and wants it for one more Christmas.

26 : Mr. Green came out with four barrels of cyder that he has pressed from our apples. The barrels are from Mr. Minor and I think I recognize some of the hoop-pole material that Robert and I sold to him.

27 : Father is making a smaller pinion wheel for the saw machinery.

Boring through white oak must have taken a great deal of strength, yet there never seemed to be much complaint from the old-time builders. When you think that the pointed screw was not thought of until the mid 1800's, it seems remarkable that metal bits could be made to bore through the toughness of seasoned oak. The drawing shows a smith's beam drill such as Izaak Blake must have used in his shop. With such a contrivance, you could put more weight on the drill than the complete weight of your body. Below you may see some of the bits used a century or more ago with the beam drill. Bits of this type can now be bought for use with electric drill sets; they are called "new high speed bits," but Noah Blake knew them well.

Although wooden gear wheels, like those in the machinery of old water mills, were not perfectly made, they became perfect through actual wear.

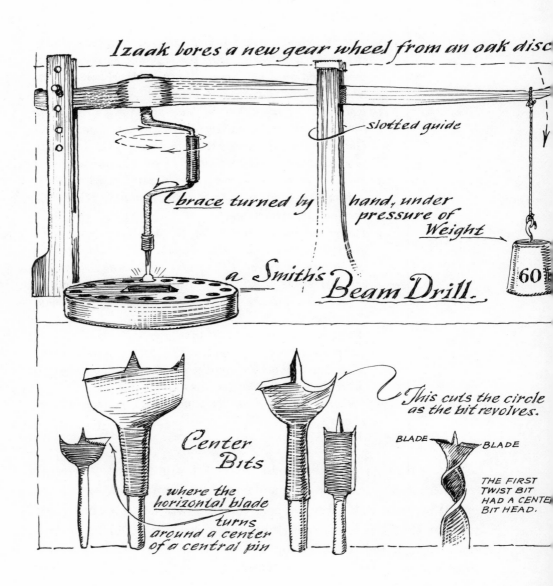

Izaak bores a new gear wheel from an oak disc

slotted guide

brace turned by hand, under pressure of Weight

a Smith's **Beam Drill.**

60

Center Bits

This cuts the circle as the bit revolves.

where the horizontal blade turns around a center of a central pin

BLADE   BLADE

THE FIRST TWIST BIT HAD A CENTER BIT HEAD.

Before very long, a set of noisy gears would wear themselves into smoothness and quietness, which is something metal gears will not do.

28 : Snow! The first white of the year. We are looking to the sleds which are in sad repair.
30 : Spent the day in the mill helping Father.

Chapter 9

1 : December has arrived with another fall of snow—just enough to cover the ground. Went to Meeting in the wagon but we soon look forward to introducing Bang to runners. Father says it shall be my job to keep the bridge floor in snow. The bridge bears my name, he reminded me.

Very few people stop to think how important it was to keep snow shoveled into the old covered bridges. In fact, some believe they were built just to keep out the snow. Yet because most road traffic was during the winter (because of the impassability of muddy summer or spring roads, and the ease with which heavy loads could be sledded over snow), the covered bridge's busiest time was sled time. A load of logs stuck in a bridge for lack of snow on the floor could tie up the traffic badly.

"We shall miss Daniel this winter," said Noah. "He pulled the snow roller as if he were two oxen. I don't think Bang could even budge it!"

"Well, this year we'll have to leave the snow rolling up to the village.

We've given them a good new bridge; I guess they won't mind helping with the roadway now."

> *2 : Banked the house with cornstalks and pompion vines.*

It seems a little late to bank the house, yet Noah has had a busy time of it, and better late than never. A thick matting of cornstalks around the bottom of the house will keep some of the winter cold and wind out. "Pompion" was the old name referring to the pumpkin which was used mostly for cattle fodder. It is a little confusing to learn that the old picture of the pioneer American with his pumpkin pie and his Thanksgiving dinner, is quite incorrect. You will notice that Noah's diary went completely through November without a mention of Thanksgiving. Only when Lincoln set aside a Thanksgiving day in 1863, did the almanacs begin to list the holiday. Thanksgiving began as a Puritan day, but because the Puritans were opposed to Christmas as a holiday, the American farmer looked down upon anything Puritan, and he was content with his harvest thanksgiving feasts in August.

> *3 : I had a long talk with Mother about Sarah. Mother is go-*
> *ing to ask Sarah to stay for Christmas. The weather is*
> *warmer and the snow has disappeared.*
> *4 : I have started making rockers for a chair to give Sarah for*
> *Christmas.*

"Do you think she will like to have her own chair?" asked Noah.

Rachel herself had always wanted a rocker, so she was being honest. "I cannot imagine a nicer present!"

Rockers were not exactly new in 1805, but nearly all of them were converted chairs. Most of the rockers at that time were slat-back chairs with oversize rockers exactly like those beneath a child's cradle. It is quite possible that in 1805 the rocking chair was only twenty-five years old. It's origin is not certain, but it is American—possibly the only completely American piece of furniture.

102

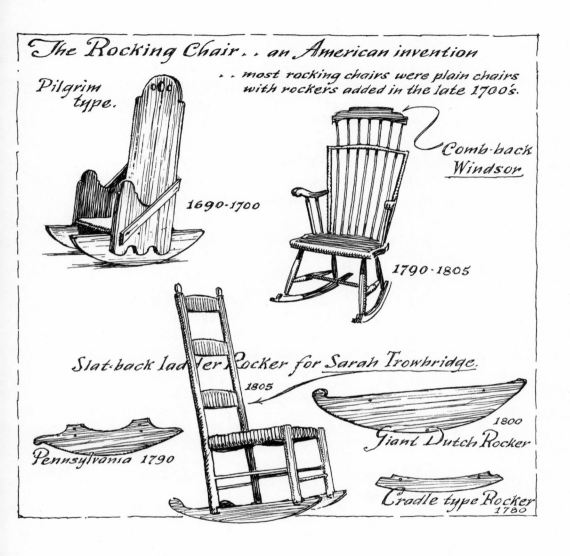

The Rocking Chair... an American invention

... most rocking chairs were plain chairs with rockers added in the late 1700's.

Pilgrim type.

1690-1700

Comb-back Windsor

1790-1805

Slat-back ladder Rocker for Sarah Trowbridge.

1805

Pennsylvania 1790

Giant Dutch Rocker

1800

Cradle type Rocker

1780

Noah had taken his share of the hoop-pole money and while in the village he had bought the kind of a chair he thought Sarah would like; the rockers were an afterthought.

5 : The saw mill machinery is complete. Father and I have begun to close in the walls and start a brick chimney in preparation for a stove. The forge fire will pipe into the same chimney.

103

6 : *Same work. It is almost too cold for the plaster.*

7 : *Chimney-building still!*

8 : *Mother spoke with Sarah at Meeting today. I do not know what she said and she will not say. The Meeting was cold. I wish they would place a stove there. They need that more than a bell.*

Noah did not know who was buying it, but it was announced that a bell had been ordered for the village Meeting House, and some day soon it would arrive, having come all the way from Boston. It was Izaak's secret idea when he first began building his house; he was away from the village and that was good—but he wanted to be near enough to hear an alarm. In those days the town bells told of fires and deaths and funerals and holidays and feasts and church events and Indian attacks. Bells were not just for the pleasure. Yet to hear a fine bell peal across the rich countryside is the greatest music to the farmer, and Izaak was a farmer. He had seen an advertisement in the *Massachusetts Spy* or *Worcester Gazette.* "Church bells," it had read, "of all sizes." So he had

"*He had seen an advertisement*"

HERE are a few old time Church Bell Codes

↳ Church bells rang at 7 A.M., at 12 noon and 9 P.M. (CURFEW)

↳ Deaths were tolled: 6 bells for a woman, 9 for a man. After a pause, the deceased's age was tolled in bells.

↳ Births tolled after 7 A.M. tolling.

↳ After 9 p.m. (curfew toll) the day of the month in bells was rung (10 bells for the 10th etc.)

CHURCH BELLS.

PAUL REVERE & SON,

No. 13, Lynn Street, North End, BOSTON,

HAVE conftantly for fale, CHURCH and ACADEMY BELLS, of all fizes, which they will warrant *equal* to any made in Europe, or this *country.* From perfonal information obtained in Europe, and twenty years experience, they are affured they can give fatisfaction, and will fell, on as good terms, as they can be imported for, or obtained in this country.

sent in an order for a smallish bell, and it was to be inscribed: "To the village from Rachel and Izaak Blake and from their son Noah." Even now it was being so inscribed at Number 13 Lynn Street, North End, Boston, by a very expert bell maker named Paul Revere. And if it arrived before December 25th, it would be a Christmas surprise.

9 : Wonderful news! Robert Adams came over with a note from Sarah. She has received word from her home that she may stay over the Christmas days, and that her Mother and Father are already on their way here. I went to see Sarah after my work and I expressed my joy.

"Why didn't you tell me you'd asked to stay?" asked Noah.

"I wanted to wait till the reply came," said Sarah. "And besides, I wanted to surprise you. If I'd gone back home, I would have had to stay the whole year, and I should not care for that at all."

10 : Began building a sled for Bang to pull. Father is using four of the wide oak boards that he intended for the new house flooring, to make the sled floor.

"Won't it need seasoning?" asked Noah. "I thought you said it would take about a year to season those boards."

"No" said Izaak, "not if they are to stay out in the weather continually. Only boards for placing indoors need seasoning. These boards will season nicely right on the sled. But do help me with the metal runners. They are almost ready for me to put onto the sled skids."

They went into the "under-room" of the mill, where for two days Izaak had been feeding a small fire in the forge basin just to warm the new chimney and help the plaster to harden and keep it from freezing. It wasn't a fire big enough to warm the place, but there were still glowing embers. Reaching out of a window after swinging open its wooden shutter, Izaak pulled a rope and fastened the end to a peg. This opened the gate in the sluice. At once there was a splashing of water somewhere

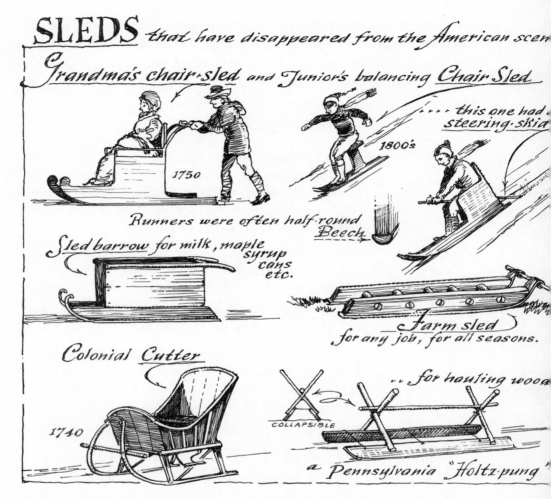

SLEDS *that have disappeared from the American scene*

Grandma's chair-sled and **Junior's balancing Chair Sled**

...this one had steering-skis

1800's

1750

Runners were often half-round Beech

Sled barrow for milk, maple syrup cans etc.

Farm sled for any job, for all seasons.

Colonial Cutter

...for hauling wood

COLLAPSIBLE

1740

a Pennsylvania "Holtz-pung"

outside, and before another minute, there came the groan and squeak of wood turning against wood. The mill wheel was "under way." The wood was not old enough to have worn itself into the smoothness of a nearly perfect wheel, so there were unnatural rumblings and shudderings now and then that caused Izaak to cock his head and listen. It was like listening to the breathing of a first-born child. Then he stopped listening, and his face assumed a pleased expression.

"Before long she will turn as slick and easy as any wheel!" he said.

He swung a wooden lever over against an oaken cog that protruded from the big main axle beam, and twice during each revolution, just as

106

Izaak had planned, that cog lifted the bellows and then released it. The strong breathing of the bellows wakened the embers in the forge basin, and before the mill wheel had revolved a dozen times, the coals were alive and hissing.

> *11 : Our first business at the mill! An order for sawing some pine floor boards, for Mr. Thoms.*
> *12 : Worked at the saw mill. Pine wood cuts beautifully.*
> *13 : do.*
> *14 : We took off the day. General Washington died this day six years ago. We could hear a cannon salute all the way from the village, and Robert told me there was a service held there.*
> *15 : At Sunday Meeting I came across a Biblical verse which I copied and gave to Sarah. I asked her not to open it until she arrived at her room. Now I am very worried about it.*

All the way home from Meeting, Noah had thought of nothing but what he had done. His father noticed a faraway look on Noah's face.

"Keep the wagon out of those ruts, son," he said. "You must be thinking of something a long way off!"

Noah set his mind back to driving Bang as a horse should be driven from Meeting of a Sunday. Still he did keep trying to remember the quotation that he had copied from The Second Epistle of John. It went:

"And now I beseech thee, lady, not as though I wrote a new commandment unto thee, but that which we had from the beginning, that we love one another."

> *16 : No word from Sarah. A soft snow fell today and I worked at making firewood before the snow becomes too heavy.*
> *17 : The snow stopped and I still am at splitting wood. No word from Sarah yet.*
> *18 : Mr. Thoms' order has been done. It has been loaded upon a sled and is waiting for a snow.*

"I think we should make a small offering at Sunday service," said

107

Izaak, "out of what Mr. Thoms pays us. It was our first sawmill job and I am exceedingly proud of the water wheel and its machinery. That saw went through pine much easier than it did with the oak for our flooring. Yet I would not have pine for a floor, because it should not be nailed down until a year or more after it is laid. My father had a pine floor, and I shall always remember that year of toe-stubbing that I endured.

Indeed, it was the old custom to lay floor boards down loosely and to nail them only after they had dried completely in the warmth of a winter household. Often when the boards dried and shrank, the whole series of floor boards would need sliding over until they were all tight. Then a new narrow board would have to be added to complete the floor before the final nailing took place. "Random widths" do mark an ancient floor, but random shapes mark them even more distinctly, for the early boards were seldom the same width at one end as they were at the other.

The early random-floors were random more in Shapes, than regular width.

wide   narrow

18"   2

16"   1

20"   1

Square nails are still best (and are used) for floors (THEY WON'T

The old PLANCHER Nails had clinching heads for floors.

19 : *Mother has begun Christmas baking and the smell is wonderful. It snowed, though not enough to sled Mr. Thoms' boards. No word yet from Sarah.*

20 : A great surprise today! The bell that Father ordered arrived in the village. It was drawn by a waggon with four horses, and it took eight men to lift it down.

"It is a beauty!" said Izaak when he arrived with Noah to help. "We must not tell Mother until she hears it ring. When do you think we can get it into a belfry?" he asked.

from here up is the "Spire."

This place will be the "Belfry." with open louvres.

derrick

The "watch"

... "on a temporary frame, for tomorrows Service."

Mr. Simon, the town framer and carpenter, said a derrick would be needed. "We will hoist it up on the watch-tower platform," he said, "and then we shall build a belfry wall around it. Some folks will want to see a spire on top of the belfry, but we can't do that for a while."

"We'll get it up on a temporary frame," said another man, "and we shall ring it for services tomorrow."

21 : What a day! They started ringing the bell as we drove to the village. Mother was most surprised and everyone con-

gratulated Father. I saw Sarah and when the Service was
finished she gave me a folded paper asking me to open it
when I got home, which I did. It just said first chapter of
Ruth, *16.*

Noah had known that the piece of paper held good news, for Sarah
smiled through what seemed to be a blush when she gave it to him. And
all during the service, whenever he looked at Sarah, she had that same
strange expression upon her face.

Noah didn't wait until evening to read his note. As soon as they were
home, after he had unhitched Bang and had the harness hung, he went
to that corner of the barn where an open window cast a ray of light
into the hay-filled room. Then he opened the note and read its message.
It mystified him and he went to the house, still wondering.

"Mother," he asked, "where is our Bible?"

"It is where it should be, in the Bible box," said Rachel. "Are you going to read it?"

"Well," said Noah, "I just wanted to look up something. I want to
see the sixteenth verse of the first chapter of Ruth."

"You don't have to look that up," said Rachel, "I know it by heart!"

"You do?" asked Noah, looking very surprised, "How does it go?"

"It is what Ruth said, and it goes: 'Entreat me not to leave thee, or to
return from following after thee: for whither thou goest, I will go: and
where thou lodgest, I will lodge: thy people will be my people, and thy
God my God.' "

"Is *that* what it says? Are you sure?" Noah didn't wait for a reply.
He had already left the room.

"Where are you going?" called Rachel. "Dinner is almost ready!"

"I'm going over to the Adamses," shouted Noah, who was already out
of the house and heading down the path.

"What in the world is wrong with Noah?" asked Izaak, who had
just turned into the doorway. "He seems in a great hurry to leave."

"Nothing is wrong. I guess everything is right. I guess Sarah told him.
Are you ready for a bit of dinner, future father-in-law?"

110

the winter of 1805...

THE BARN

IZAAK

LOG CART

Bonking

CELLAR

RACHEL

SARAH

NOAH

the new mill

The old water wheels froze tight during winter.

THE BRIDGE

SLED

RN FIELD

Snow rolling to make a smooth highway for sleds.

22 : Shortest day of the year, Midwinter Day. Finished Sarah's rocking chair. Made Mother a candlestick.

Noah had gone to the under-room of the mill to start up the fire, only to find his father already working at the forge. Both had the same idea— to make a Christmas candlestick for Rachel.

"You have already started one!" said Noah in disappointment.

"I didn't know that you were going to give Mother the same thing," said Izaak, "but why don't you make a matching stick? Then she could have a fine pair of candlesticks for Christmas. I'm sure she'd like nothing better."

> *23 : Draped the room with laurel leaves on a string. Every-thing is set for Christmas. Sarah's parents should arrive tomorrow.*
> *24 : It was a fine Day Before Christmas. Sarah's parents ar-rived and I met them. They are good people and I hope they approve of me.*

Noah left off with that thought. He snuffed out the candle and suddenly the smell of bayberry filled the room. He knew then that his mother had put this special candle in his room for the holiday occasion. Everything seemed perfect now. He could hear the crackling of the fire in the next room and his father returning from the barn after putting Bessie and Bang "to bed." He remembered how on this night all animals were supposed to speak. On Christmas Eve the livestock are supposed to discuss their master, after the manner in which they were said to have done of the Great Master in the manger at Bethlehem. He wondered what Bessie and Bang might say.

He looked out of his window, but there was no moon. A few crystals of snow blew against the glass from the dark outer world. The winter of 1805 had taken over the American landscape.

A MUSEUM
of
Early American
TOOLS

by

ERIC · SLOANE

This sketchbook is dedicated to the unrecorded pioneer Americans who fashioned their own tools. Although mass production has made their old tools obsolete, along with Early American individualism, these ancient implements are symbols of a sincerity, an integrity, and an excellency that the unionized craftsman of today might do well to emulate.

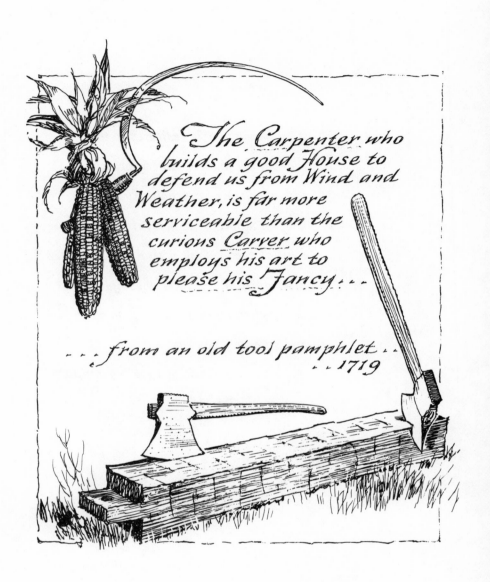

The Carpenter who builds a good House to defend us from Wind and Weather, is far more serviceable than the curious Carver who employs his art to please his Fancy...

...from an old tool pamphlet... ..1719

116

Author's Note.

I like the sound of the word museum. Perhaps because the word root refers less to an actual collection of things than to the musing, cogitating, and reflecting that one does while beholding a collection.

Nowadays we use the word museum to identify a big, housed collection, but in the days of Early America it usually meant a simple library or some printed collection of facts. There were magazinelike books, such as "Merry's *Museum*," and there were newspaperlike publications, such as "The Farmer's *Museum*," but the fine word museum has since drifted from the world of writing. Because it is my hobby to recapture what I believe to be the good things of the past, I hope the reader will accept and enjoy my title, *A Museum of Early American Tools*.

The word magazine was first used to identify what we now might call a museum; it then meant "storehouse," or "housed collection" (powder magazine, for instance). And the first printed magazines were (like the newspapers of that day) printed on one piece of paper and folded once or perhaps twice—never in the book-form of today's magazine.

In presenting my collection of drawings as a museum, I hope that it will, like a scrapbook, induce musing and reflecting, and that it will draw the reader back into the quite different world of Early America. The rambling sequence of subjects is no accident: I would like my reader to "stroll" through this book as he would through a museum.

We might regard some of the old tools as clumsy or ugly unless we look at them in terms of the century in which they were used. Many of today's tools would have been considered ugly, clumsy, and completely undesirable by the early craftsmen. The steel and plastic handles we now have, for example, lack the spring and "feel" of seasoned wood that experts know. Shovels were made of wood not because of a lack of metal (as many assume) but because it was supposed that grain and apples were harmed by contact with metal. You might think of a wooden shovel as being short-lived, yet, although thousands of wooden shovels are to be found in antique shops and collections, almost no early metal shovels remain.

Most of today's tools have the cheapness of mass production; the old hand-made tools often had design that made them examples of fine art. Lumber cut and sold as a "two by four" was once an honest two inches by four inches; even today there are people who are shocked to learn that our lumber, because it is measured before being trimmed and planed, is sold at a quite untrue measurement. Builders who constructed rooms that were not accurately square (and why should they be?) are now regarded as slipshod and careless; yet the old buildings have stood the test much better than will many we are now building, for the joints and braces were made with much greater care than today's craftsmen consider "necessary." Floor boards were never the same width at one end as they were at the other. Quaint or poor workmanship? Not at all. The finished effect is finer than the monotony of today's narrow-width floor boards. A building pinned together with hand-whittled wooden pins? We don't have to do that sort of thing today! But if we built for lastingness and for handing down to future generations we would do so, for wooden pins work much better than nails: they hold tighter, they don't rust and rot the beams.

While I was putting this book together, my neighbor bought a good new saw and left it out overnight in the dew. Its shiny newness had given way to the orange of rust, and he telephoned me to ask for help in removing it. I took it to clean and loaned him one of my early saws to use in the meantime. The old saw was one I found in the stone wall of an ancient barn. It is still sharp and clean of rust.

And so it goes. The craftsman of yesterday might look like a poorly informed man only before we take a longer and a better look. His tools might appear pathetically poor, but his ways were honest and lasting and beautiful to an extent that is today deemed over and above requirements. How poor and dishonest and ugly and temporary are the results

118

so many modern workers whose constant aim is more to make the
ost money from their profession instead of producing the most honest
d beautiful and lasting things. I feel that a good way of studying the
onscience and personality of the anonymous pioneer American—so
at I may emulate some of his ways—is by collecting and analyzing the
ols with which he worked.

As a collector of early tools, I have also been a collector of informa-
n. Antique implements have a price tag on them, but for the in-
rmation that has been priceless and gratis, I am indebted to the men at
ylestown, Shelburne, Winterthur, Cooperstown, Sturbridge, Wil-
msburg, and Saugus. I learned much from two excellent books,
ercer's Ancient Carpenters' Tools *and Wildung's* Woodworking
ols, and from the Early American Industries Association's publication,
he Chronicle.

Eric Sloane

eather Hill

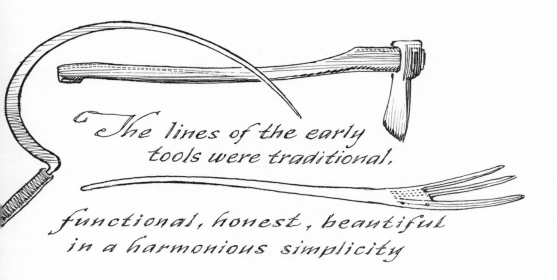

The lines of the early tools were traditional, functional, honest, beautiful in a harmonious simplicity

Contents

a Museum of
of
Early
American
Tools

The Romance of Tools.

Finding an ancient tool in a stone fence or in a dark corner of some decaying barn is receiving a symbol from another world, for it gives you a particular and interesting contact with the past. Men used to build and create as much for future generations as for their own needs, so their tools have a special message for us and our time. When you hold an early implement, when you close your hand over the worn wooden handle, you know exactly how it felt to the craftsman whose hand had smoothed it to its rich patina. In that instant you are as close to that craftsman as you can be—even closer than if you live in the house that he built or sit in the chair that he made. In that moment you are near to another being in another life, and you are that much richer.

Why an ancient tool should be closer to the early craftsman than a modern tool is to a modern workman is not readily understood by most people. Even the ardent collector is sometimes unaware of the reason an ancient tool meant so much to its user. But reason there is. Henry Ward Beecher said it nicely when he explained that "a tool is but the extension of a man's hand." Whereas today's implements are designed with the idea of "getting a job done quickly," there was an added quality to the early implements and an added quality to early workmanship too. For, like the nails on a beast's paws, the old tools were so much an extension of a man's hand or an added appendage to his arm, that the resulting workmanship seemed to flow directly from the body of the maker and to carry something of himself into the work. True, by looking at an old house or an old piece of furniture, you can imagine the maker much more clearly than you can by beholding anything made today.

The early implement was also a piece of art, as much as the work it

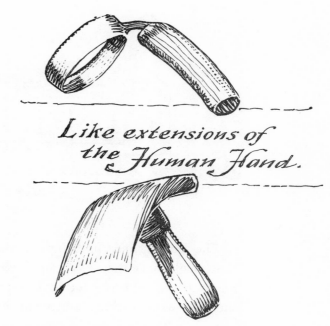

Like extensions of the Human Hand.

fashioned, for the worker designed his tools too. In Early America the ironworkers forged only the cutting blade; they gave no thought to the design of the wooden handle and the rest of the finished tool. Plane blades and even knife-blades were hand-forged and sold like axe heads, and the craftsman was left to make his own wooden "hand" to hold the "fingernail," or cutting part. A small hand needed a small handle and a big hand needed a big handle; the man who used an apprentice had notches in his big plane that enabled the apprentice to help push it along with a stick.

A man whose architectural creations followed the Greek or Roman tradition would find it natural to include Greek or Roman artistic touches in the ornamentation of his implements. Decoration on the early tool, however, sprang from the pride of the maker rather than from any custom.

The feeling that certain tools had souls of their own was not unusual; an axe might be marked "Tom" or "Jack" simply because the owner felt it was a companion worthy of a pet name. All this sounds strangely superstitious. Yet today motor trucks are often named "Sally" or "Babe"; boats almost always have names; even large machine tools, such as presses or bulldozers, are graced with pet names.

125

Sacred initials on one side, the date on the other.

The religious man probably felt that sacred initials or Biblical quotations might have their effect upon the work done by that tool. Perhaps mindful that the carpenter Jesus once worked with such tools, some of the early woodworking implements have crosses carved upon them.

One of the finer pieces in a recent showing of modern art was a piece of steel that curved like a bird's wing. It was set into a square block of wood and its title in the catalogue was "Number 1760." The artist had an even more honest sense of beauty than a sense of humor, for if you looked closely and with an informed eye, you could recognize the piece as the head of an Early American "goose wing" broad axe. In the back of the blade, the year 1760 had been marked, which, of course, explained the title. To many it was, at first, the most beautiful piece of art there

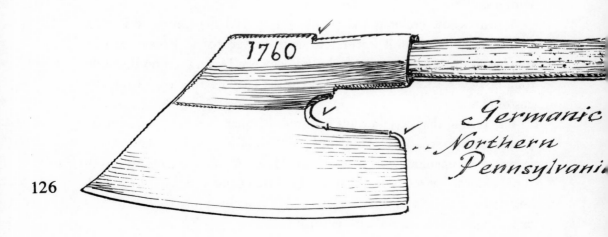

Germanic
Northern
Pennsylvania

but when they learned that it was only an old axe head, they felt as if they had been hoaxed. How, after all, could an axe head be considered a work of art!

The Civil War period marked a turning point in tool design, as it did for so much Americana. Before that time, the word tool meant an implement that could make one thing at a time; mass-production tools then entered the scene, and the word tool, which had meant only "hand tool," took on many added meanings. Finally the word tool came to mean any item having to do with the production of an item; it could be the machine and also the building that housed the machine. Even the salesmen, the advertising gadgets, and the business offices are "tools of the trade."

Generally speaking, hand tools made after the Civil War period lacked the simple beauty of those of the ante-bellum period. Things were made to sell quickly, things were made in large quantities so that they could be catalogued identically, and hand-made implements began to disappear. Wooden handles became "fancier," more curved and ornamental, but the severe beauty of folk art and primitive usage was lost. Saw handles became "trickier"; they were designed to appeal to the eye instead of to fit the hand. Axe handles, which had always been almost straight, as a good club should be, took on curves such as the "fawn foot" and the "scroll knob." By 1885, handles on axes and adzes had become almost too curved, but by the 1900's they settled down to a sensible and standard design, such as that of those you can buy now at the hardware store.

Before the Civil War, most axe handles (like the handles of all tools) were made by the man who would use the axe. A pattern was cut from a piece of flat wood and saved as the model from which future handles would be fashioned. Axe patterns (which you can still find in old barns) were so subtly curved and proportioned that they were as distinctive as a man's signature; you could take one look and say "This tool belongs to Jones" or "That tool belongs to Smith." Very often an axe-handle pattern was handed down from generation to generation, and it was considered counterfeit for another family to copy it.

While we are on the subject of the handles of old tools, I would like to point out that the collector should understand something of the philosophy about the connection between the workman's hand and that

127

part of a hand tool that he touches. Most modern workmen will scoff at the idea, but any fine craftsman will tell you that the right wooden handle (let us say, on a hammer) helps you along with your work. A metal or plastic handle or even an incorrect wooden handle can feel "dead" and not "spring back" against pressure, thus causing blisters and slowing your work. The proper handle's "feel" or "heft" is the unexplainable quality that a fine violin has to the musician. *The Oxford History of Technology* quotes Christian Barman's comments on an exhibition of early hand tools: "Everybody who appreciates the qualities of materials loves wood, and here was wood formed into a special kind of tactile sculpture made to be felt with the hand. I remembered that old craftsmen, when they buy a new set of modern chisels, throw away the handles and carefully fit their own. These handles, polished bright by a lifetime of use, became part of their owners' lives."

Always in the fine art of working with wood, the old-time craftsman's laboratory was in his head and his hands and his heart. He called it "knack"; some now believe it was a "sixth sense" or an extrasensory power. Elusive as this "knack" may be, it is the most important part of those small differences that distinguish the master craftsman from the good workman.

When we consider tools, we are dealing with human benefactors of the most primary sort. Tools increase and vary human power; they economize human time, and they convert raw substances into valuable and useful products. So when we muse on historic tools as symbols, we are always analyzing the romance of human progress.

Although Early American tools were traditional in design to such an extent that one can usually tell the nationality of the maker, there are almost always subtle differences and decorative touches in design that equally identify the region of American countryside from which the tool came. A collector can easily tell a piece coming from Pennsylvania from one originating in Connecticut. This distinctiveness was often intentional; the Early American's urge for identification was born of pride both in himself and in his time. An extraordinary awareness of life and time permeated our early days; when something was made and the maker was satisfied, it wasn't complete until his mark and the date were added.

Nowadays things are almost obsolete before they leave the drawing board. How lucky we are that so many of the old tools and the things that were made with them were dated and touched with the craftsman's art.

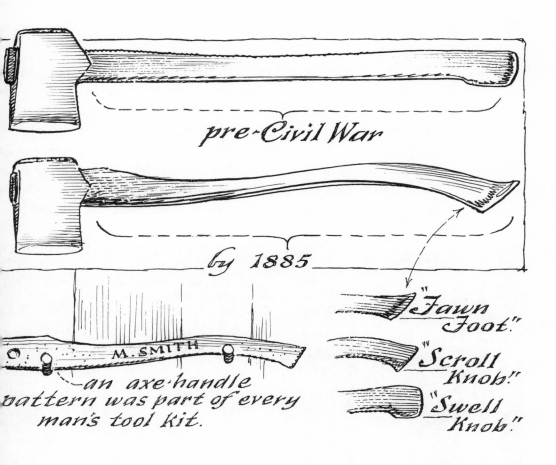

pre-Civil War

by 1885

"Fawn Foot."

"Scroll Knob."

"Swell Knob."

M. SMITH

an axe-handle pattern was part of every man's tool kit.

Crude Shops, Magnificent Results.

After the Civil War, factory-made things became popular and the t[...]
house was limited to such minor work as farm repairs. The Dominy Sh[...]
(shown below) was used by Nathaniel Dominy IV (1737–1812) a[...]
his son Nathaniel V (1770–1852). This entire shop, including man[...]
script accounts covering the period from 1762 until 1829, has been ke[...]
intact at the Henry Francis du Pont Winterthur Museum in Delawa[...]
The visitor's first reaction is usually "What a primitive shop!" Yet t[...]
magnificent table standing in the center of the room was made in it.

130

Courtesy, Henry Francis du Pont Winterthur Museum

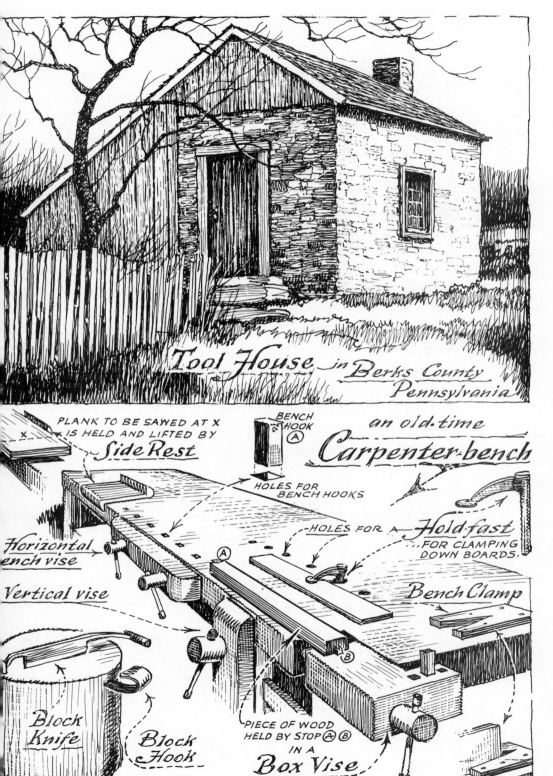

Tool House in *Berks County Pennsylvania*

PLANK TO BE SAWED AT X
IS HELD AND LIFTED BY
Side Rest

BENCH
HOOK
Ⓐ

an old-time
Carpenter-bench

HOLES FOR
BENCH HOOKS

HOLES FOR A *Hold-fast*
FOR CLAMPING
DOWN BOARDS.

Horizontal bench vise

Ⓐ

Bench Clamp

Vertical vise

Block Knife

Block Hook

Ⓑ

PIECE OF WOOD
HELD BY STOP Ⓐ Ⓑ
IN A
Box Vise

131

An Ax is an Axe!

No matter how you spell it (both ways are correct), it is natural to start off a sketchbook of Early American implements with this tool. America was a new world of unending wood where a man armed with only a felling axe could enter the forest and survive. With his axe he could clear the land of trees, cut fuel, build a bridge, a house, and furniture. With his axe he could fashion snares for game and, in a pinch, use it to protect himself against marauding Indians or wild beasts. No wonder the first settlers carried axes in their belts and treated them with a respect like that of a soldier toward his sword or side arms.

As was true of all first American artifacts, our earliest axes were like those from abroad. They had well-curved, gracefully fashioned blades, and they lacked the bulky polls such as those that identify the pure American design. The heavy poll appears to be for hammering (indeed it could have been used for such), yet it was devised to serve as a weight to give more momentum to chopping. Few early polless axes have survived except those traded with the Indians (trade axes).

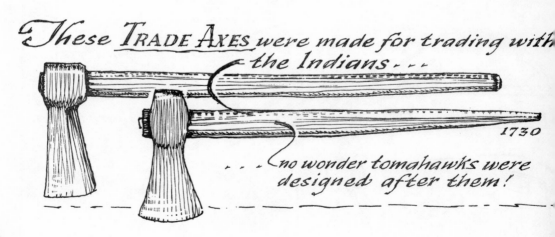

These TRADE AXES were made for trading with the Indians ...

1730

... no wonder tomahawks were designed after them!

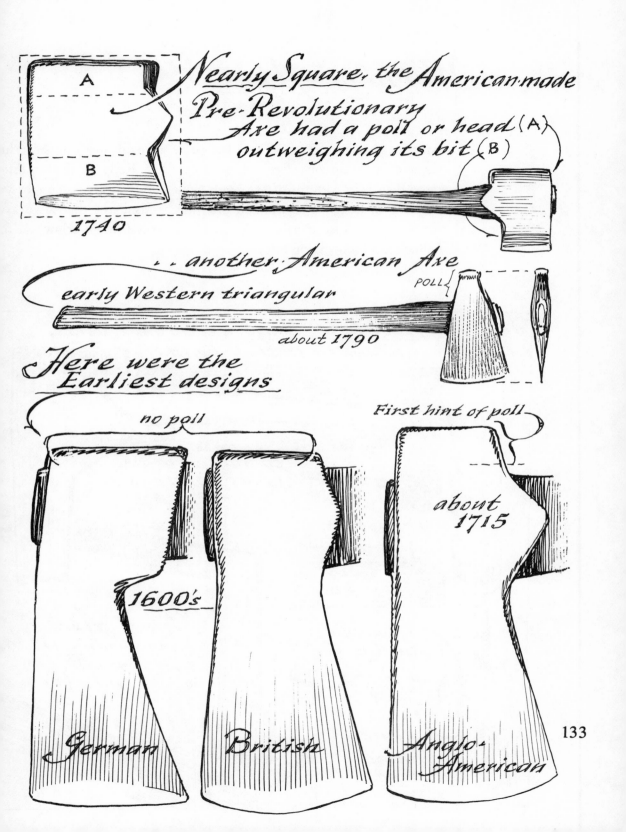

Nearly Square, the *American made*
Pre-Revolutionary
Axe had a poll or head (A)
outweighing its bit (B)

A

B

1740

. . . *another American Axe*

early Western triangular

POLL

about 1790

Here were the
Earliest designs

no poll

First hint of poll

about 1715

1600's

German

British

Anglo-
American

133

A World of Axes

America's wealth of wood and her pride in carpenter craftsmansh[ip]
resulted in an amazing array of specialty tools. Early catalogues list[ed]
more than fifty patterns of axe heads alone, all doing the same jobs y[et]
differing in design. Farmers and blacksmiths fashioned their own ax[es]
for framing and for mortising the beams of barns (shown below) or f[or]
felling trees (shown opposite).

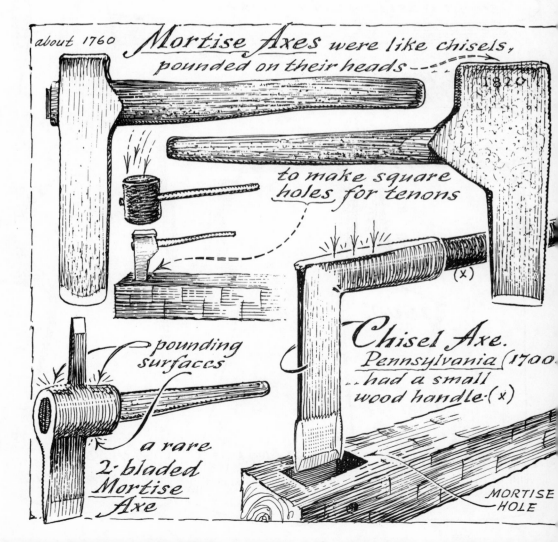

about 1760

Mortise Axes were like chisels, pounded on their heads ---

1820

to make square holes for tenons

pounding surfaces

(x)

Chisel Axe.
Pennsylvania (1700[)]
...had a small
wood handle·(x)

a rare
2·bladed
Mortise
Axe

MORTISE HOLE

134

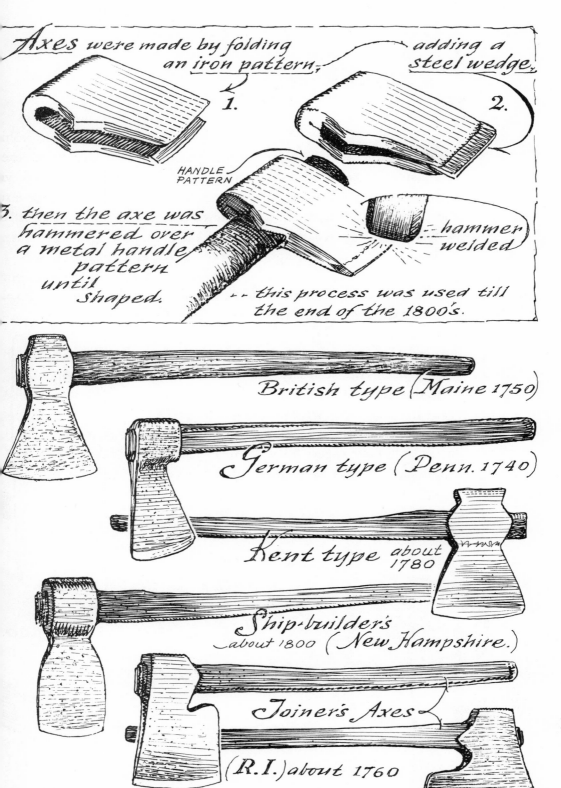

Axes were made by folding an iron pattern, adding a steel wedge.

1.

2.

HANDLE PATTERN

3. then the axe was hammered over a metal handle pattern until shaped.

hammer welded

-- this process was used till the end of the 1800's.

British type (Maine 1750)

German type (Penn. 1740)

Kent type about 1780

Ship-builder's about 1800 (New Hampshire.)

Joiner's Axes

(R.I.) about 1760

135

The Broad Axe:

A most essential Early American tool was the chisel-edged broad axe. Thousands of them are still around, but people seeing this broad axe often take it for a very big and clumsy felling axe. Because few museums bother either to include the tool or to explain its use, few people really know how it was used. Actually, it was a kind of plane or striking chisel that early Americans used for hewing round logs into square beams.

More than twice the size of a felling axe, this tool had a short bent handle protruding outward from the side of the axe head with the bevel (basil or chisel-slant) on that same side. Two hands were used; the process was called "squaring" or "hewing."

The American-style broad axe had a fair-sized squarish head, or poll (as the other American-style axes did); European types had none.

Although hand-hewn timbers in old buildings are commonly called "adzed beams," they were usually broad-axed.

Although some odd people hack up beams "to make them appear hand done," the most expert broad-axe man cut the fewest axe marks, and those that were left were spaced nicely—never haphazardly.

Never haphazard!

136

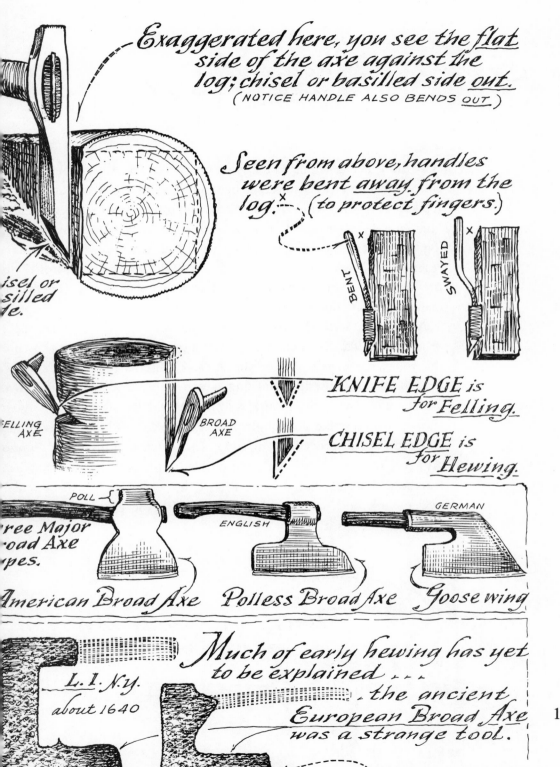

Exaggerated here, you see the flat side of the axe against the log; chisel or basilled side out.
(NOTICE HANDLE ALSO BENDS OUT.)

Seen from above, handles were bent away from the log. × *(to protect fingers.)*

BENT

SWAYED

isel or silled de.

ELLING AXE

BROAD AXE

KNIFE EDGE is *for Felling.*

CHISEL EDGE is *for Hewing.*

POLL

ENGLISH

GERMAN

ree Major road Axe pes.

American Broad Axe   Polless Broad Axe   Goose wing

L.I.N.Y. *about 1640*

Much of early hewing has yet to be explained ...

... the ancient European Broad Axe was a strange tool.

DUG UP AT JAMESTOWN

137

How the Broad Axe was Used

Any old-timer is willing to tell you how to use a broad axe, but each on is bound to describe a different method. Trying to ferret out the tru I asked everyone who visited my collection—if the visitor claimed knew the art—to demonstrate broad-axing. Some "used to stand upon t log, hewing as they walked along it." "But you wouldn't be able reach the log with so short a handle! You'd chop your toes off!" w my reply. But they insisted, and offered to demonstrate. The doct managed to sew one toe back on very nicely.

Actually, a walk-along-the-log method was used, but with a speci broad axe unlike the ancient ones with bent handles. (This is shown the following page.) As for the ancient chisel-edged broad axe, yc walked *alongside* the log, working as you went. One man would swir horizontally (with the grain); another would hit straight downward another would strike at an angle. As for me, I contend there was no ger erally accepted procedure. Mercer (in *Ancient Carpenters' Tools* says that the broad axe was usually "held with both hands, right han foremost. The leg face was set against the workman's left side and hewed with both hands, not longways with the grain but diagonall *downward* across it."

"DOGS" were used to fasten logs to be worked upor

two types

138

Broad-axing began with a *Chalk-Line*, as the
log was bark-stripped
to the brown under-bark
and "twanged" with a
Squaring Cord.

MAKING CHALK-LINE AT A

①

CHALK

② *First standing on the log
with a long-handled
Felling Axe*

"Scoring to the Line"

nd scoring
eep vertical
ts.

ften the pieces between
tervals
        were split off.

Dog

③

.. then standing *alongside*.

"Hewing to the Line."

*Holding the Broad axe
with two hands, right
hand foremost*———— *and
eft knee close to the log.*
the final smooth-hewing was done

139

A Giant and a Midget.

The straight-handled broad axe—a knife-edged axe beveled on both side —was usually used to hew railroad ties. Logging railroads that make thei ties out of softwood hew just two sides of the log. A tree was felled a a slight angle (held at one end by its own branches), and the hewe walked first up and then down, flattening the sides as he went. The sam axe was used both for scoring and hewing! This process seems difficul but it was fast.

Because this axe has a straight handle, it is often mistaken for som re-handled ancient broad axe, ground on two sides to convert it into felling axe. The only clue to its true use is that its ponderous head i much too heavy to swing sideways as an axe must be swung in felling

The smallest version of the hewing axe is the carpenter's hewing hatchet (below). It sometimes looks like a toy model of the big one Never used to split wood or to drive nails, these hatchets were used for shaping.

a tiny Carpenter's Hewing Hatchet

about 1725

side view.

140

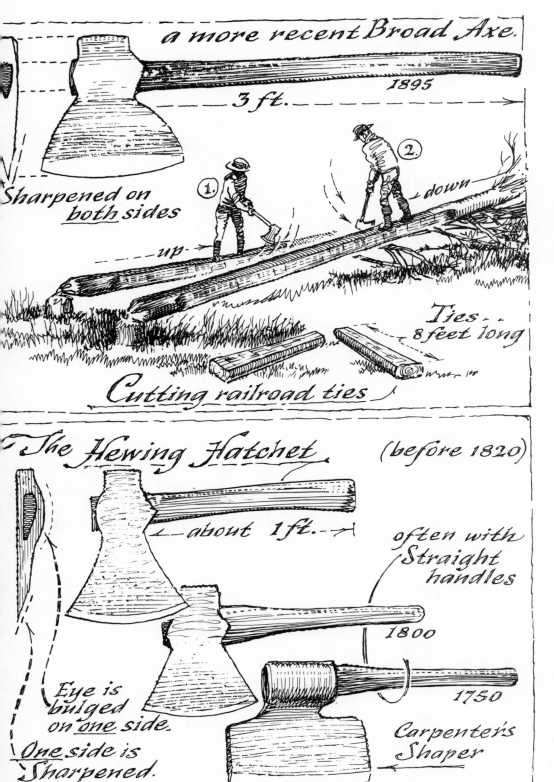

a more recent Broad Axe.

1895

3 ft.

Sharpened on <u>both</u> sides

1.

2.

down

up

Ties...
8 feet long

Cutting railroad ties

The Hewing Hatchet (before 1820)

about 1 ft.

often with
Straight
handles

1800

Eye is
bulged
on <u>one</u> side.

One side is
Sharpened.

1750

Carpenter's
Shaper

141

The Hatchet.

Today's household hatchet began as the "shingling hatchet." This had a flared shape with slightly rounded nail-hammering head and a nail-pulling notch in the bit. Because the first New World roofs were thatched, shingling hatchets were unknown to the early settler. Shingling hatchets so often fell from roofs being worked on that roofers frequently had them strung for hanging at the wrist.

The "lathing hatchet" is recognized by its flat outside contour, made so nails could be struck near a ceiling without hitting it. If the axe head flared, the flare was on the inside of the bit. It soon became the favorite carpenter's tool to replace the awkward cooper's hatchet. (See opposite. The cooper rounding off a barrel head is using a cooper's hatchet; notice how it was held close to its head rather than by the end of its handle.)

The 1790 American axe-hatchet (shown below) was a miniature model of the square-headed American axe with the poll that outweighed the bit.

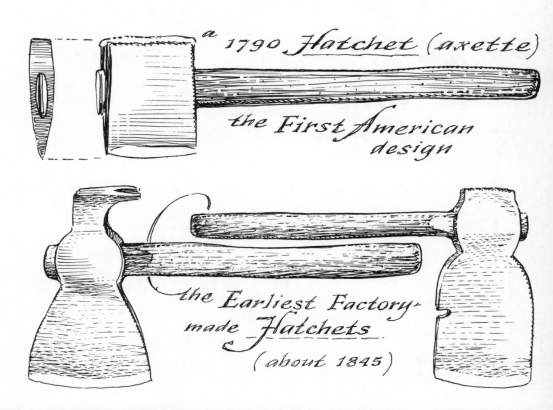

a 1790 *Hatchet* (*axette*)

the *First American design*

142

the *Earliest Factory-made Hatchets*

(*about 1845*)

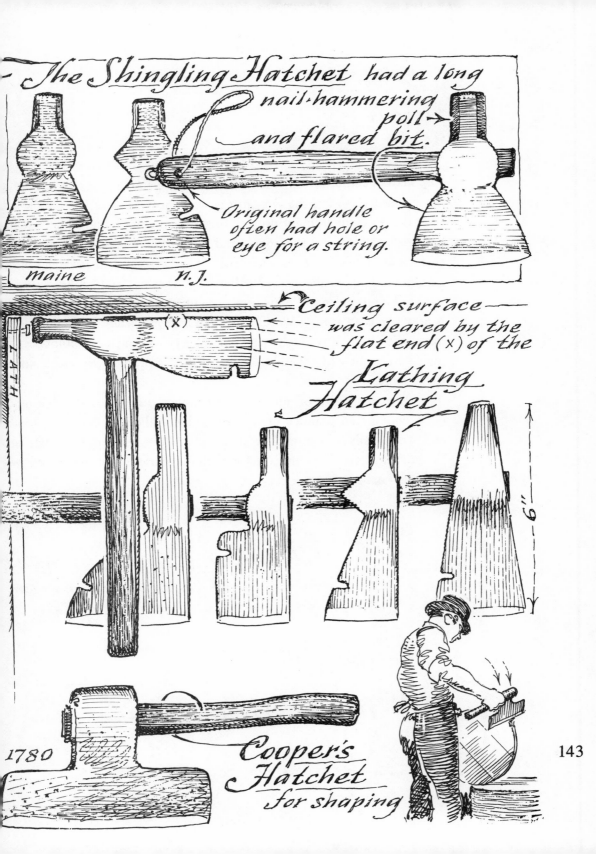

The Shingling Hatchet had a long nail-hammering poll and flared bit.

Original handle often had hole or eye for a string.

Maine

n.J.

Ceiling surface was cleared by the flat end (x) of the _Lathing Hatchet_

LATH

(x)

6"

1780

Cooper's Hatchet for shaping

143

Hammers

The claw hammer hasn't changed much since about 75 A.D. Aside from its aesthetic qualities, the Roman example shown below has a most efficient design (which might do well to show up any day now).

The use of nails in the 1600's and the 1700's was more efficient then than now. The early square-cut nails, for instance, had greater holding power than our round nails; furthermore, they retarded splitting of the wood. The practice of "clinching" (bending over the protruding point) is now regarded as poor workmanship, but its efficiency is obvious. Early batten doors with wrought nails on the outside and bent points on the inside are cemented together so well that it is next to impossible to pry them apart.

Perhaps the rarity of ancient iron hammers in America is due to the once widespread practice of using wooden mallets to drive in wooden nails (tree-nails or trunnels), even wooden nails of a tiny toothpick size. Wooden mallets were also used as striking chisels; iron hammers, only for metal nails.

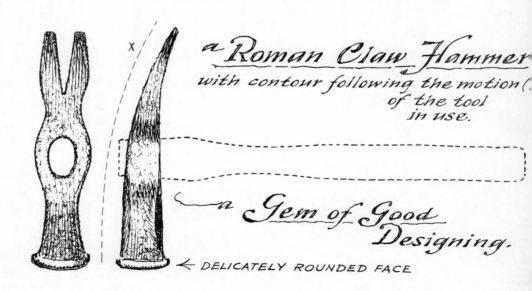

X

a Roman Claw Hammer
with contour following the motion
of the tool
in use.

a Gem of Good Designing.

← DELICATELY ROUNDED FACE

144

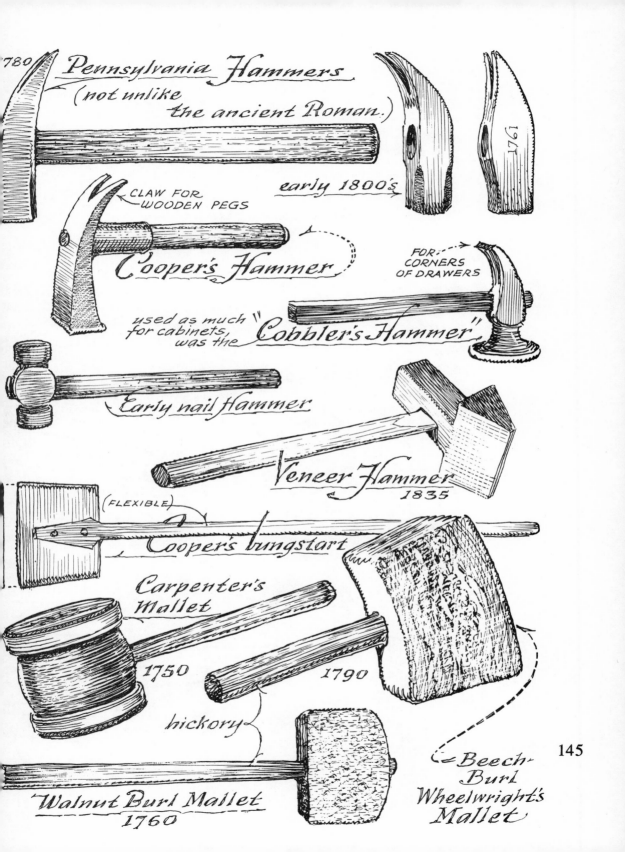

'780

Pennsylvania Hammers
(not unlike
the ancient Roman.)

1761

early 1800's

CLAW FOR
WOODEN PEGS

Cooper's Hammer

FOR
CORNERS
OF DRAWERS

used as much
for cabinets,
was the "Cobbler's Hammer"

Early nail Hammer

Veneer Hammer
1835

(FLEXIBLE)

Cooper's bungstart

Carpenter's
Mallet

1750

1790

hickory

145

Beech-
Burl
Wheelwright's
Mallet

Walnut Burl Mallet
1760

The Axe and the Log House.

Before we leave the subject of axes, the reader will be interested in seeing just what was expected of the axe. Here are some standard log-house notches often made with only the axe.

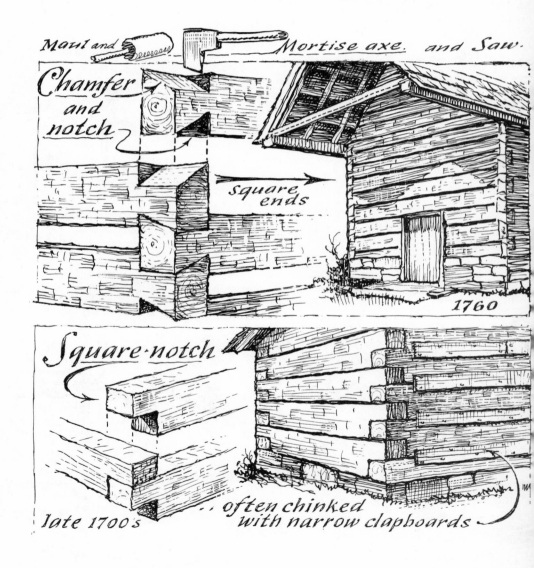

Maul and
Mortise axe. and Saw.

Chamfer and notch

square ends

1760

Square·notch

late 1700's

..often chinked with narrow clapboards

Saddle-notch

1. Axe cut

2. Gutter Adze to round out

Sharp-notch · could be done with axe alone.

2 slashes and notch below 3

1 2

3

Dovetail-notch   came from Sweden (c.1640)

Lip adze and axe.

upper notch slants out to drain rain.

147

The Adze

The idea of a sharp tool with its blade at a right angle to the handle is most ancient. The Early American version was swung in the curvature of the blade, with the arm and tool forming the radius.

Because of its flaring square end, the adze head had to be removable (as the bevel to be sharpened was on the inside and inaccessible to a grind stone). Some of the earliest adzes, however, had nonremovable heads which had to be sharpened with a whetstone.

The shipwright's adze had a long peg-poll for driving down broken nails (and to prevent the blade from being nicked).

As shown below, the right-angle cuts on old beams are make-ready scorings for broad-axe work, not so-called "adze marks." Only on special "parlor beams" (these were made to be exposed) was the adze introduced; then the surface effect was from a delicate ripple to almost complete smoothness.

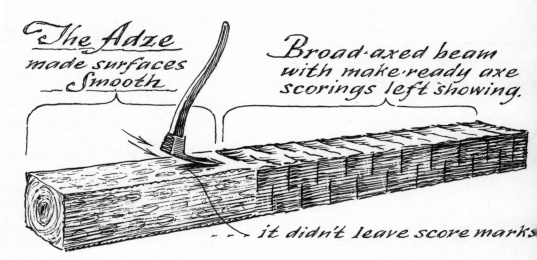

The Adze made surfaces Smooth

Broad-axed beam with make-ready axe scorings left showing.

- - - it didn't leave score marks

148

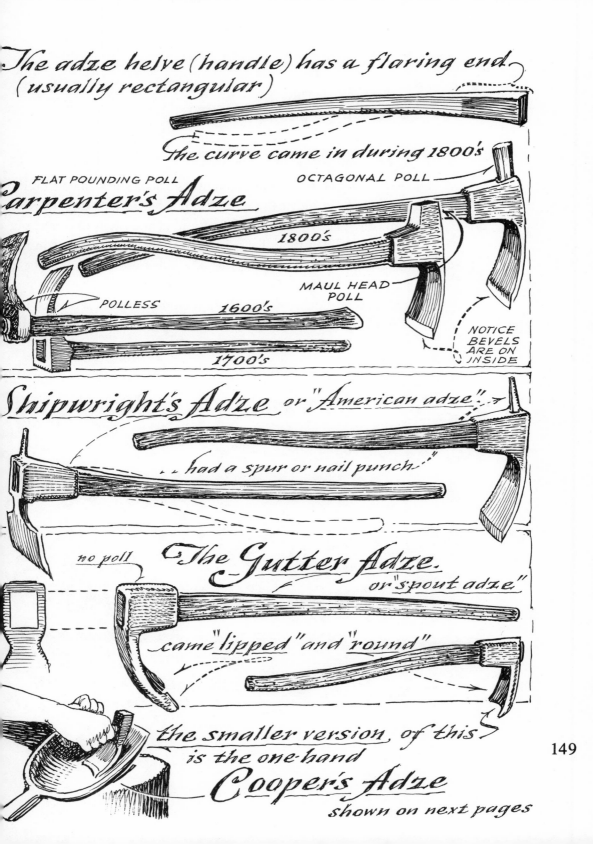

The adze helve (handle) has a flaring end.
(usually rectangular)

The curve came in during 1800's

FLAT POUNDING POLL   OCTAGONAL POLL

Carpenter's Adze

1800's

POLLESS   1600's

MAUL HEAD POLL

1700's

NOTICE BEVELS ARE ON INSIDE

Shipwright's Adze or "American adze"

...had a spur or nail punch...

no poll   The Gutter Adze.

or "spout adze"

came "lipped" and "round"

the smaller version, of this
is the one-hand
Cooper's Adze
shown on next pages

149

Canoes and Bowls

The word canoe (canow and canoo in the 1600's) described a hollow[ed] out log. Until the Indians saw the English hand adze, they used fire [to] burn out the hollow portion and flint knives and shells to scrape out [the] burned wood. Then they devised their own adze, using flint instead [of] metal for the blade. The scoop, or scorp, became refined as the ye[ars] went by, and, finally, it became a finishing tool.

Maple and ash burls (wartlike bumps on tree trunks) were first burn[ed] and then scorped out, making the toughest and most durable of all bow[ls]

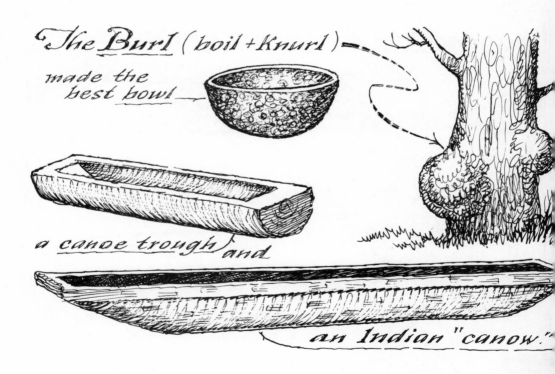

The Burl (boil + knurl) made the best bowl

a canoe trough and

an Indian "canow."

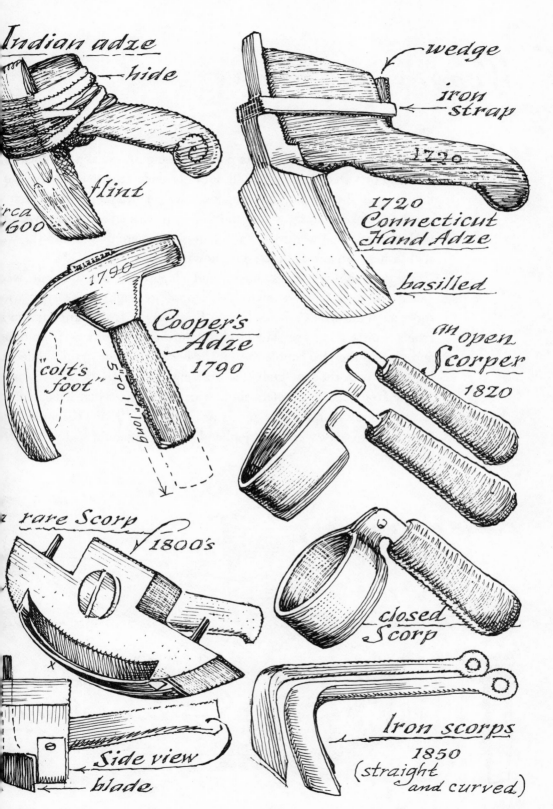

Indian adze

hide

flint

circa 1600

wedge

iron strap

1720

1720
Connecticut
Hand Adze

basilled

1790

Cooper's
Adze
1790

"colt's foot"

5 to 11" long

an open
Scorper
1820

a rare Scorp

1800's

closed
Scorp

Side view

blade

Iron scorps
1850
(straight
and curved)

151

Wedges and Froes

A good woodsman would never consider using his axe as a hammer to [drive?] the head of a wedge. That would not only widen the eye but also wo[uld] finally split the cheeks, finishing off the axe head forever. Yet ma[ny] paintings of Lincoln show him splitting rails with an axe. Rails were s[plit] with wedges. Iron wedges (or wooden gluts) were driven into the wo[od] with a heavy maul or beetle (as shown below).

To split shingles, laths, staves, and clapboards, a knife-type wed[ge] called a froe or frow (shown on the opposite page) was struck wit[h a] short maul known as a froe-club. In England the froe is known also a[s] fromard or rending-axe. The clapboard-maker struck away from hims[elf] and twisted the froe handle to split the board with the grain, while str[ik]-ing away with the froe-club (see drawing).

The froe became obsolete about a century ago, when it became c[us]-tomary to saw-cut shingles and laths. Till then, "riving" shingles wa[s a] favorite rainy-day woodshed job, and every household had several fr[oes] on hand.

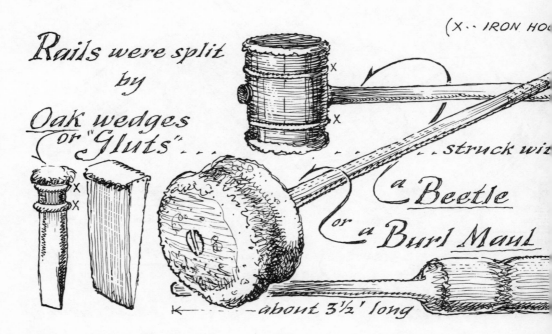

Rails were split by Oak wedges or "Gluts"...

(X·· IRON HO[OP?]

...struck wi[th] a Beetle or a Burl Maul

about 3½' long

152

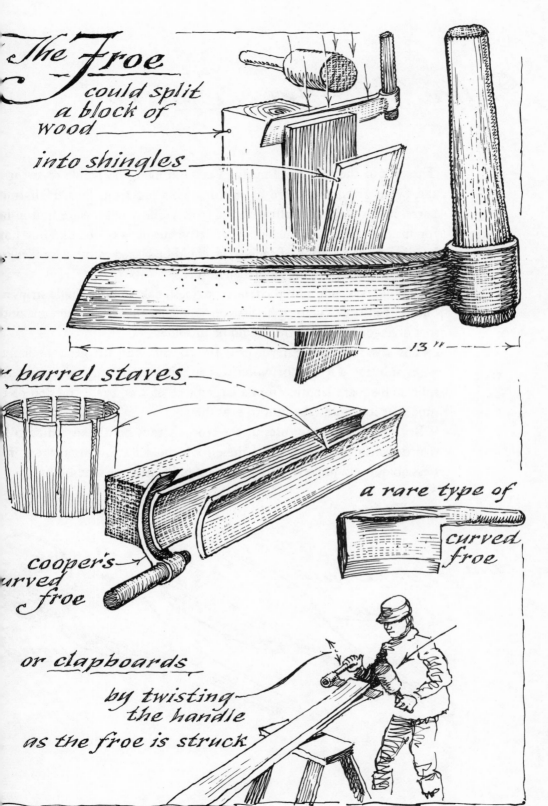

The Froe

could split
a block of
wood

into shingles

13"

barrel staves

cooper's
curved
froe

a rare type of

curved
froe

or clapboards

by twisting
the handle

as the froe is struck

153

The Fine Art of Splitting.

The uses of the froe were many. Very old men, too feeble to swing [an] axe, were given the chore of splitting kindling from logs. Half-rou[nd] barrel hoops were also split with the froe. Willow poles were split in h[alf] for making gates and hurdles. The early hurdle was not like our ho[rse] hurdle; it was a section of fence that could be lashed to other similar se[c-] tions to make a portable animal enclosure.

Lathing was split with the froe from fresh oak, in both single strips a[nd] "flats." Lath flats were split first on one side, then the other, making [a] sort of accordion piece that could be unfolded.

The saw was almost never used for cutting with the grain or leng[th-] wise: splitting a length of wood was so much easier. A craftsman co[uld] split inch-square lengths from a large piece of wood in a fraction of t[he] time that it would take him to saw them.

Because of the many uses of the froe, there is hardly an old barn l[eft] that doesn't have a number of these tools tucked away somewhere in [it.] Less ubiquitous, however, are their battered mates, the froe-clubs.

the Froe-Club
new
used

154

No need for a saw! Want a 1" by 2" or a 2" by 3"?

Just split a pole, twist the froe and with three more rives

you've got it!

Early "accordion lath" was made by splitting an oak slab

and pulling it apart

a rare froe is the **Knife Froe**

14"

155

All wrought metal . . . New Hampshire about 1740

Tools with Legs

Chairmaking was one of the earliest industries of the Shakers, so i[t] natural that they were also pioneers in installing their wonderful mech[an]ical appliances onto benches so that operators could sit while worki[ng]. The first American shingle bench may have been made in Maine or Pe[nn]sylvania, but it reached its peak in design with the Shakers.

One Lebanon (New York) shinglemaker filled a request for 5,0[00] shingles in December of 1789, which, apparently, was a usual sort [of] output for one operator. Shaker-made broom-vices, apple parers, na[il] benches, and herb-cutters were installed on legs and attached to stools [of] one kind or another or designed so that the buyer could affix the app[li]ance to a bench he made himself. To sit at work was, all of a sudden[, a] new American pleasure.

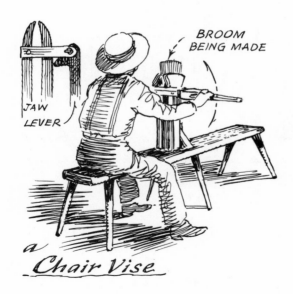

JAW LEVER

BROOM BEING MADE

a *Chair Vise*

PLUNGER

BLADES

an *Apple Quarter*[er]

To Sit at your Work . . .

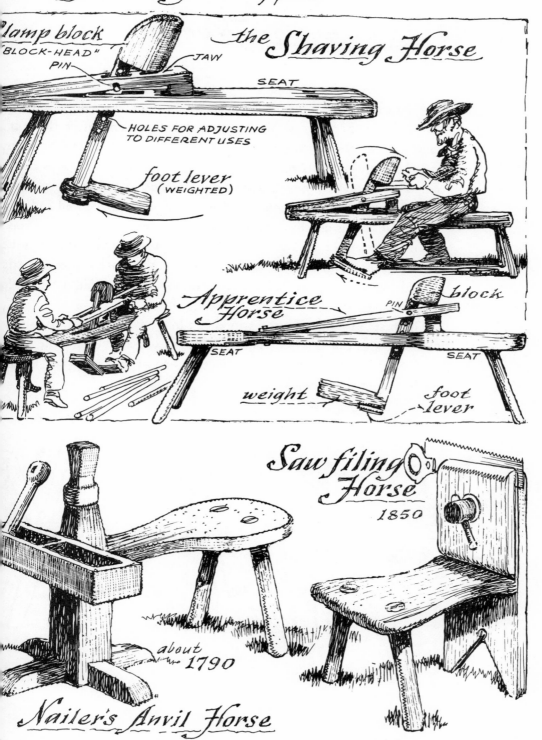

the Shaving Horse

Clamp block "BLOCK-HEAD"

PIN

JAW

SEAT

HOLES FOR ADJUSTING TO DIFFERENT USES

foot lever (WEIGHTED)

Apprentice Horse

block

PIN

SEAT

SEAT

weight

foot lever

Saw filing Horse
1850

about 1790

Nailer's Anvil Horse

157

The American Horse

The American saw-horse is now usually carpenter-made and hasti[l]
knocked together by the workman to be discarded "after the job [is]
done"; it can also be bought ready-made, put together with "two-by[-]
fours" and metal fasteners. Either way the modern saw-horse is more [a]
temporary prop than a well-designed table. The early saw-horse, whic[h]
had a flat top, was wide enough to hold the wood being sawed and oth[er]
things too; it was usually a handy and permanent part of the tool roo[m].

An Early American sawyer's prop was made of two clubs pushe[d]
against a raised log. A later arrangement was the "tackle prop," a stic[k]
pushed through a forked bough; two of these could hold a whole l[og]
in place.

The first "saw-buck" was a tripod (a tilted cross with a stick throug[h]
it) and it was called a "saw-goat" instead of a "saw-buck" (the Dutc[h]
word *zaag-boc* means saw-goat). So the three-legged *zaag-boc* becam[e]
our four-legged saw-buck!

Zaag-boc to

1600's

Saw-buck 1700's

"Sawhorses" were saw-tables

1750

for carpenters...

or when **Logs** were to be sawed, you used a **Sawyer's Prop**.

made of **two "clubs"**

hole

or a **Sawing Tackle**

Single or double

159

"For Making Snitzels"

First called the "drawing knife" because you drew it toward you, the drawknife (or snitzel-knife, as some Pennsylvanians called it) came to America before the Pilgrims. But only with the emergence of the snitzel bank, or shaving horse, which made it simpler to hold the article being shaved, did the drawknife become a most favored tool. There are probably more ancient drawknives extant than any other antique tool.

The drawknife was used to taper the sides of shingles, to rough-size the edges of floor boards and rough-trim paneling before planing them, to fashion axe, rake, and other tool handles, and to make stool legs, ox yokes, pump handles, and wheel spokes. It is easy to see why the drawknife was so popular! The final finishing on much drawknife work was done by our next tool, the spokeshave and scraper.

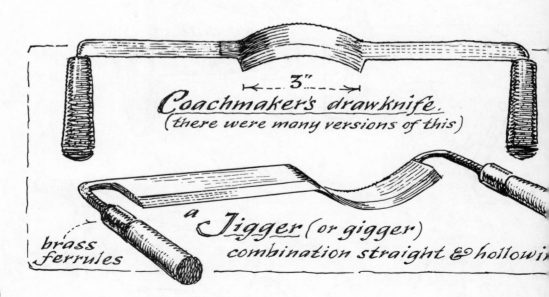

|← - - 3" - - →|
Coachmaker's drawknife.
(there were many versions of this)

brass ferrules

a Jigger (or gigger)
combination straight & hollowi[ng]

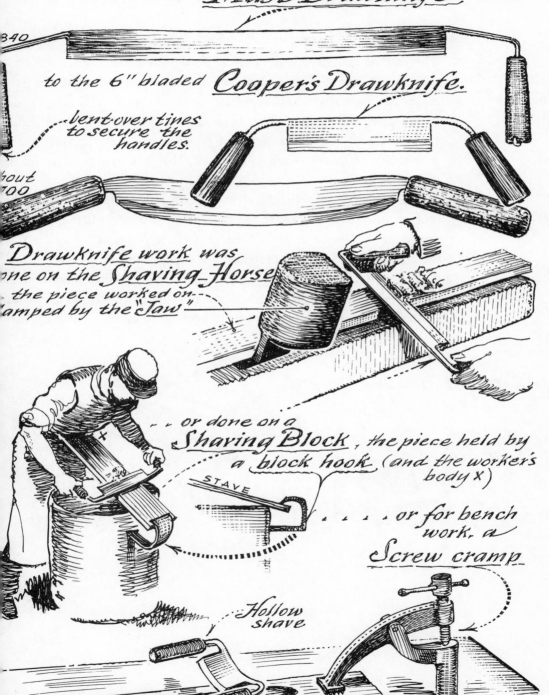

The <u>Drawknife</u> *first called Draft Shave ranged from the* 24" *Mast Drawknife*

840

to the 6" bladed <u>Cooper's Drawknife.</u>

bent over tines to secure the handles.

bout 700

<u>Drawknife work was</u> one on the <u>Shaving Horse</u> ... the piece worked on clamped by the "Jaw"

. . done on a <u>Shaving Block</u> *, the piece held by a* <u>block hook</u> *(and the worker's body X)*

STAVE

. . . . . or for bench work. a <u>Screw cramp</u>

<u>Hollow</u> shave

161

Little Shavers and Big

The difference between the drawknife and its little brother the spok[e]
shave is like the difference between the old open razor and the safe[ty]
razor. The spokeshave has a regulated depth of cut. Tap the tangs and t[he]
cut deepens; tap the face of the blade back and it becomes more shallo[w].
Often a screw held the adjustment in place. All-metal spokeshaves a[p]
peared just before the Civil War; before that, the variety of wood ha[n]
dles seems endless.

The biggest shaver was the chamfer knife, sometimes all metal, whic[h]
is often misrepresented (even by the experts) as a kind of froe. The sha[rp]
upper surface, however, shows that it was not designed for striking; a[nd]
the curve-beveled blade is certainly not for splitting.

Although the tiny tools shown below were called "top and si[de]
shaves," they were really planes. They were designed for the use of stai[r]
makers, but coachmakers found them even more useful.

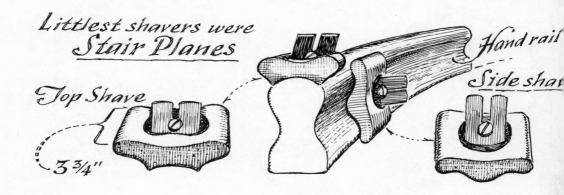

Littlest shavers were **Stair Planes**

Top Shave

3 ¾"

Hand rail

Side sha[ve]

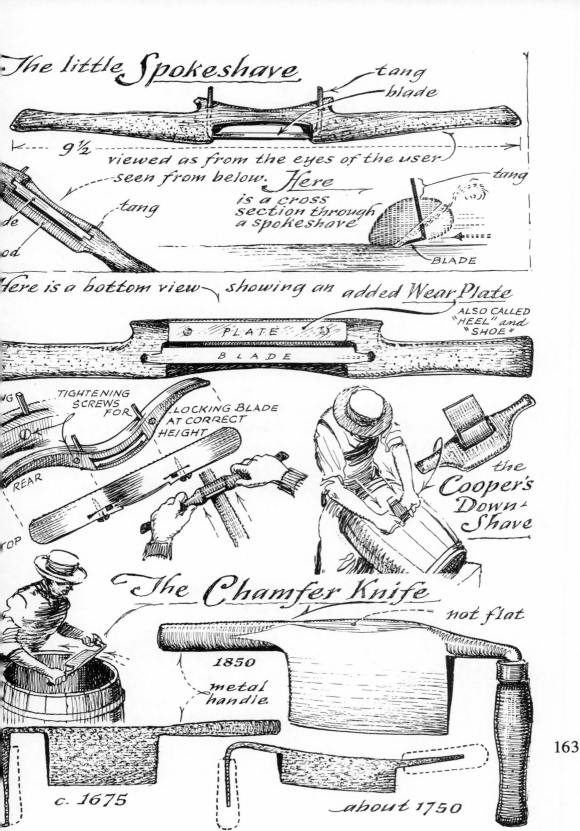

The little **Spokeshave**

tang
blade

9½ — viewed as from the eyes of the user
seen from below. Here is a cross section through a spokeshave

tang

de
od

tang

BLADE

Here is a bottom view — showing an added *Wear Plate*

ALSO CALLED "HEEL" and "SHOE"

PLATE
BLADE

TIGHTENING SCREWS FOR LOCKING BLADE AT CORRECT HEIGHT

REAR

TOP

the *Cooper's Down Shave*

The Chamfer Knife

not flat

1850 metal handle

c. 1675

about 1750

163

The Days of River Rafting

In many wooded areas of eighteenth-century America, farmers raised crops mostly for their own use and derived cash only from the sale of wood. Timber was floated to its destination by means of fastening logs into giant rafts. Three or more "platforms" were fastened, one behind the other, to make one long raft; steering was done by long oars. When rafts were sold and dismantled at the mill, irons and fastening devices were put into kegs, loaded on wagons, and hauled back to the farm. Most farmers ran at least one raft a year in late winter (when rivers were high) and busied themselves a good part of each winter with making or repairing lumbering implements.

White pine for masts and spars was a prime American export in the early 1800's and up until the Civil War. On such rivers as the Delaware were floated more than a thousand rafts each spring. The largest one on record was 215 feet long, and it contained 120,000 feet of lumber.

Below is a device known as a "bow-and-pin fastener." The square pins were driven into holes in the log; the wooden bow held the lash pole in place.

LASH POLE

LOG

wood bow
wood pin

lash pole

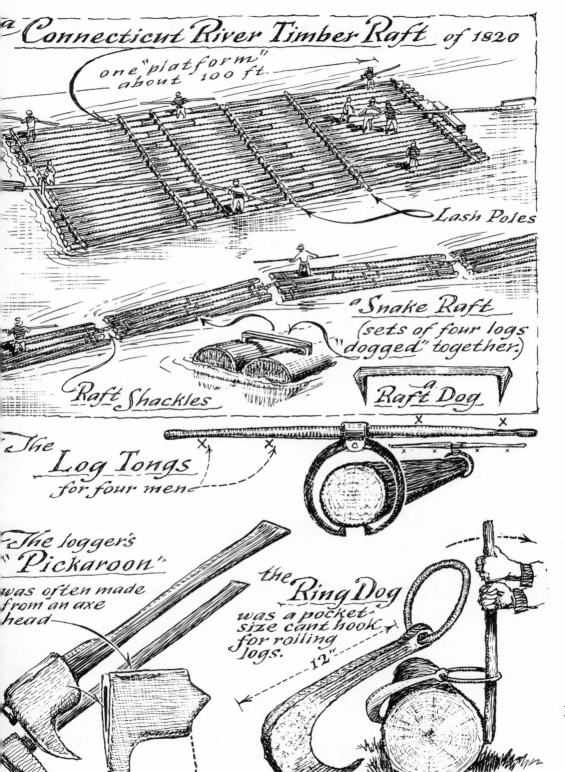

a Connecticut River Timber Raft *of 1820*

one "platform" about 100 ft.

Lash Poles

a "Snake Raft (sets of four logs "dogged" together.)

Raft Shackles

a Raft Dog

The Log Tongs *for four men*

The logger's "Pickaroon" was often made from an axe head

the Ring Dog was a pocket-size cant hook for rolling logs. 12"

165

Tools of the River Lumberman

*The American word "lumberman" came before our present
use of the word lumber. "Lumber" at one time (and still does in England)
meant "anything useless or cumbersome."*

The so-called "ship augers" you find in antique shops had not, as yo
might think, anything to do with ships; they were really used for log
rafts, or log-ships. The length of these augers allowed a man to bore
hole while standing.

The lash-pole and wooden-pin method of building rafts was later re
placed by iron raft shackles and "dogs."

Loose logs were "herded" into "corrals" by the owners at the m
(branded with the owners' marks). The marking axe was also an inspec
tion axe with a special bark-lifting poll.

Below you may see how the cant hook was made (in 1870 by a black
smith named John Peavey) into the "American peavey" by wedding it t
the jam pike. The jam pike pried, the cant hook rolled, but the peave
did both.

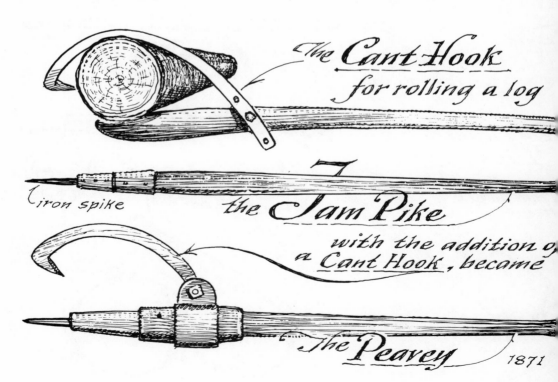

The *Cant Hook*
for rolling a log

iron spike — the *Jam Pike*

with the addition o
a *Cant Hook*, became

The *Peavey*   1871

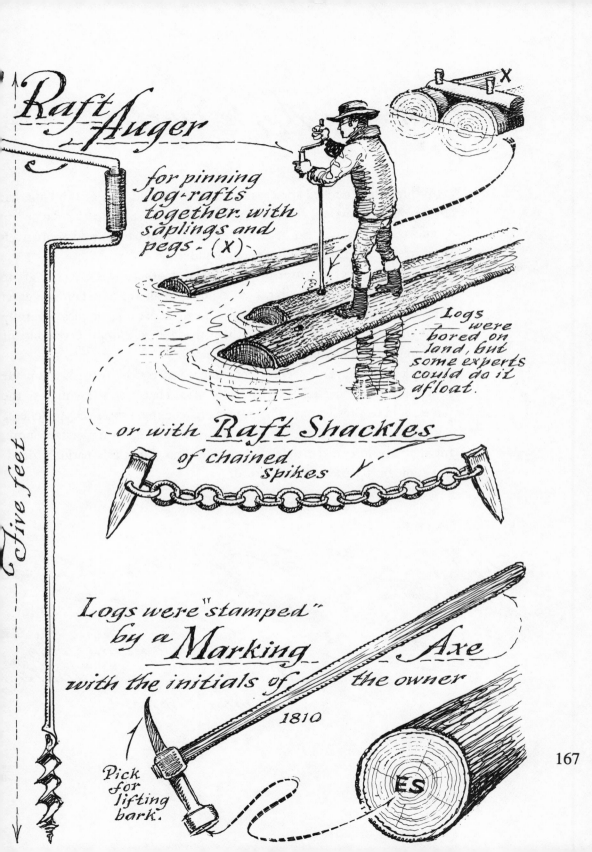

Raft Auger

for pinning log-rafts together with saplings and pegs - (X)

Logs were bored on land, but some experts could do it afloat.

or with **Raft Shackles** of chained spikes

Logs were "stamped" by a **Marking Axe** with the initials of the owner

1810

Pick for lifting bark.

ES

Five feet

167

Of Cider and Apple Butter

Anything that touched apples, according to the old way of thinking, had to be made of wood. Even a nail would "risk spoiling the flavor" or "quicken a souring." So heavy treen-ware (appliances and tools made from trees) was necessary in the apple industry.

Cider was never a matter of just squeezing—there was a special art to "bruising" apples and leaving them exposed to air for a certain and exact time before pressing. Oddly, those who picked eating apples carefully from the tree to avoid bumping them made an elaborate ceremony of crushing the same fruit when making cider.

Apples were never squeezed: "pomace was pressed." A mash was made into pomace or "cheese," then carefully placed between straw mats so the juice could be pressed out. The pomace rake, apple butter scoop, "cheese cutter," and apple shovel are tools that are difficult to understand now, for they are lost to the times when cider was America's national drink and apple butter the national spread.

Apple butter Scoop   1790

Combination Scoop and paddle (both Shaker)

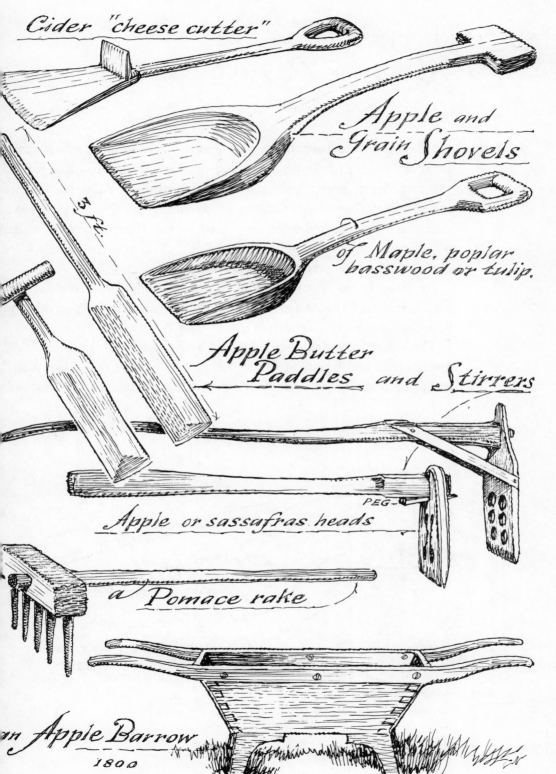

Cider "cheese cutter"

Apple and Grain Shovels

3 ft.

of Maple, poplar basswood or tulip.

Apple Butter Paddles and Stirrers

Apple or sassafras heads

PEG

a Pomace rake

an Apple Barrow
1800

169

To Remove Bark

Until recently the main source of tannin for treating hides was obtained from oak bark, and the production of oak bark was an essential part of the economy of many American farms. In April and May, bark peeled easily, and this was done with the spud, barking iron, and barking axe. The peeling chisel and adze were used mostly for "debarking" cedar posts and cleaning logs before broad-axing. The irons and spuds were true tanbark tools, usually blacksmith-made to order.

At first, chunks of oak bark were ground under massive stone mill wheels that turned into a trough of stone, but as early as 1797 the iron bark mill entered the scene to create a major American industry.

The liquor for tanning was obtained by pouring cold water on finely ground bark and leaving it to stand for a few days. Then it was passed from one leaching pit to another till the desired strength was reached.

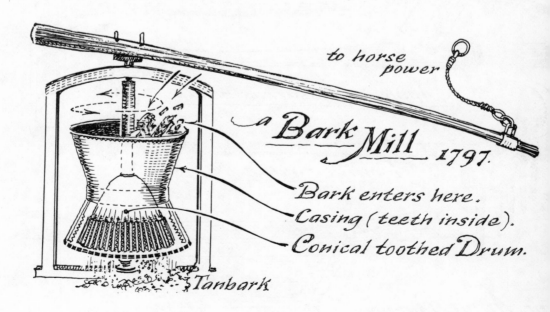

to horse power

a Bark Mill 1797.

Bark enters here.
Casing (teeth inside).
Conical toothed Drum.

Tanbark

170

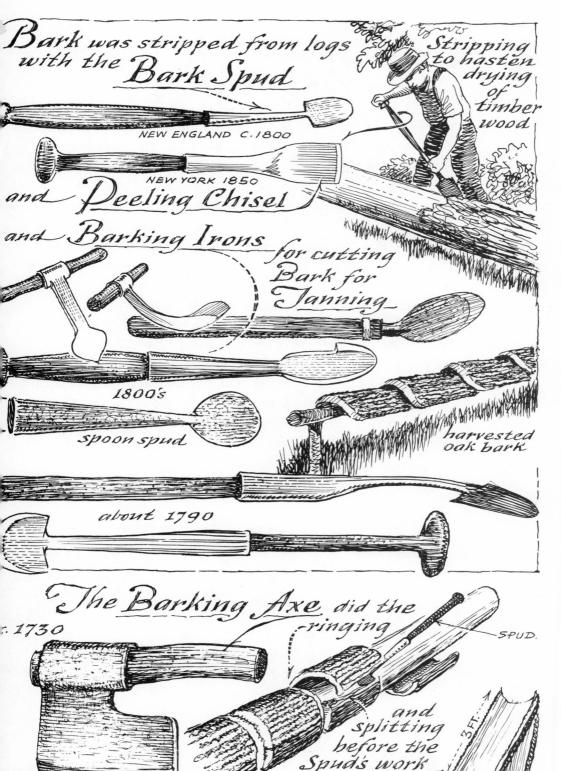

Bark was stripped from logs with the *Bark Spud*

Stripping to hasten drying of timber wood

NEW ENGLAND C. 1800

NEW YORK 1850

and *Peeling Chisel*

and *Barking Irons* for cutting Bark for Tanning

1800's

spoon spud

harvested oak bark

about 1790

The *Barking Axe* did the ringing

c. 1730

SPUD.

and splitting before the Spud's work

3 FT.

171

Two Heads are Better than One.

Except for the double-bitted axe, these tools are rare. So rare in fact, that there is doubt about their true names. One of the first dictionary mentions of the "twibil" calls it "an iron tool used by Paviers" (road-builders). This would make it a sort of grubbing hoe. Another describes it a twin-billed hoe-and-knife for beans and peas. One old dictionary says the "twivel" is "among Carpenters, a tool to make Tortoise Holes." We must assume this definition was dictated to a printer who mistook "mortise" for "tortoise."

I would guess that all two-bitted hatchets might have been at some time called "twin-bills," "twibils," or "twivels." Still used in England to cut hurdle mortises, the twivel there is called "tomyhawk," "dader," or "two-bill."

The ice hatchet, adze-hatchet, and hatchet-adze were American, but only the Yankee double-bit remains. From Maine (about 1840) it was designed with one razor-sharp bit that could do fine work and one less sharp for rough work. It also provides a means for being held (by sinking it into a stump) for filing either bit.

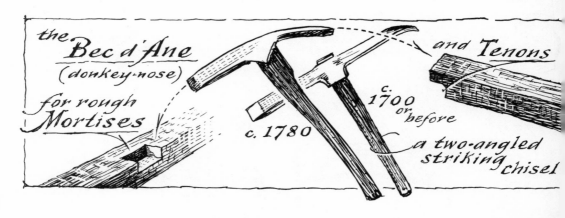

the Bec d'Ane (donkey-nose)
for rough Mortises

c. 1780

c. 1700 or before

and Tenons

a two-angled striking chisel

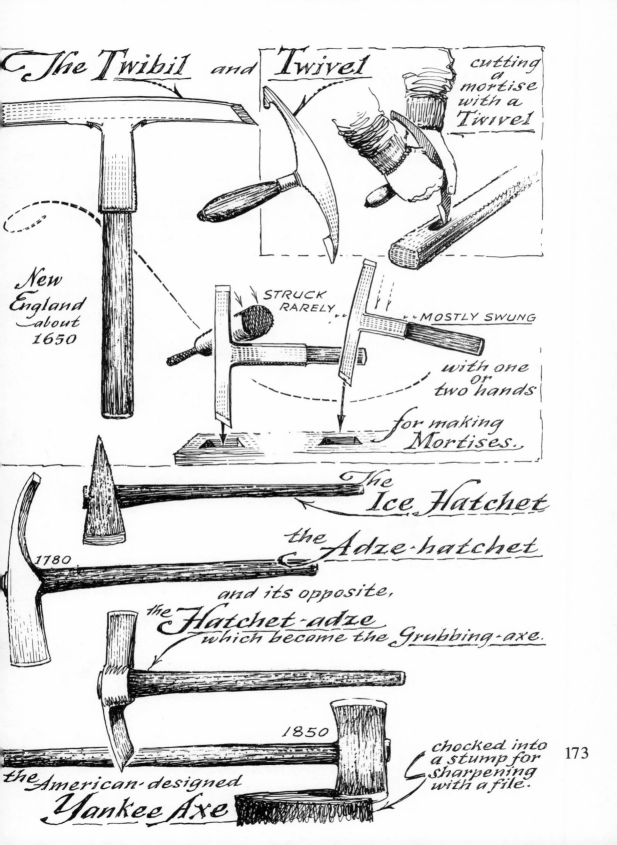

The Twibil and Twivel

cutting a mortise with a Twivel

New England about 1650

STRUCK RARELY

MOSTLY SWUNG

with one or two hands

for making Mortises.

The Ice Hatchet

the Adze·hatchet

1780

and its opposite,

the Hatchet·adze which became the Grubbing·axe.

1850

chocked into a stump for sharpening with a file.

173

the American·designed Yankee Axe

The Chisel

There are so many kinds of chisels that it is difficult to establish definite nomenclature; yet, on the opposite page, we have attempted a general classification. The firmer (or firming or forming) chisel is the basic chisel design; it did a great many jobs, but one special use was to cut the superfluous wood from two auger holes to make a mortise. The framing chisel is a heavier version, and it was used largely in the cutting of tenons to fit the mortises. Both of these tools are wood-handled (usually socketed) and were designed to be struck with a mallet. The socket-end can be struck bare, without the handle, though a good craftsman seldom did this.

The short, stout mortise chisel is almost square, a one-purpose tool. The giant paring chisel, known as a slick, has a big blade that curves very slightly toward the bevel; it was designed, not for striking, but to be used with two hands (often with some shoulder help) like a giant plane. Big framing chisels are often misnamed slicks; if the curve is evident, it is a slick; if not, it is a giant framing chisel.

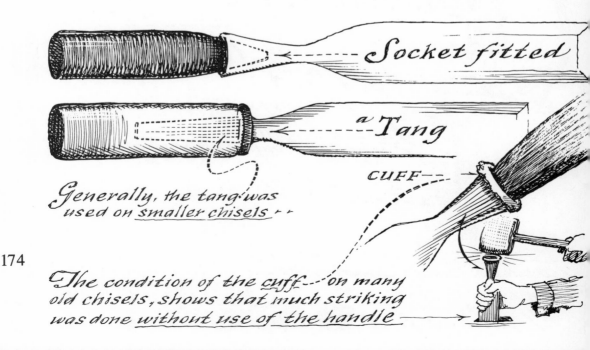

Socket fitted

a Tang

CUFF

Generally, the tang was used on smaller chisels

The condition of the cuff on many old chisels, shows that much striking was done without use of the handle

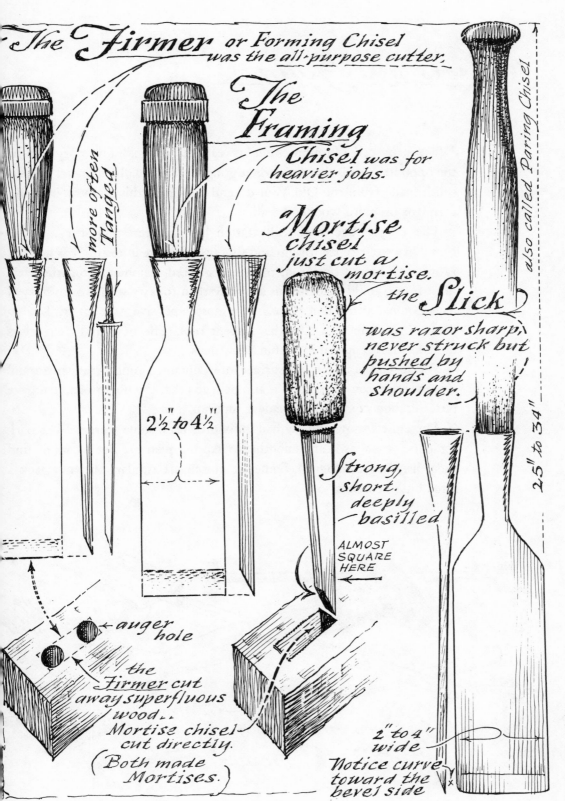

The *Firmer* or Forming Chisel was the all-purpose cutter.

more often *Tanged*

The **Framing** Chisel was for heavier jobs.

"*Mortise* chisel just cut a mortise.

the **Slick**

was razor sharp, never struck but pushed by hands and shoulder.

also called Paring Chisel

2½" to 4½"

Strong, short. deeply basilled

ALMOST SQUARE HERE

25" to 34"

← auger hole

the *Firmer* cut away superfluous wood ..
Mortise chisel cut directly.
(Both made Mortises.)

2" to 4" wide

Notice curve toward the bevel side

175

Chisels and Gouges

What many call a "round chisel" is really a "gouge." The story told on the opposite page is that the earliest gouges were usually all metal (blacksmith-made from the Old World) and copied in this country in larger form for use with wooden handles.

The 1775 gouge in the illustration has an interesting story. It was found in a stone fence. Bright and silverish, its edge is keen; it has no rust. How farm-bound bog iron, privately smelted, hammered together at a farm forge, could be better in any way than today's steel is a mystery. I have compared the best chisels (the most expensive, that is) by leaving them in the rain alongside this ancient tool. The new tool's edge was dulled, and rust appeared within a few days.

The legend is that early surface ore contained much manganese and was purer in iron content. It is also believed that the use of charcoal gave purer carbon content and made a superior iron.

The chisels shown below had individual uses; some were used as bark scrapers, others as beam smoothers (like big planes). But I cannot find them listed or catalogued. Some ice chisels are similar, but they lack a tilted bit (see below—*x*).

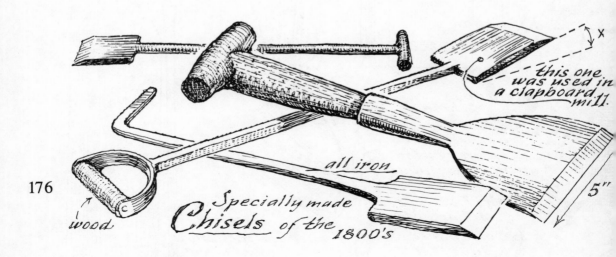

x

this one was used in a clapboard mill.

all iron

wood

Specially made Chisels of the 1800's

5"

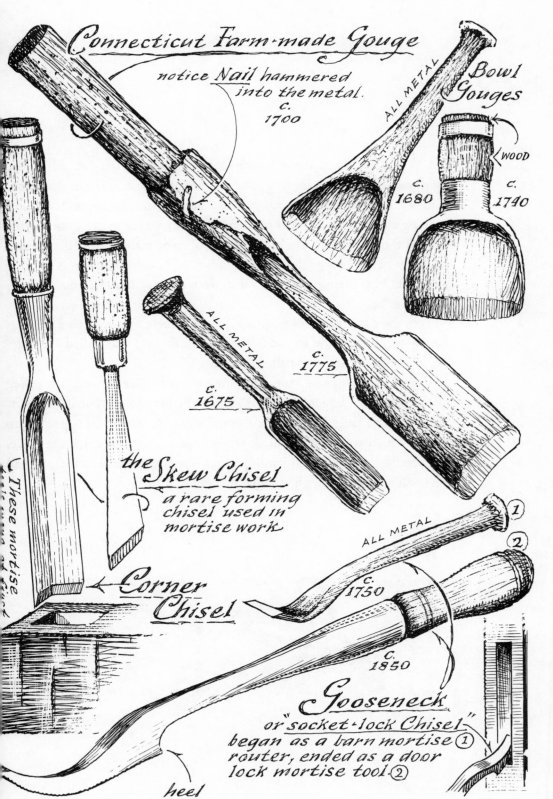

Connecticut Farm-made Gouge

notice <u>Nail</u> hammered into the metal.
c. 1700

Bowl Gouges

ALL METAL

c. 1680

WOOD

c. 1740

ALL METAL

c. 1775

c. 1675

the *Skew Chisel*
a rare forming chisel used in mortise work

→ *Corner Chisel*

These mortise

ALL METAL

c. 1750

①

②

c. 1850

Gooseneck
or "socket-lock Chisel"
began as a barn mortise router, ended as a door lock mortise tool ①②

heel

177

Planes

Old World planes, made as much to look at as to do a job, often had inscriptions and floral carving. But the completely utilitarian American plane, except for an occasional graceful handle, usually resembled a box. Looking alike, a nest of small planes in the average carpenter's chest often reached thirty or more. Perhaps because of their plainness, or their quantity, they never caught the collector's fancy. Not long ago in Vermont, you could buy them by the barrel as firewood for five dollars. That included the barrel!

From the big ones ("long" planes) down, these either leveled the surface or fit pieces (side by side) together. Leveling was called "trying" and "trueing"; fitting was called "jointing."

With the trying plane (top, opposite) was a smaller bench plane called a jack plane and a larger (now rare) mate, the long jointer, or floor plane. But all other planes bow to their granddaddy in size, the cooper's long jointer, which was used upside down on a pair of legs to work the piece. Restricted in use mostly to joining barrel staves, this plane sometimes had two blades—one for rough, one for fine cut.

a Favorite — Hand-made Plane

Natural Handle of oak

"bit or Iron" made from an old file

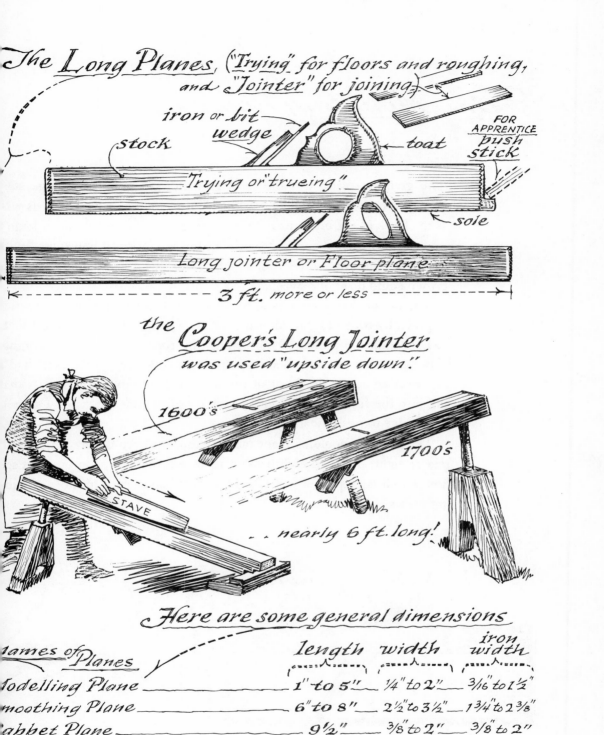

The **Long Planes**, ("Trying" for floors and roughing, and "Jointer" for joining)

iron or bit wedge

stock

toat

FOR APPRENTICE **push stick**

"Trying or "trueing""

sole

Long jointer or Floor plane

← ----- 3 ft. more or less ----- →

the **Cooper's Long Jointer** was used "upside down".

1600's

1700's

STAVE

. . . nearly 6 ft. long!

Here are some general dimensions

Names of Planes	length	width	iron width
Modelling Plane	1" to 5"	¼" to 2"	3/16 to 1½"
Smoothing Plane	6" to 8"	2½ to 3½"	1¾" to 2⅜"
Rabbet Plane	9½"	⅜" to 2"	⅜" to 2"
Jack Plane	12" to 17"	2½ to 3"	2" to 2¼"
Long or Trying Plane	20" to 26"	3½"	2½" to 2⅝"
Jointer Plane or Floor Plane	28" to 36"	3¾"	2¾"
Cooper's long Jointer	60" to 72"	5" to 5½"	3½" to 3¾"

179

The Moulding Plane

The grandest plane was the crown moulding plane. That large strip between the wall and ceiling was the identification of a fine room as well as the mark of the craftsman. No workman even carried about so large a tool and few owned one; instead the ordinary workman improvised with the basic "hollow" and "round" planes to make a moulding that the crown could do at one sweep.

The big crown plane was so heavy that it had bars for the apprentice to pull it by rope (1). Or, looped once or twice around a mill-wheel shaft (2), it could be pulled by tightening the rope, released by loosening.

Some crown planes had an apprentice pulling stick (3); others had a bar screwed across the front of the stock (4); others had two bars that slid into the front and back of the stock (5), with a notch for a second apprentice to push by stick.

The simplest moulding plane made a bead, but even this design came in sets of eight (from an eighth of an inch to a full inch), so you can see how a well-equipped carpenter's chest often had twenty or more moulding planes.

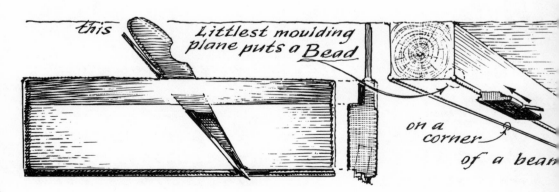

this

Littlest moulding plane puts a _Bead_

on a corner

of a beam

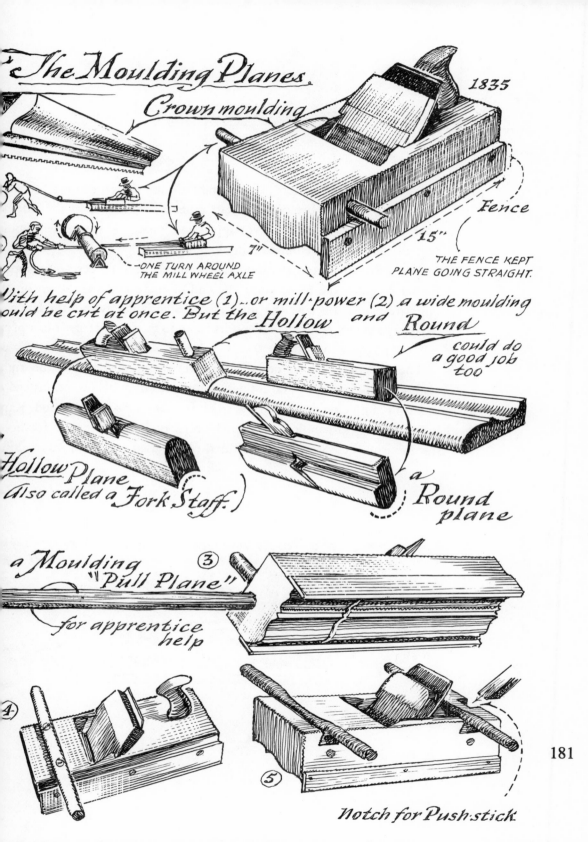

The Moulding Planes

Crown moulding

1835

ONE TURN AROUND
THE MILL WHEEL AXLE

7"

15"

Fence

THE FENCE KEPT
PLANE GOING STRAIGHT.

With help of apprentice (1)...or mill·power (2) a wide moulding could be cut at once. But the *Hollow* and *Round* could do a good job too

Hollow Plane
(Also called a *Fork Staff.*)

a **Round** plane

a *Moulding* "Pull Plane"

③

for apprentice help

④

⑤

Notch for Push-stick.

181

The Rabbet

Most American carpenters call it a "rabbit"; the British call it a "rebate." It is really the "rabbet plane" that "rabbets" out a cut in the sides of boards, so that they may be overlapped and joined. This was the popular way of joining before milled tongue-and-groove.

The first rabbet and the long rabbet plane have fences (overlapping strips) to guide the plane along the end of the board (as shown on the opposite page). Because the little rabbet stands flat without a fence, it needs a strip of wood nailed along its route to guide it before it can properly cut a rabbet in a board.

These planes vary in design, some throwing shavings to the right, some to the left, some to both sides. Some irons have blades set, instead of at a right angle, on a skew to the stock to avoid tearing the wood. Rare is the pistol-grip-handled rabbet, which lacks the usual wedge for holding the iron. Below is the rabbet saw, rarely used except in stairmaking.

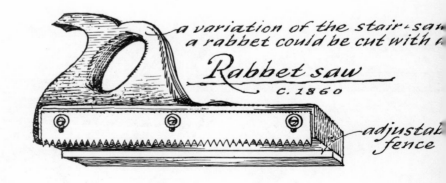

a variation of the stair-saw
a rabbet could be cut with it

Rabbet saw
c. 1860

adjustable fence

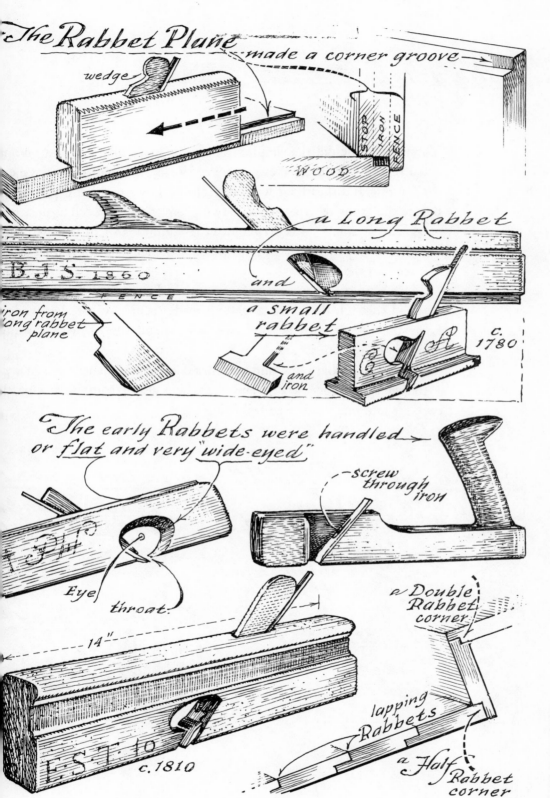

The Rabbet Plane

wedge

made a corner groove

STOP · IRON · FENCE

WOOD

a Long Rabbet

B. J. S. 1860

FENCE

and

iron from long rabbet plane

a small rabbet

and iron

c. 1780

The early Rabbets were handled or flat and very "wide-eyed"

screw through iron

Eye   throat.

14"

a Double Rabbet corner

lapping Rabbets

E. S. T. 10   c. 1810

a Half Rabbet corner

183

The Plow

The plow plane did the simplest job, yet it looks like the most compl[i]cated of tools. It just makes a groove. We use tongue-and-groove cu[t] for flooring and sheathing without realizing how recent this practice i[s]. Before the "tongue" was popular, two grooves were placed against eac[h] other, and a "spline" was driven into the "tunnel" to join the two piec[es] together. For paneling, a tongue was not planed, but a "feather edge[" was set into the groove.

The adjustable plow had its fence attached to the plane by two arm[s] that slid through the plane stock and made secure by wooden wedge[s]. Later the square arms became two long round screws with threade[d] knobs to hold them secure.

The unadjustable plow and unadjustable tongue plane came in pai[rs] ("tongue-and-groove sets"), and there was also a combination of th[e] two, set into one stock (see following pages).

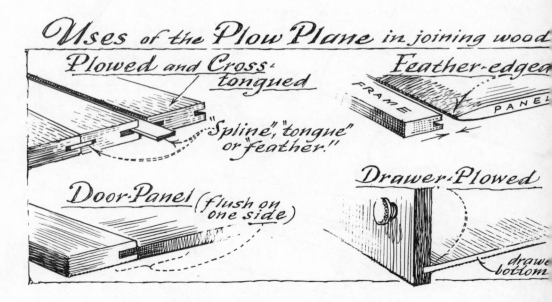

Uses of the Plow Plane in joining wood

Plowed and Cross-tongued

"Spline", "tongue" or "feather."

Feather-edge[d]

FRAME

PANEL

Door-Panel (flush on one side)

Drawer-Plowed

draw[er] bottom

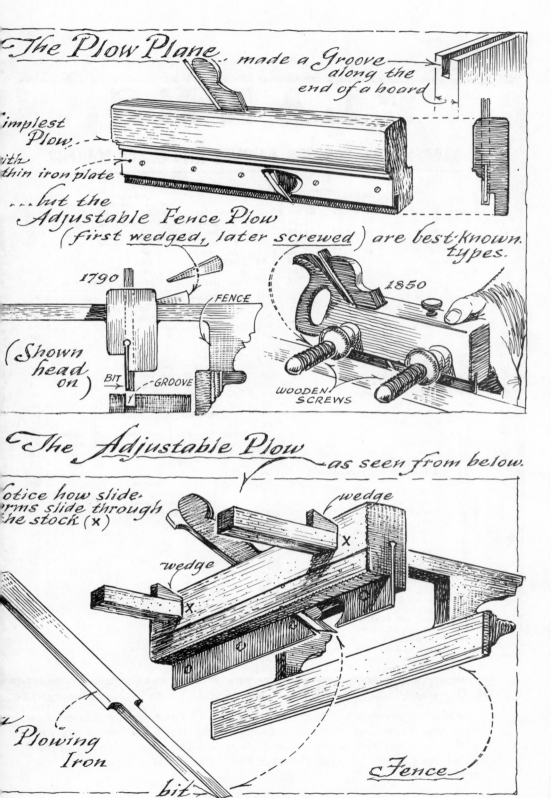

The Plow Plane .. made a Groove along the end of a board

Simplest Plow...

with thin iron plate

...but the Adjustable Fence Plow (first wedged, later screwed) are best·known types.

1790

FENCE

(Shown head on)

BIT — GROOVE

1850

WOODEN SCREWS

The Adjustable Plow as seen from below.

Notice how slide arms slide through the stock (x)

wedge

wedge

X

X

Plowing Iron

bit

Fence

185

PLANES,

FOR

CARPENTERS, COOPERS, CABINET AND COACH MAKERS.

	Cast Steel. Irons. Single.	Cast Steel. Irons. Double.	German Steel. Irons. Single.	German Steel. Irons. Double.
Jointers 30 inch	$1 70	$2 17	$1 58	$2 05
do 28 "	1 64	2 08	1 52	1 96
do 26 "	1 58	2 00	1 46	1 88
do 22 "	1 50	1 92	1 38	1 80
do 21 "	1 42	1 84	1 30	1 72
Jack Planes	96	1 37½	88	1 30
Smooth Planes	87½	1 25	80	1 17
do Circular	92	1 31	84	1 23

	Cast Steel. Irons. Single.	Cast Steel. Irons. Double.	German Steel. Irons. Single.	German Steel. Irons. Double.
Cooper's Jointers	$2 50	$3 50	$2 88	$3 88
do stock howel	2 50	pl'd 3 00	2 38	2 88
do circ. leveler	1 50	" 2 00	1 38	1 87
do with handles	2 00	2 50	1 88	2 38
do crows	2 50			
Tooth Planes	1 25			
Miter Planes	1 00			

Ogees for Cabinet Makers, $1 00 per inch.

Astragals ¼ to ½ inch	62½
do ⅝ to 1 inch	75
Beads ⅛ to ¾ inch	75
do over 1 inch	87½
do full boxed ⅛ to ⅜	92
do do ½ to ¾	1 00
Coves to ⅝ inch	62½
do ⅞ to 1 inch	75
Cove and Beads ⅜ to ½ inch	75
do do ⅝ to 1 inch	87½
do do over 1 inch	1 00
Center Beads to ⅜	87
Dadoes, slide stop	1 37
do screw stop	2 00
Fillisters	1 50
do with stop	1 75
do do and cut	2 00
do do cut and boxed	2 25
do with screw stop, cut and boxed	3 00
Guages	20
do oval head	25
Gothic Beads	1 25
Grecian Ovolos ⅜ by ¾ inch	1 00
do do ½ by 1 inch, ⅝ by 1¼	1 12½
do do ¾ by 1½ inch	1 25
do do Beads ⅜ by ⅞ in., ½ by 1⅛ in.	1 25
do do do ⅝ by 1⅜.—¾ by 1¼ in.	1 50
do do do ⅞ by 1¾ and 2 inch	1 75
do Ogee and Bevel sq. ⅜ by ⅞ in. ½ by 1⅛ in.	1 25
do do do ⅝ by 1⅜ in. ¾ by 1½ in.	1 50
do do do ⅞ by 1¾ and 2 inch	1 75
Halving planes	62½
do do plated	87½
do do with handles	1 00
do do plated, with handles	1 25
Hollows and Rounds 9 pair to No. 18.	10 50
Match Planes for Boards ⅝ to 1 inch	1 75
do fence plated	2 00
do for Plank 1¼ inch	2 62½

Match Planes, fence plated		3 00
do moving fence		4 00
do screw arms		6 00
Plows, 1st rate, 8 irons		7 00
do 2d " "		6 00
do 3d " "		5 00
do 4th " "		4 50
Extra for boxing fence		50
Extra for side screws		50
do screw arms and 8 irons		7 00
do box fence		7 50
do side screws		8 00
do solid box		8 00
do do side screws		8 50
Rabbet Planes to 1 inch square	62, skew	75
do 1¼ inch	68, skew	87½
do 1½ inch	75, skew	92
do 1¾ inch	78, skew	1 00
do 2 inch		1 12½
do with handles		2 00
Extra for boxing		25
Extra for adding cut		25
Raising Planes, common		1 75
do moving fence		3 25
do do 3 in. iron		4 00
do do 3½ "		4 50
do do 4 "		5 00
Reeding Planes ⅛ to ½ inch		1 00
Sash Planes, 1 iron	1 00, boxed	1 50
do 2 "	1 50, "	2 00
do double	2 50, "	3 00
Snipe Bills		75
do full box		1 00
Side Rabbets		62½
Torus Beads to ¾ inch		75
do from ¾ to 1 inch		87½
do over 1 inch		1 00
Table Planes, pair		1 50
do boxed		2 00

Omitting various moulding planes and special planes (such as those illustrated on the opposite page), the above advertisement of the 1800's lists some of the basic planes that the average carpenter was likely to have in his chest. As many of these planes came in sets of eight, the army of old-time wooden planes seems overwhelming.

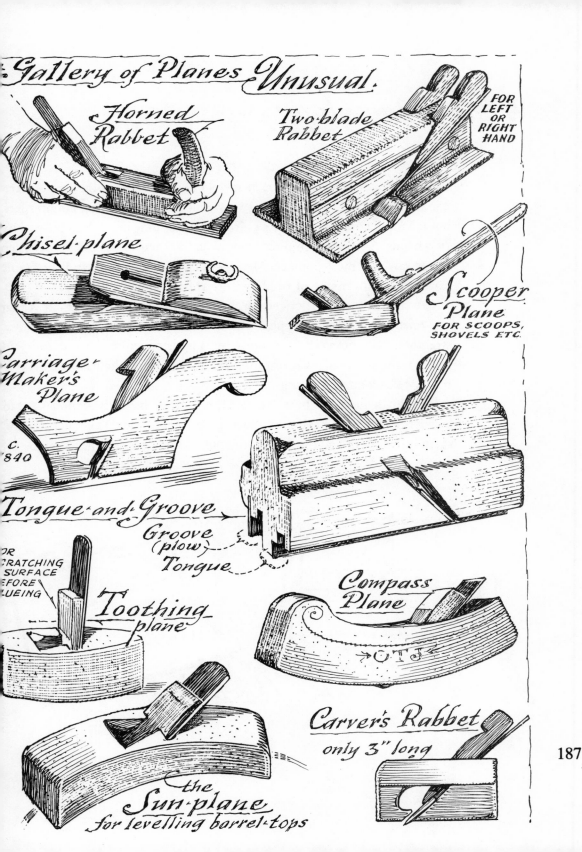

Gallery of Planes Unusual.

Horned Rabbet

Two-blade Rabbet

FOR LEFT OR RIGHT HAND

Chisel-plane

Scooper Plane
FOR SCOOPS, SHOVELS ETC.

Carriage-Maker's Plane

C. 1840

Tongue-and-Groove

Groove (plow)
Tongue

FOR SCRATCHING SURFACE BEFORE GLUEING

Toothing plane

Compass Plane

O.T.J.

Carver's Rabbet
only 3" long

the Sun-plane
for levelling barrel-tops

187

Early American Saws

Both the frame saw and the open saw were in use during the first American settlements. The open saw is very much like its modern counterpart but it had a handle like that of a knife and it was long enough to be used by two hands. Americans enjoyed using wood in their tools, and the wooden frame saw was most popular. Metal was hard to come by, and the frame saw had the advantage of needing only the narrowest blade.

Saw nomenclature is uncertain, but the most common division is that of "open" and "frame" types. The bow saw (again a frame type) was stretched taut between two arms by a twisted cord (or by rod and screw); the saw blade was readily turned by twisting the handles, making it easy to saw curved pieces.

The buck saw is a bow frame type, but its blade is stationary and heavier, and a long handle has been added. To "buck" logs was to saw them into proper lengths; hence, the buck saw is a woodsman's saw.

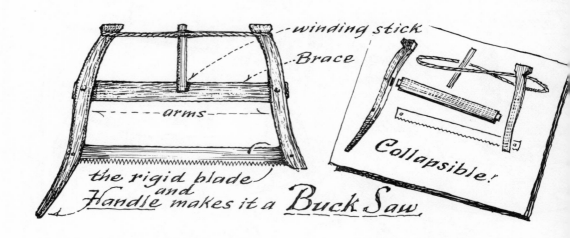

winding stick

Brace

arms

the rigid blade and Handle makes it a Buck Saw

Collapsible!

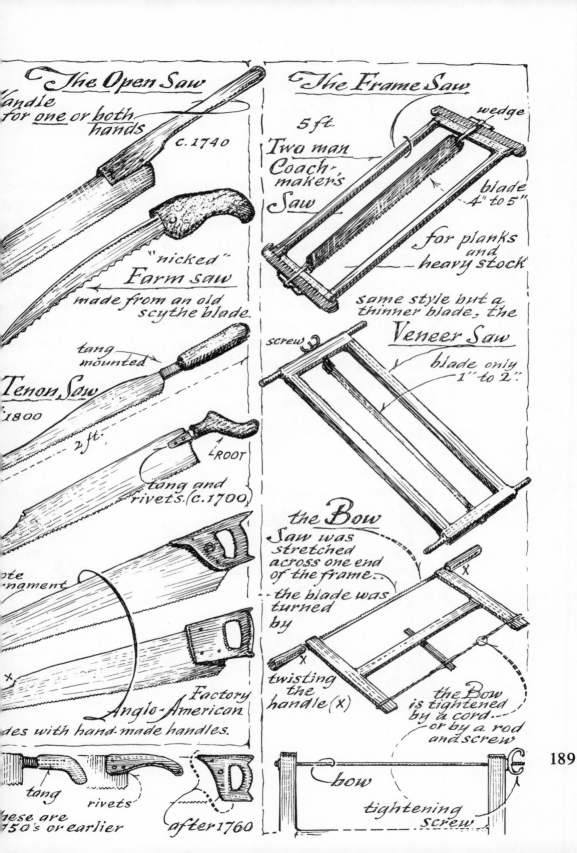

The Open Saw

Handle for <u>one</u> or <u>both</u> hands

c. 1740

"nicked" **Farm saw** made from an old scythe blade.

tang mounted

Tenon Saw 1800

2 ft.

ROOT

tang and rivets. (c. 1700)

ote nament

x

Factory Anglo-American des with hand-made handles.

tang   rivets

ese are 50's or earlier

after 1760

The Frame Saw

5 ft. Two man Coach-maker's Saw

wedge

blade 4" to 5"

for planks and heavy stock

same style but a thinner blade, the

screw

Veneer Saw

blade only 1" to 2"

the Bow

Saw was stretched across one end of the frame.

the blade was turned by

x

x

twisting the handle (x)

the Bow is tightened by a cord or by a rod and screw

bow

tightening screw

189

a Gallery of Frame Saws

The frame saw looks clumsy to us now, but actually it was much mo[re] of "an extension of the craftsman's hand" than the modern saw. You c[an] cut straight or around corners with it and always see where the bla[de] was cutting. The modern saw blade is wide, always covering the sp[ot] it is cutting, and is restricted to a straight cut.

The terms "chairmaker's saw," "felloe (also "felly") saw," "turnin[g] saw," etc. are difficult to pin to one model because each design over lapped the other in size or shape at one time or another. The frame saw "strained" in the center and two stretchers keep it taut; the bow saw strained on one end, with a stretcher cord (or rod) on the other.

The finer the work to be done the finer the saw; some frame saws a[re] pieces of art both to work with and to look at.

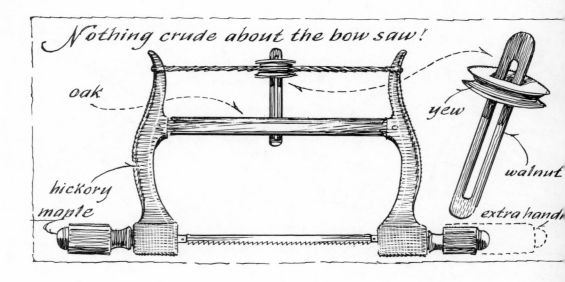

Nothing crude about the bow saw!

oak

yew

hickory
maple

walnut

extra hand[le]

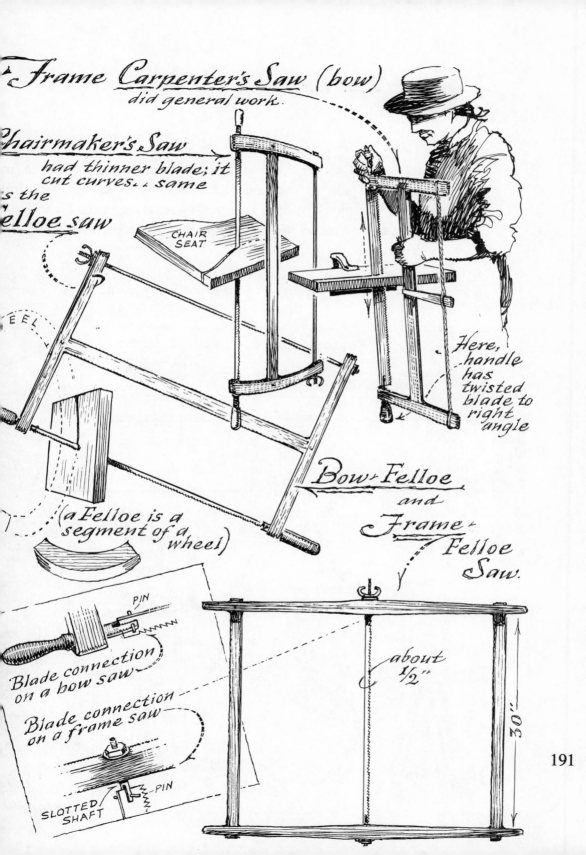

Frame Carpenter's Saw (bow)
did general work.

Chairmaker's Saw
had thinner blade; it cut curves — same as the

Felloe saw

CHAIR SEET

Here, handle has twisted blade to right angle

(a Felloe is a segment of a wheel)

Bow-Felloe
and
Frame-Felloe Saw.

PIN

Blade connection on a bow saw

Blade connection on a frame saw

PIN

SLOTTED SHAFT

about 1/2"

30"

191

The Biggest Saws

Its teeth raked to cut downward, the long pit saws (both open and framed) did most of the earliest American plank-sawing both from trestles and in pits. The open type was more recent in the New World than the framed model. Factory-made, the open pit saw was used until the late 1800's.

There was an ancient open plank saw (see below) that some collectors regard as an open pit saw, but the curved blade and matching handles indicate otherwise.

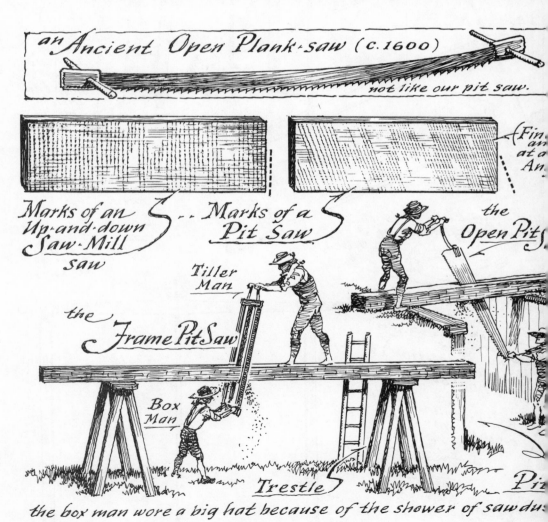

an Ancient Open Plank-saw (c. 1600)

not like our pit saw.

Marks of an Up-and-down Saw-Mill saw

Marks of a Pit Saw

(Fin... an... at a An...

the Open Pit...

Tiller Man

the Frame Pit Saw

Box Man

Trestle

Pi...

192

the box man wore a big hat because of the shower of sawdu...

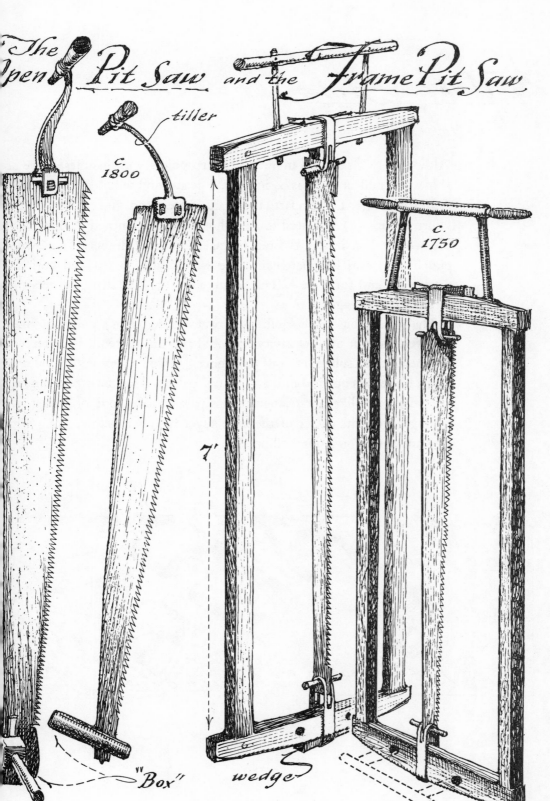

The *Open Pit Saw* and the *Frame Pit Saw*

tiller

c. 1800

c. 1750

7'

"Box"

wedge

193

to Make a Hole

Although awls seem no more than sharp points with handles, there are those who collect them as basic tools. The awl and punch enter wood by "spreading" the fibers apart; the ream, auger, and gimlet "cuts." The "burn auger" (1) was fired to a red-hot point that burned its opening in the wood; then it was twisted to make the hole deeper. The "wood punch" (2) was hammered into the wood, and was twisted both for deeper cut and for release. The "ream awl" (3) had sharp corners that acted as cutting agents.

The "gouge bit" (split-quill) was round-ended, like a gouging chisel; if water was put into its cavity it would run out the end. If water was dropped into a "spoon bit" or "pod auger," it would stay in, for the nose of the bit scoops upward into a twist (A and B). The "twisted cylinder" bit, neither podlike nor triangular, has parallel sides, one of which is a cutting edge. The cutter of the nose auger is shown below, along with the same device on a spiral-ribbon bit.

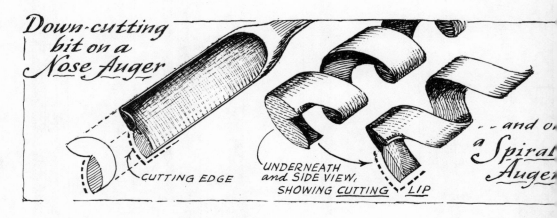

Down-cutting bit on a Nose Auger

CUTTING EDGE

UNDERNEATH and SIDE VIEW, SHOWING CUTTING LIP

...and on a Spiral Auger

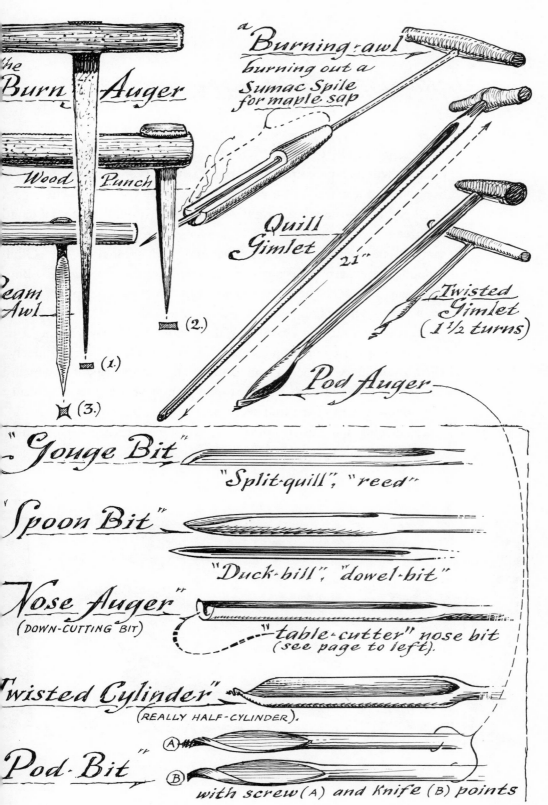

The Burn Auger

Wood Punch

"Burning-awl
burning out a
Sumac Spile
for maple sap

Quill
Gimlet

21″

Twisted
Gimlet
(1½ turns)

Pod Auger

Seam
Awl

(2.)

(1.)

(3.)

"Gouge Bit"

"Split-quill", "reed"

"Spoon Bit"

"Duck-bill", "dowel-bit"

Nose Auger"
(DOWN-CUTTING BIT)

"table-cutter" nose bit
(see page to left).

"Twisted Cylinder"
(REALLY HALF-CYLINDER).

Pod-Bit"   Ⓐ
           Ⓑ

with screw (A) and Knife (B) points

195

To Make a Hole Bigger

To enlarge a hole, you may "ream" it with a tapered blade; to be sure the hole will be tapered too, but often (as when you are cutting a barrel bung-hole or a wheel hub-hole) this is just what you want. The biggest of all reamers is the wheelwright's hub reamer; often it reaches a length of three feet and weighs as much as twenty-five pounds. Some of these can still be found without handles and with strange hooks. Oddly enough, the experts have not decided just how these were used. But I rigged up a wagon wheel on a wheelwright's bench, then put a hooked reamer through the hub, which I had weighted with seventy-five pounds. With two men turning a very long detachable handle (which might explain the missing handles on so many of these blades it worked nicely). With an ordinary reamer, a man exerts about half his weight downward; this can be bettered with a seventy-five-pound weight plus the twenty-five-pound weight of the tool itself.

Tap augers and hub reamers were usually sharpened on one blade (on the inner side).

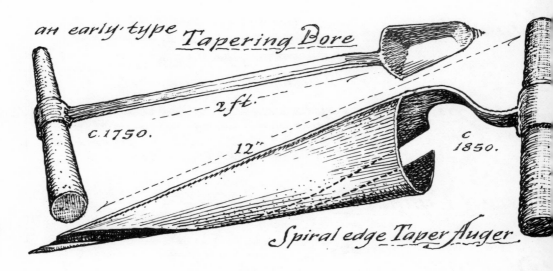

an early type Tapering Bore

2 ft.

C. 1750.

12"

c 1850.

Spiral edge Taper Auger

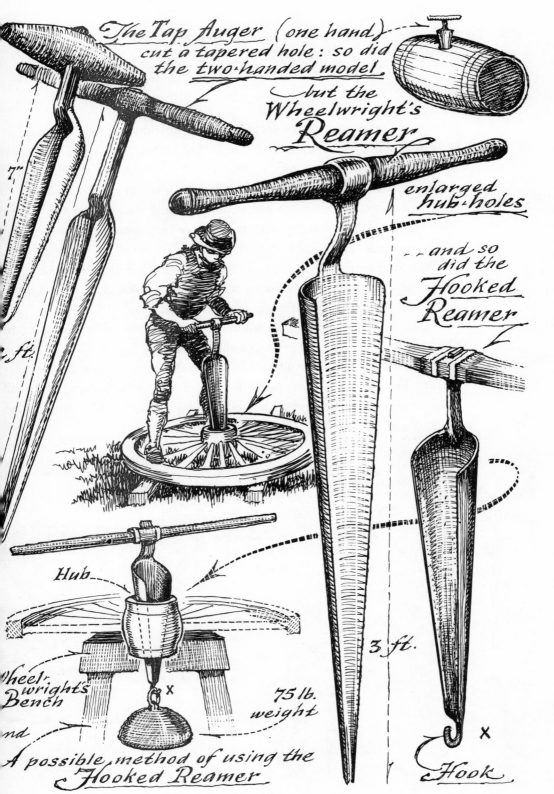

The Tap Auger (one hand)
cut a tapered hole: so did
the two-handed model

but the
Wheelwright's
Reamer

enlarged
hub-holes

--and so
did the
**Hooked
Reamer**

7"

ft.

Hub

3 ft.

Wheel-
wright's
Bench

75 lb.
weight

nd

Hook

A possible method of using the
Hooked Reamer

197

to Make a Bigger Hole

Recently a "revolutionary speed bit" was introduced for electric drills. Actually it is an adaptation of an early "button bit" (A) and (B) and has the same design as the "center bit" (c. 1794) with which the pioneer American started trunnel holes in his buildings. For shallow holes or to start a boring, it cut downward without pulling shavings upward as the big spiral bit does. Center bits, therefore, which were never put on bar handles, were used with a brace.

The four typical wooden bar handles shown are generalizations; because so many men made their own handles, it is difficult to pinpoint the date of a handle from its design. I have worked out these estimates, from the handles in my own collection, in the hope that this information might be helpful in dating tools in other collections.

It seems incredible that a man could turn the huge bits that some augers have. The job was made easier in the 1800's by a two-handled drill (shown opposite); an adjustable model came out in the 1860's that drilled at any angle.

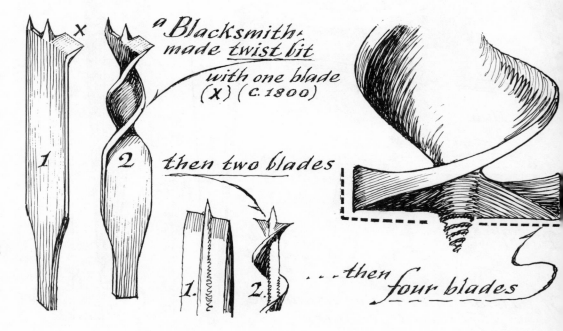

X

"Blacksmith made twist bit with one blade (X) (c. 1800)

1

2

then two blades

1. 2.

...then four blades

198

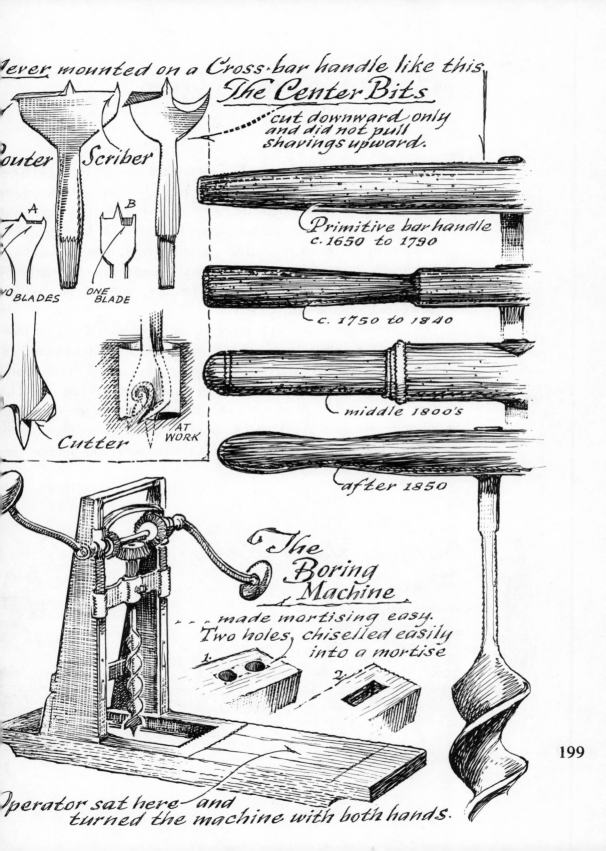

never mounted on a Cross-bar handle like this.

The Center Bits

cut downward only
and did not pull
shavings upward.

Router Scriber

A   B

TWO BLADES   ONE BLADE

Cutter   AT WORK

Primitive bar handle
c. 1650 to 1790

c. 1750 to 1840

middle 1800's

after 1850

The Boring Machine

made mortising easy.
Two holes, chiselled easily
into a mortise

1.   2.

199

Operator sat here and
turned the machine with both hands.

The Brace or Bitstock

The early American bitstock or brace was made of native seasoned hard
wood. Some of the earliest were made of natural-shaped roots or bough
(see drawing in center, opposite page). Oak and hickory were mos
commonly used although the burl-wood bitstock was also prized.

Most early braces (particularly in New England) were "bitted" in
permanent manner; the bit was moulded into a metal wad and fitted tightly
into a square wooden chuck (sometimes ferruled), and this square chuck
was wedged into the stock to stay.

The revolving buttons were masterpieces of woodworking, for mos
of those on the earliest braces still work nicely and are not even cracked
The button was either "stayed" by a wooden pin through the shaft and
head (A), or the shaft was "stayed" by a "Cotter-pinlike" peg (B). The
natural-shape stock's button was loose, staying in just by pressure. (As
some braces were rested against the chest—and therefore needed a bigger
and flatter button—this brace may have had interchangeable buttons, one
for the hand and one for the chest.)

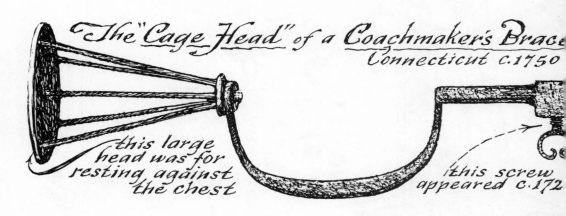

The "Cage Head" of a Coachmaker's Brace
Connecticut c.1750

this large
head was for
resting against
the chest

this screw
appeared c.172

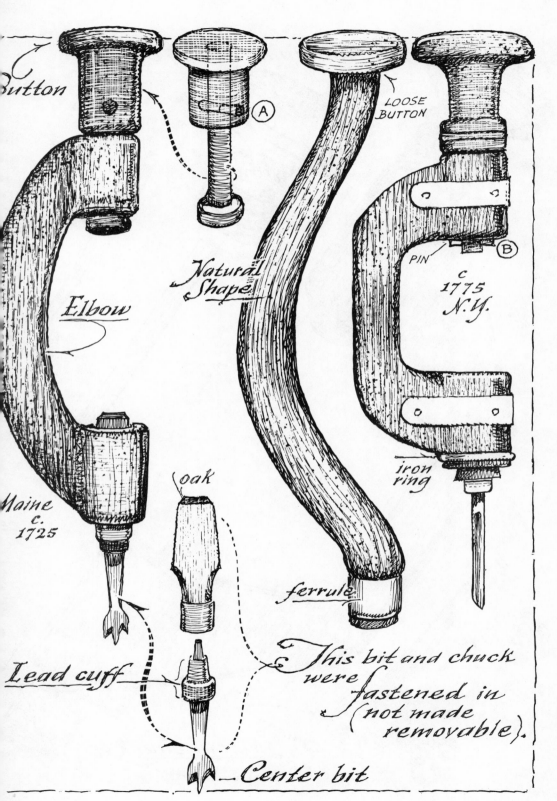

Button

Natural
Shape

Elbow

Maine
c.
1725

Lead cuff

oak

ferrule

This bit and chuck
were fastened in
(not made
removable).

Center bit

(A)

LOOSE
BUTTON

PIN

(B)

c
1775
N.Y.

iron
ring

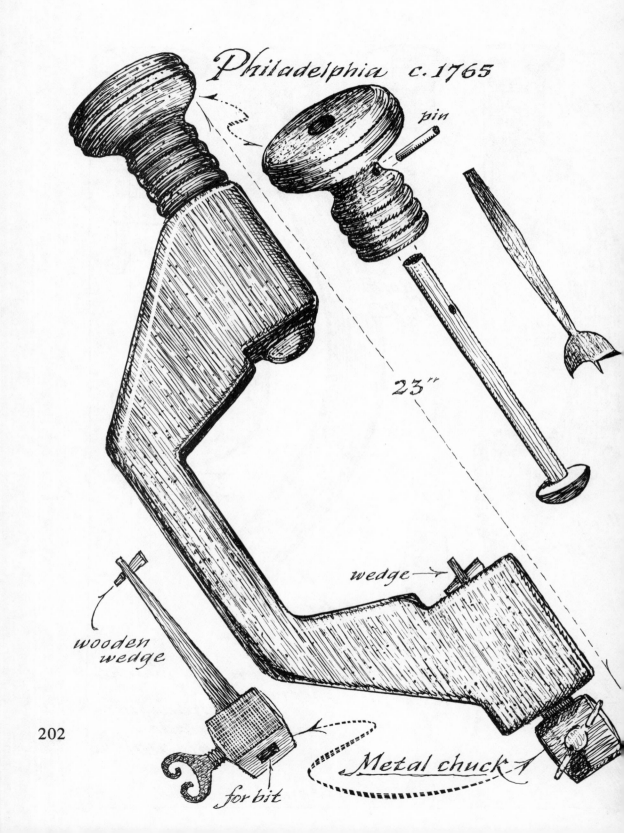

Philadelphia c.1765

pin

23″

wedge

wooden
wedge

for bit

Metal chuck

202

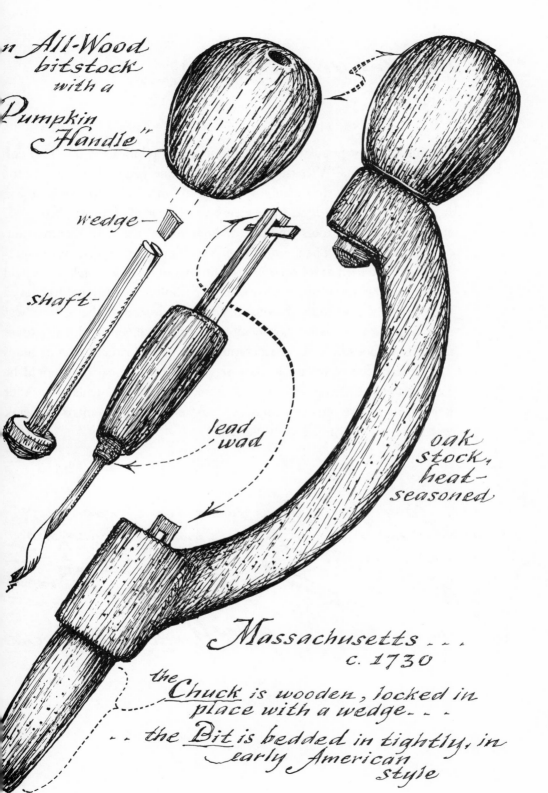

n All-Wood
bitstock
with a

*Pumpkin
Handle*"

wedge—

shaft—

lead
wad

oak
stock,
heat-
seasoned

Massachusetts . . .
c. 1730

the **Chuck** is wooden, locked in
place with a wedge. . . .
. . the **Bit** is bedded in tightly, in
early American
style

203

The THINGS you'll find in a Barn!

One of the most popular pages of the monthly publication of a tool collectors' club is its "Whatsis Column." Antique gadgets that stump the experts are frequently turning up. In the era of hand-made tools, it was logical that one-of-a-kind implements were created—the man who custom-made his own tools could allow himself the luxury of making tools to meet *his* needs. Then, too, there were devices that had many uses. Ladders were used as tobacco driers; the bars of a ladder-back chair held candleholders; meat hooks doubled as grappling hooks that retrieved things from the bottoms of wells. If you think it strange that a hook was so necessary to a household, remember that the well was used many times a day, that foods needing refrigeration were often lowered into it. Items lost beneath the water could not, of course, be seen, so they could be retrieved only by groping. The well hook was used as much as any other implement of the old-time household. After all, who wanted to drink water from a well filled with old pails?

These tiny Hammers were not Carpenters'... they were hung on sleds..... They knocked snow from horses' hoofs.

— all iron — 5½" called Yankee Snow Knocker

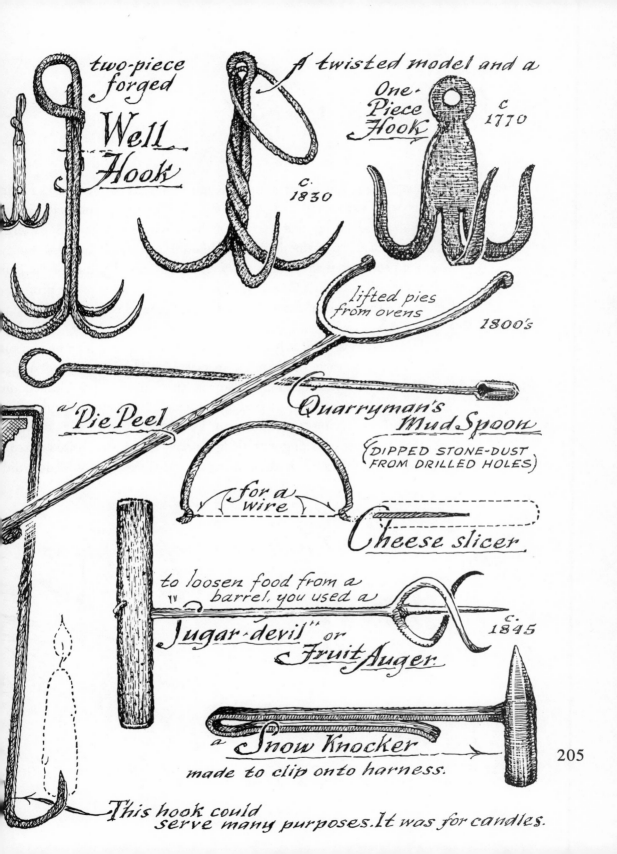

two-piece forged
Well Hook

A twisted model and a
One-Piece Hook
c. 1770

c. 1830

lifted pies from ovens
1800's

"Pie Peel

Quarryman's Mud Spoon
(DIPPED STONE-DUST FROM DRILLED HOLES)

for a wire

Cheese slicer

to loosen food from a barrel, you used a
Sugar-devil" or Fruit Auger.
c. 1845

a **Snow Knocker**
made to clip onto harness.

205

This hook could serve many purposes. It was for candles.

Some were Special

Although nails and hooks and tacks and hundreds of other iron imple
ments were hammered out by farmers all over the countryside, it wa
recognized as fitting that each item have its own sizes and patterns
The nails made in Maine look quite like the nails made in New Jersey
both in proportions and design; only an expert can tell a difference. Peo
ple were religious about conforming to tradition; they had a profoun
reverence for accepted design that we nowadays feel is decadence.

Here are a few things that are of the past that you might find in ol
attics or barns, each thing for a special use. The stock-knife shaped
wood, the mill pick dressed millstones, the barrel-scrape cleaned ou
barrels, the "commander" pushed beams "home" and into their mortises
When I was trying to move a barn, I found a "commander" of bette
use than two men working with sledgehammers, and was pleased to see i
sending beams into place without disfiguring them as the iron sledges did

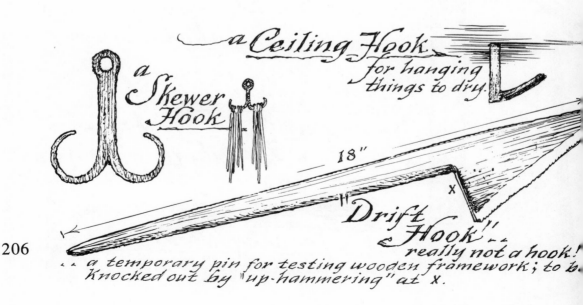

a *Skewer Hook*

a *Ceiling Hook* for hanging things to dry.

18"

Drift Hook" ... really not a hook!

... a temporary pin for testing wooden framework; to b
knocked out by "up-hammering" at x.

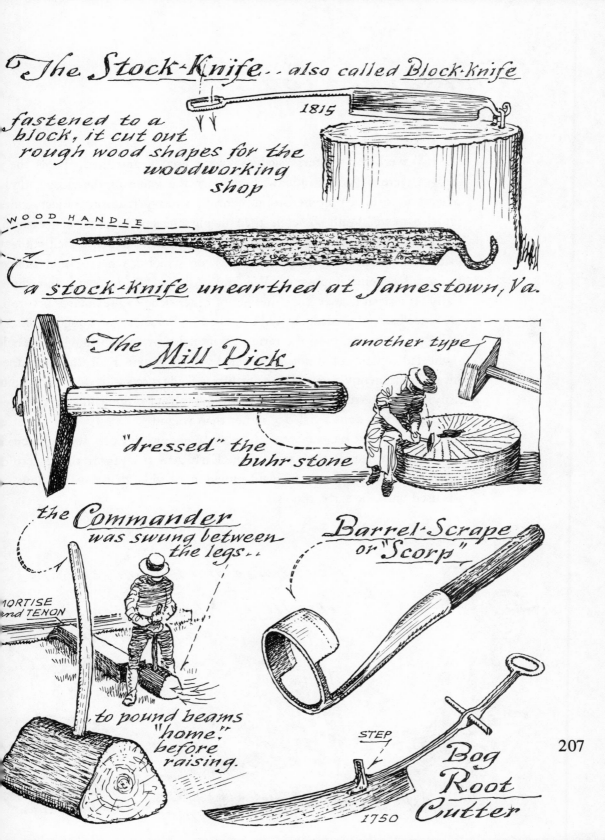

The **Stock-Knife** — also called **Block-Knife**

1815

fastened to a block, it cut out rough wood shapes for the woodworking shop

WOOD HANDLE

a <u>stock-knife</u> unearthed at Jamestown, Va.

The **Mill Pick**

another type

"dressed" the buhr stone

the **Commander** was swung between the legs

MORTISE and TENON

to pound beams "home" before raising.

Barrel-Scrape or "Scorp"

STEP

1750

Bog Root Cutter

207

These were *Tools too!*

"Sleds" were for winter; "sledges" were used year round. Tools the sledges were. If you would wish to learn the value of the sledge, try putting an ordinary house broom beneath a heavy trunk or object you wish to move. With someone then lifting one end, a child can easily pull the broom and its load across the floor. Farmers pulled unbelievable loads (on wooden runners) across grass on which a wheel would have sunk and become impossible. We know of the "stone boat," but the Early American farmer had a number of other sledge-type devices before the wheelbarrow. A sledge could be pulled by horse or ox through forest, and over rocks and onto the farm in winter ice or spring mud, whereas a wheeled vehicle could not. A wheeled vehicle is higher off the ground; this makes it inconveniently high for lifting loads *into* and it does tip over easily. So, harvesting and haying and moving rocks, dung, maple syrup barrels, etc. was done by sledge rather than wagon.

Here you may see a few of these early sliding devices. It might be safely said that for every wagon on the Early American farm, there were three to ten sledges. Even the hand-pulled model, like that shown below, was used until the early 1800's.

Even after horse and wagon vehicles, the *Tumbril Sledge* remained as a handy farm tool.

1650

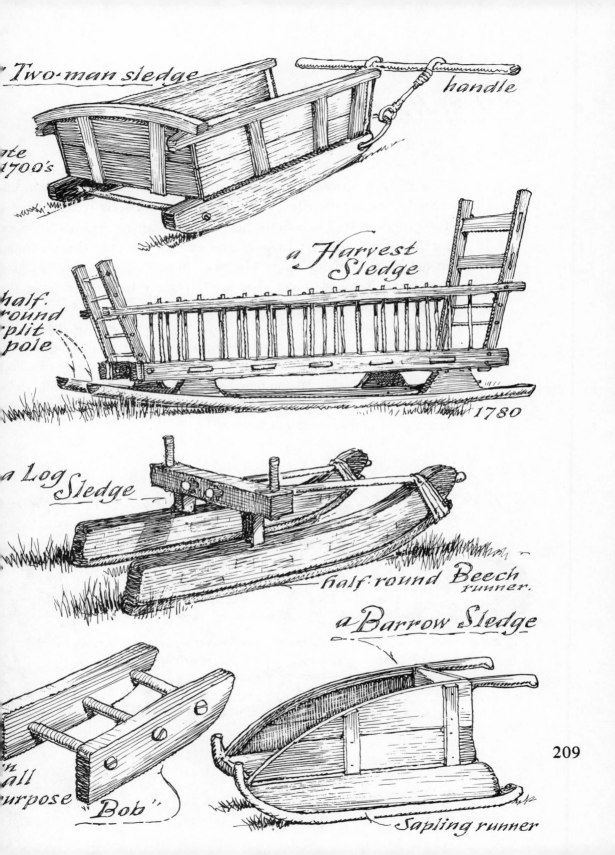

Two-man sledge

handle

ate
1700's

a *Harvest
Sledge*

half.
round
split
pole

1780

a *Log Sledge*

half-round *Beech*
runner.

a *Barrow Sledge*

n
all
urpose

"Bob"

Sapling runner

209

Jacks

The Early American was an artist at lifting and moving heavy objects
Foundations and stone fences were built with the lever principle and a
few gadgets as well as with the help of oxen. Experts are often stumped
by the strange hooks and loops of iron with teeth in them that are found
in old barns. But these were blacksmith-made jack hooks for moving
beams and logs and stones. The lever was any handy tree limb; the
longer, the more leverage.

The "wagon jacks" you find in antique shops were used for many purposes. Carpenters, framers, blacksmiths, and wheelwrights included these
jacks in their list of shop tools. Some of them are made entirely of wood
(usually ash or hickory); and they have outlasted many automobile jacks
that have rusted away and ended in the junk pile while the wooden jacks
are as good as they were a century ago.

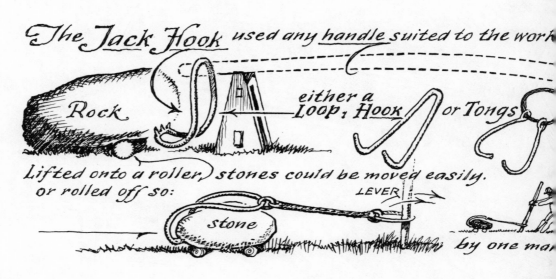

The Jack Hook used any handle suited to the work

Rock

either a
Loop, Hook or Tongs

Lifted onto a roller, stones could be moved easily.
or rolled off so:

LEVER

stone

by one man

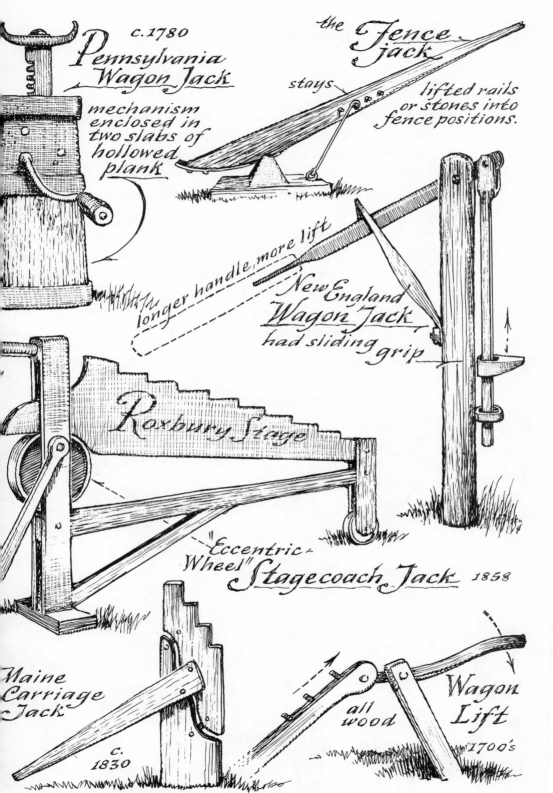

c.1780
Pennsylvania Wagon Jack
mechanism enclosed in two slabs of hollowed plank

the *Fence Jack*
stays
lifted rails or stones into fence positions.

longer handle, more lift

New England Wagon Jack had sliding grip

Roxbury Stage

"Eccentric Wheel" *Stagecoach Jack* 1858

Maine Carriage Jack
c. 1830

all wood

Wagon Lift
1700's

211

The Blacksmith

"Smith" from "smite," "black" from "black metal" (as distinguished from silversmith brightwork), the "blacksmith" was the Early American handyman. He made nails, hinges, sled runners, anchors, scythes, hoes, utensils, axes, hooks, and every kind of tool. In the middle 1800's he began taking over the farrier's work of horseshoeing; till then the farrier was veterinary too.

Blacksmith tool design has not changed very much except for the hazelwood withes that held all upper tools (chisels and swages). Hardly an implement or utensil cannot be traced to the early blacksmith.

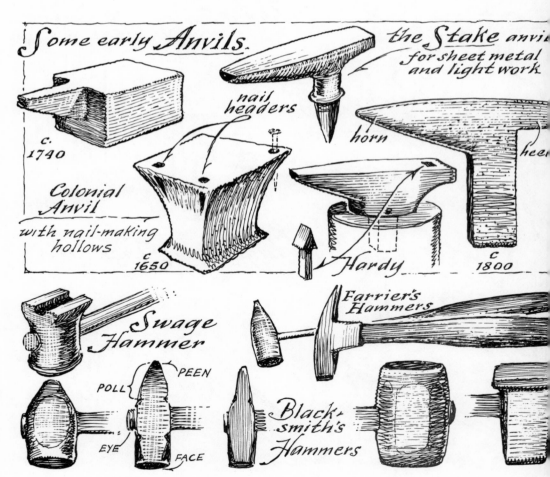

Some early *Anvils.*
the *Stake* anvil for sheet metal and light work

nail headers

horn

heel

c. 1740

Colonial Anvil

with nail-making hollows

c 1650

Hardy

c 1800

Swage Hammer

Farrier's Hammers

PEEN

POLL

Black-smith's Hammers

EYE

FACE

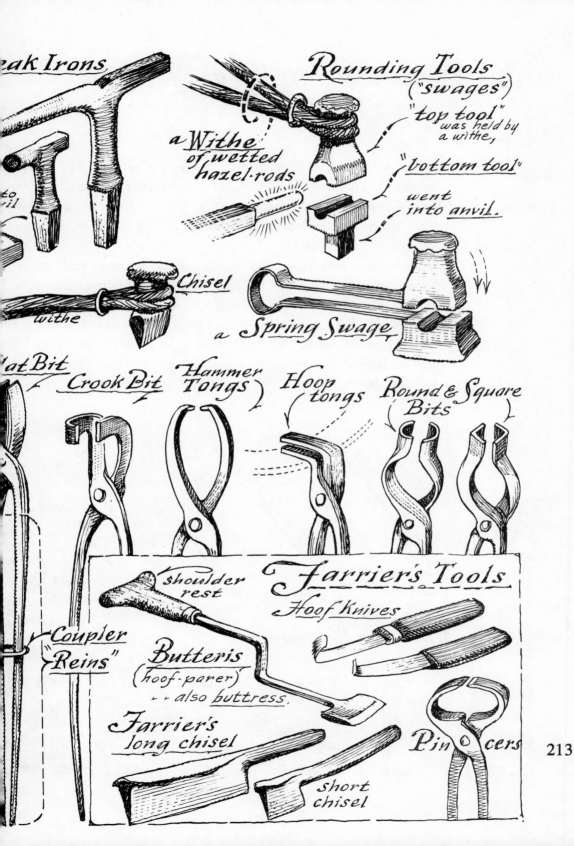

...eak Irons,

Rounding Tools
("swages")

"top tool" was held by a withe,

"bottom tool" went into anvil.

a Withe of wetted hazel-rods

Chisel

withe

a Spring Swage

...at Bit

Crook Bit

Hammer Tongs

Hoop tongs

Round & Square Bits

Farrier's Tools

shoulder rest

Hoof Knives

"Coupler Reins"

Butteris
(hoof-parer)
-- also buttress.

Farrier's long chisel

short chisel

Pincers

213

Wrought Nailmaking

MACHINE-CUT   WROUGHT

Lacking in beauty, the "nail header" is hardly a collector's prize, yet i[t]
plainness does not adequately explain its infrequent appearance in antiqu[e]
shops. Considering how farmers made nails by the thousands durin[g]
winter months around the forge or fireplace, the rarity of headers is [a]
mystery.

Machine-cut nails taper only on two sides; wrought nails on fou[r].
The most common "rose nail" had four hammer hits (if done by an expert)[;]
the head of the "clasp nail" had sharp downward sides to cut into th[e]
surface; "plancher nails" had T-shaped heads to hold down flooring; th[e]
"scupper" nailed leather (as for a bellows). Though our "brad" is [a]
small-headed nail, the word once meant "broad" and the "brad" was suc[h]
a nail for planks.

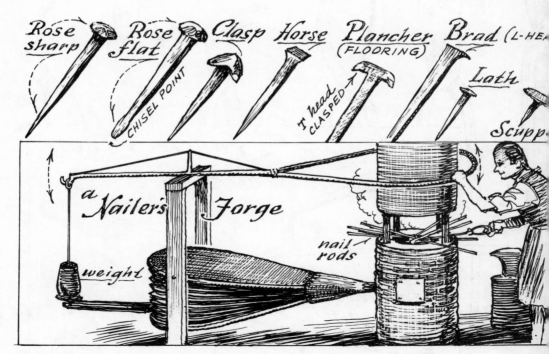

Rose sharp   Rose flat   Clasp   Horse   Plancher (FLOORING)   Brad (L-HE[AD])

CHISEL POINT   T head CLASPED   Lath   Scupp[er]

a Nailer's Forge

weight

nail rods

214

Nail Headers (bores)

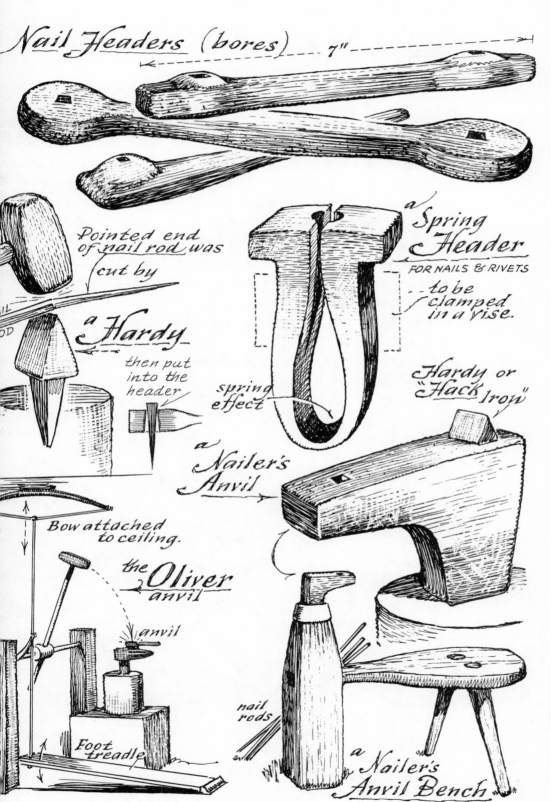

7"

Pointed end
of nail rod was

cut by

a *Hardy*

then put
into the
header

a *Spring Header*

FOR NAILS & RIVETS

...to be
clamped
in a vise.

spring
effect

Hardy or
"*Hack* Iron"

a *Nailer's Anvil*

Bow attached
to ceiling.

the *Oliver* anvil

anvil

Foot treadle

nail rods

a *Nailer's Anvil Bench*

215

Tanners and Curriers

A currier did *not* curry horses. His craft was to scrape and soften the rough hides after the tanner had treated them. The tanner's tools, so wet and messy when being used, were seldom things of beauty, but their lines were traditional and graceful. The tanner's knives had delicate curves to fit the curve of the tanner's beam.

The currier's beam was flat, just as his knife was. The shaving knife (also called beamer or head-knife) had a soft steel blade with its fine edge burred over (recurved) into a minute scraper form. This delicate edge needed constant turning with a "turning steel" and lifting with a "finger steel," which was kept handy between two fingers as the beams-man worked. (This recurved edge will have disappeared from wear and corrosion on ancient tools.)

Farmers made their own leather for shoes, hinges, and harness, so old barns often have such tools about.

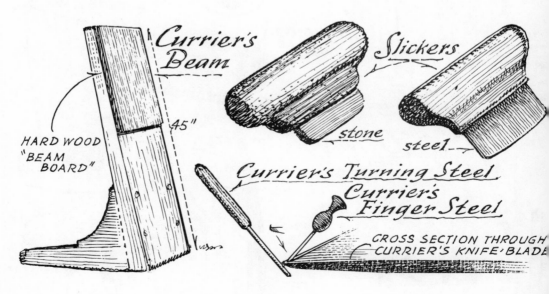

Currier's Beam

HARD WOOD "BEAM BOARD"

45"

Slickers

stone

steel

Currier's Turning Steel

Currier's Finger Steel

CROSS SECTION THROUGH CURRIER'S KNIFE·BLADE

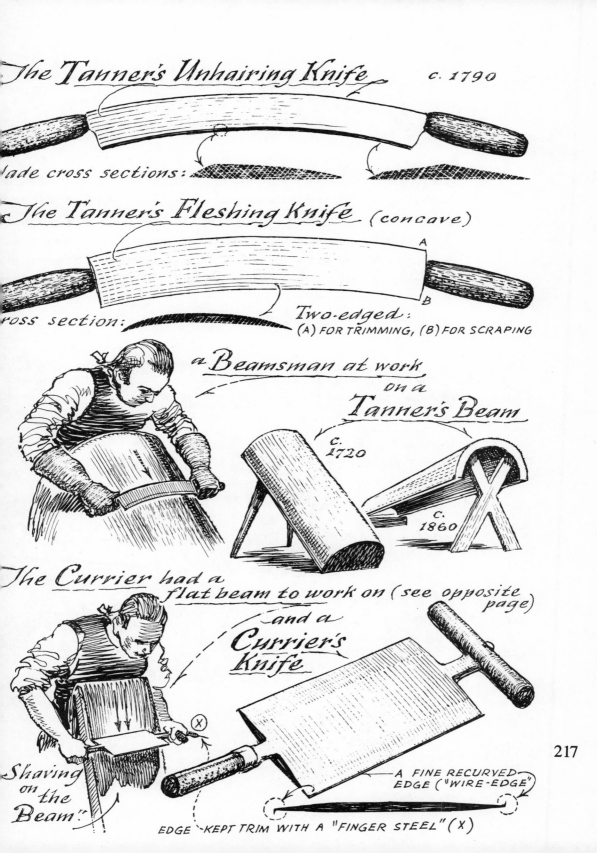

The Tanner's Unhairing Knife

c. 1790

Blade cross sections:

The Tanner's Fleshing Knife (concave)

A

B

cross section:

Two-edged:
(A) FOR TRIMMING, (B) FOR SCRAPING

a Beamsman at work
on a
Tanner's Beam

c. 1720

c. 1860

The Currier had a flat beam to work on (see opposite page)

and a
Currier's
Knife

X

Shaving
on
the
Beam".

A FINE RECURVED EDGE ("WIRE-EDGE")

EDGE KEPT TRIM WITH A "FINGER STEEL" (X)

217

About Wheels

Early wheelwright tools were not much different from those of hard-wood joinery except for those shown here. The process of putting a wheel together is illustrated below. The tire (iron outer rim) was made by the blacksmith. After the tire was made hot in a bed of ashes, it was applied to the wooden wheel, and then cooled quickly. The contraction tightened the tire, and held the whole wheel together with a tremendous force.

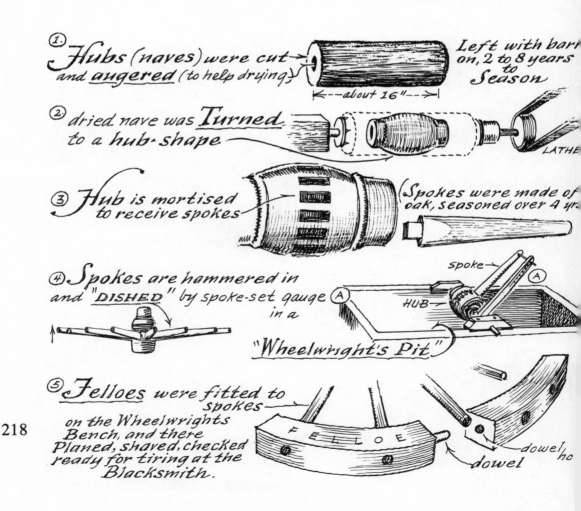

① Hubs (naves) were cut and augered (to help drying) → Left with bark on, 2 to 8 years to Season ← about 16" →

② dried nave was Turned to a hub-shape — LATHE

③ Hub is mortised to receive spokes (Spokes were made of oak, seasoned over 4 yr.)

④ Spokes are hammered in and "DISHED" by spoke-set gauge Ⓐ in a "Wheelwright's Pit" spoke → HUB → Ⓐ

⑤ Felloes were fitted to spokes — on the Wheelwrights Bench, and there Planed, shaved, checked ready for tiring at the Blacksmith. F E L L O E dowel dowel ho

218

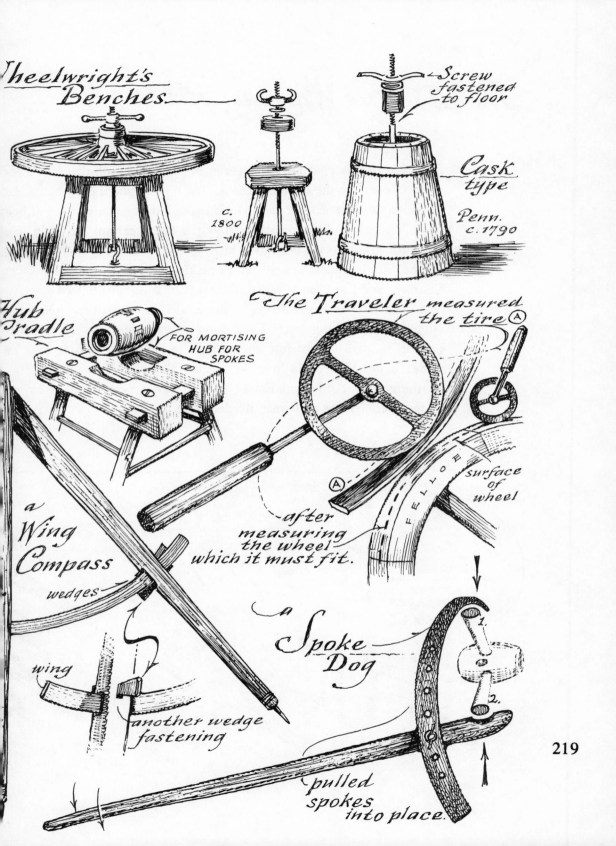

Wheelwright's Benches

Screw fastened to floor

c. 1800

Cask type

Penn. c. 1790

Hub Cradle

FOR MORTISING HUB FOR SPOKES

The Traveler measured the tire Ⓐ

after measuring the wheel which it must fit.

FELLOE

surface of wheel

Ⓐ

a Wing Compass

wedges

wing

another wedge fastening

a Spoke Dog

1.

2.

pulled spokes into place.

219

It's all in the Way you Hit it.

Today we think a hammer is a hammer—the same thing that lays a roo
cracks a nut! But the early craftsman (like a good golfer) knew that *ho*
you hit and *what you hit with* could make a difference in the job bein
done. See, in the drawing below, how the flail separates the grain whil
the pestle grinds it; yet both tools hit.

The "flinting pick" did the job of making gun flints; the "bricklayer'
hammer" and "axe" and "raker" did work that is still admired after tw
centuries. The "printing mallet" stamped designs on painted floor cloth
(popular before linoleum). The "flood gate hammer" didn't smash th
gate; its massive weight just moved it. The "zax" cut roofing slate an
made nail holes in it. The "trunnel hammer" knocked trunnels in withou
smashing them. And so on. Each "hammer" hit a special kind of blow t
do the specialty the craftsman needed done.

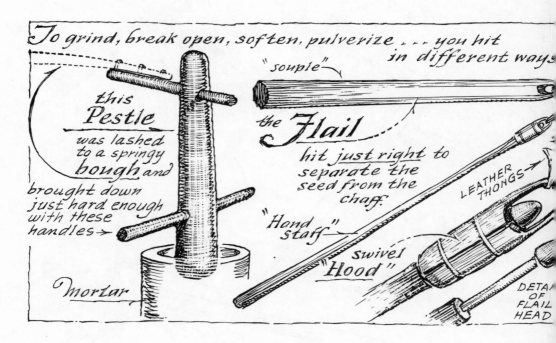

To grind, break open, soften, pulverize . . . you hit in different ways

this **Pestle** was lashed to a springy *bough* and brought down just hard enough with these handles →

Mortar

"souple"

the **Flail** hit just right to separate the seed from the chaff.

"Hand staff"

swivel "Hood"

LEATHER THONGS

DETAI OF FLAIL HEAD

220

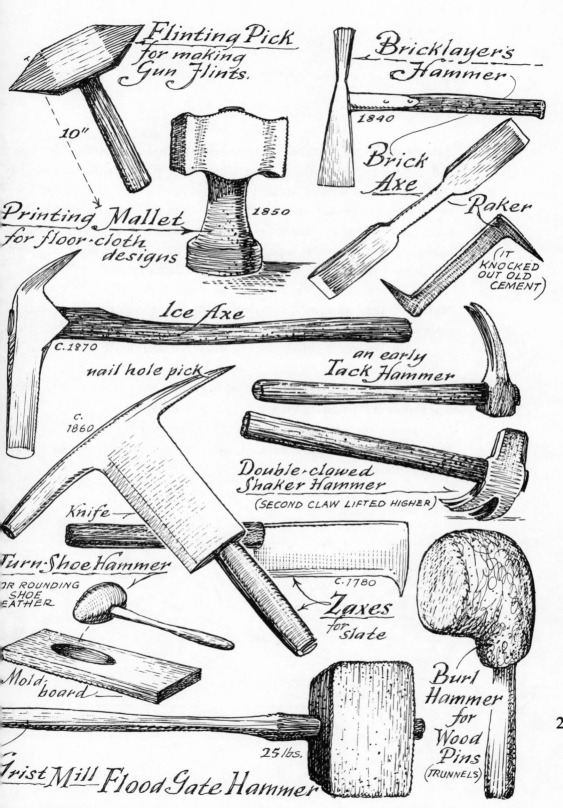

Flinting Pick for making *Gun Flints*.

10"

Bricklayer's Hammer

1840

Brick Axe

Raker

(IT KNOCKED OUT OLD CEMENT)

Printing Mallet for floor-cloth designs

1850

Ice Axe

C. 1870

nail hole pick

an early *Tack Hammer*

C. 1860

Double-clawed Shaker Hammer

(SECOND CLAW LIFTED HIGHER)

Knife

Turn-Shoe Hammer

OR ROUNDING SHOE LEATHER

C. 1780

Zaxes for slate

Burl Hammer for Wood Pins

(TRUNNELS)

Mold-board

221

25 lbs.

Grist Mill Flood Gate Hammer

Hay Implements

Among the more plentiful old barn relics is the hay knife. Wide, heavy and with the blade on the outer edge, most people wonder how hay could be reaped with it. It didn't reap—it cut out portions of hay from the haystack. The hay-spade and hay-saw did the same thing. The hay-spade knife, however, doubled as pumpkin cutter in the days when pumpkins were animal food. Pumpkin stalks tended to choke animals, so pumpkins were cut from the top and the stalks destroyed.

The slender, sharp reaping hook became an American design of rare beauty by the late 1700's. But during the late 1800's the art of cutting gave way to the art of slashing, and a sickle is a better slasher. The earliest corn knife was machetelike, but the sicklelike corn knife appeared in the early 1800's.

The sickle reaped with the aid of a grass crook (hay crook), which was also used for pulling loose hay from the stack.

Although such serrations are usually worn away in ancient tools, the early sickles were usually serrated; this sets them apart from the slender reaping hook.

This Connecticut Hay Knife c. 1850 worked like a saw.

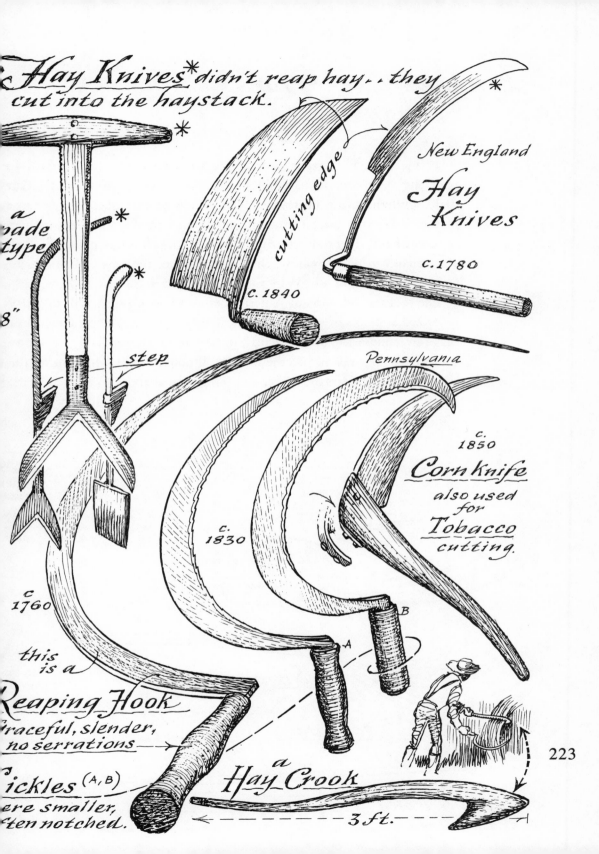

Hay Knives didn't reap hay... they cut into the haystack.

a spade type

8"

step

New England
Hay Knives
c.1780

cutting edge

c. 1840

Pennsylvania

c. 1850

Corn knife also used for *Tobacco* cutting.

c. 1830

c. 1760

this is a
Reaping Hook
graceful, slender, no serrations

Sickles (A, B) were smaller, often notched.

a *Hay Crook*

— 3 ft. —

223

Knives and Grass

The first American grass blades were from England and matched to naturally bent "snaths" (handles) without "nibs" (hand grips). Our early scythes and cradle scythes were things of rare grace. Even those of the 1800's that were factory-made retained the lines that made them different from the cruder European and English implements. The snath was usually made of willow, shaped in hot oil; the nibs and fingers of hickory; the sned of ash. Wire rods were added in the late 1800's.

The scythes and forks of America before the late 1800's will someday be prized as pieces of art, but as of now they are so large or cumbersome that few choose to collect them. You are almost never likely to see an ancient wooden rake or scythe broken, although those made during the last seventy-five years or so have an average life of about five to ten years.

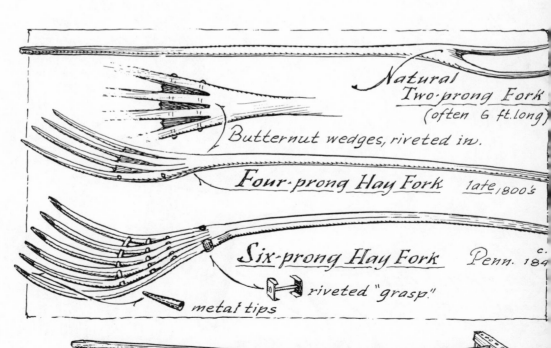

Natural Two-prong Fork (often 6 ft. long)

Butternut wedges, riveted in.

Four-prong Hay Fork late 1800's

Six-prong Hay Fork Penn. 184 c.

riveted "grasp."

metal tips

224

Bull Rake or *Hay Drag*

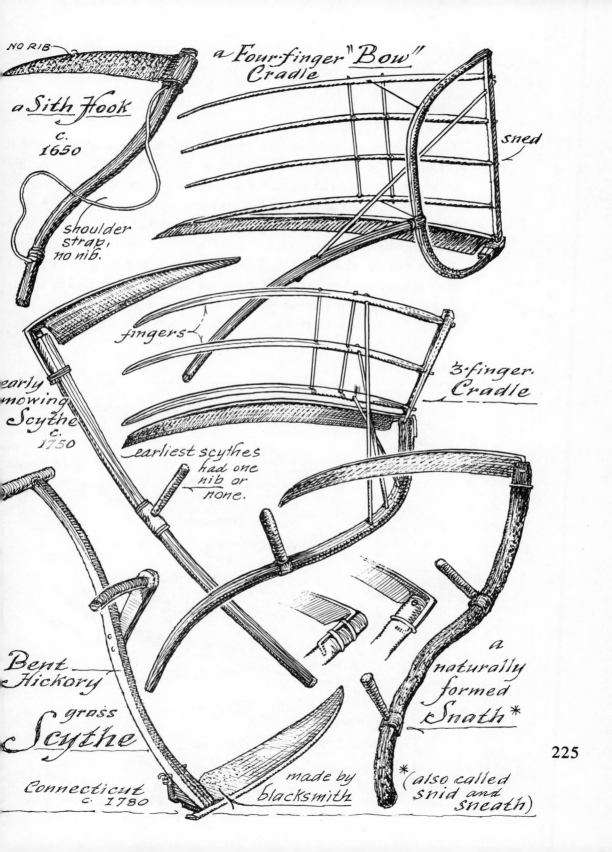

NO RIB

a *Sith Hook*
c. 1650

a *Four-finger "Bow" Cradle*

sned

shoulder strap, no nib.

fingers

3·finger. Cradle

early mowing Scythe
c. 1750

earliest scythes had one nib or none.

Bent Hickory

grass *Scythe*

a naturally formed *Snath* *

made by blacksmith

Connecticut
c. 1780

* (also called snid and sneath)

225

Found in the Barn

Oddities now, common items a century ago, here are a few things that were found in old barns and brought to me for identification. A tiny yoke for a goose, a cheesemaker's curd cutter and stirrer, a big winnowing scoop one used to throw flailed grain into the air to let the wind blow away the chaff—these are things that bring the past back vividly. Most old barns have eel spears tucked away near the rafters, although there may not be a river or lake for miles around. Yet a century ago men prized their swamp and wetlands, and stored up water in millponds for water-power instead of bulldozing over the wet places as we do now.

The American countryside was very different a century or two ago!

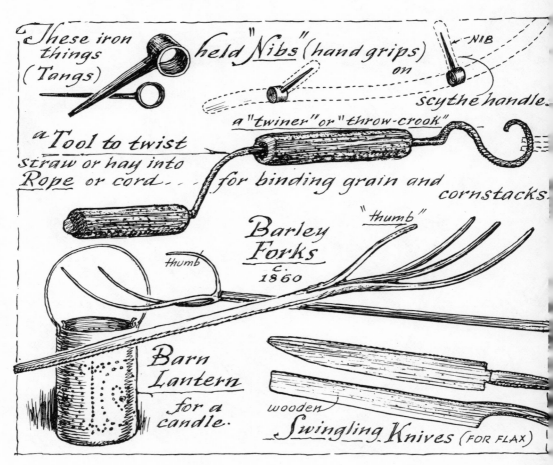

These iron things (Tangs) held "Nibs" (hand grips) on scythe handle. NIB

a "twiner" or "throw-crook"

a Tool to twist straw or hay into Rope or cord . . . for binding grain and cornstacks.

"thumb"

thumb

Barley Forks c. 1860

"thumb"

Barn Lantern for a candle.

wooden Swingling Knives (FOR FLAX)

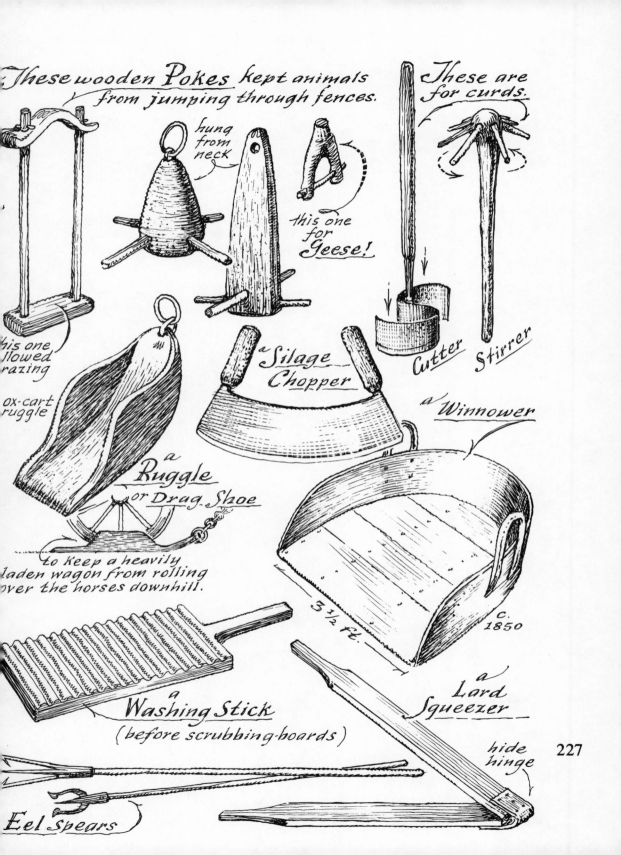

These wooden **Pokes** kept animals from jumping through fences.

hung from neck

this one for *Geese!*

These are for curds.

Cutter

Stirrer

his one llowed razing

ox-cart ruggle

a *Silage Chopper*

a *Winnower*

a *Ruggle* or *Drag-Shoe*

to keep a heavily laden wagon from rolling over the horses downhill.

3½ ft.

c. 1850

a *Lard Squeezer*

a *Washing Stick* (before scrubbing-boards)

hide hinge

227

Eel Spears

A REVERENCE for WOOD

ERIC SLOANE

To Joseph McLaughlin
the man at my publishers' office who
insisted upon my doing this book

CONTENTS

AUTHOR'S NOTE

The way this book came about, as I think back on it, is an odd one. For after having done a score of books about early American life, I found that I'd never done the one I first had in mind, the book to be called *A Reverence for Wood*.

As a painter of clouds and sky, my greater interests were in flying and in meteorology. I believe I was the first weatherman on television; I built the Hall of Atmosphere in the American Museum of Natural History (Willetts Memorial) in 1945, and later I wrote several books about weather. When World War II came along I did manuals and three dimensional models of weather phenomena for military flyers. The more research I did in meteorology, the more impressed I became with the weather knowledge of the early American. I found an amazing source of information in old diaries and almanacs, and before long my own interests in weather became submerged in the lore of the early American countryman. His manner of living with the seasons instead of battling to overcome them, his regard for natural resources, and his amazing reverence for wood seemed to be worth recording.

I was recalling this to my friend Hugh Weidinger one day as we were flying over the New England countryside. "Some day soon," I said, "I must do the book about trees and wood." Down below, the wooded hills were just turning to their autumn colors, and the shadow of our plane raced across a sea of crimson and russet.

"You'd better write it soon, while there are some trees left," said Hugh. "Look ahead." He pointed over the nose of the plane.

There on the horizon began the mathematical pattern of the metropolis. Fifty miles from its center, New York City had spilled rudely over the design of nature. It was obvious that wherever such an intrusion had taken place, there would never be a going back. Nothing can take over as completely as man: he has had many complex relationships with the forest in the course of history, but where solid concrete appears, those relationships seem to end and man's dominance becomes complete.

"You just must admit it," my friend said. "Trees and wood are on their way out. Everything is metal and plastic these days. Look at this airplane; it's not made of wood the way planes once were."

It was something to think about as we roared on. But I then realized that we were running on wood fuel! The gasoline that operated our engine came from prehistoric forests that had grown and perished when there were no men and no need for conservation.

Sometimes even I have been trapped by the illusion that the uses of wood are declining, and on one of my infrequent trips to New York, a glance around the city revealed the vast changes made there within the last ten years. What impact, I thought, could a book about trees and wood have on people living in this world of concrete and glass and steel?

Certainly we don't see as much wood as we once did, yet wood is still with us. I realized that the very contract for my book was made of materials derived from wood. Every time one picks up the telephone to call long distance, one's voice is conveyed across the country by hundreds of miles of wires strung from wooden post to wooden post; even the number you call is listed in a directory made entirely of wood pulp. We think of traveling by "railroad," yet there is far more wood in the ties than there is steel in the rails. Modern tires, plastics, medicines and paints, boxes and cartons and bags and newspapers; almost everything we use can still be traced in some way to the tree. The pencil (and its eraser) and the paper on which I am writing this book, the ink and the paints that I use to illustrate it, all are wood products. The finished book you are now reading began as a tree. My royalty checks and the envelopes they arrive in will also be wood products.

I just read in a newspaper that because of plastics and other innovations, the usefulness of the tree has diminished in the past half century. But the same newspaper (which boasts the country's largest circulation) enjoys the products of the forest; each Sunday issue destroys a sizeable grove.

It may be that after we have spent a century or two in expending our wealth of wood to seek the riches of other planets, we will realize that our greatest wealth was right here on earth after all.

I derive a certain pleasure from an awareness of our gift of wood. Besides giving me its chemical and utilitarian benefits, like the fireplace that "warms the soul as well as the body," the tree and its wood are a most necessary part of my life's aesthetic enjoyment.

Perhaps after reading this book when you hear the rustling of leaves or the wind in the boughs, smell the fragrance of a Christmas tree or the burning of a pine log in the fireplace, or see the majesty of a gnarled and ancient oak, you will revive some faint memory from our early American heritage and share with those first settlers a reverence for wood.

Eric Sloane

Weather Hill Farm
Cornwall Bridge
Connecticut

Postscript: The names and dates and places in the following story have been given accurately to the best of my ability; yet my writing is supposed to be a tale, and as in any historical novel, my own imagination has blended with fact to create poetical reality.

Perpetual modernness is the measure of merit in every work of art.

Emerson

The Old Barn

"They don't build them like that now," said Harley as he tapped his wrecking bar against one of the old pegged joints.

I was above on a ladder, ready to tackle the roof. It seemed wrong to destroy such symmetry. The ancient shingles lay haphazardly like matted grass on a hill, but from my vantage point, the wooden roof pattern stretched away with a mathematical grace that first became part of the local landscape, then of the distant horizon. Sighting along the peak I could see wavy contours that indicated the position of each rafter underneath. Old barn roofs always have a lively style and no two will settle in the same way. The long tobacco barns of Connecticut, after a century of weather, begin to slouch comfortably into the contours of the land upon which they rest. The stone barns of Pennsylvania have rigid walls, which support their roof peaks in a fairly straight posture for a number of years; then, after a brief period of picturesque decay, the middle rafters weaken, and under the weight of wet snow one certain

239

winter night, the whole covering falls at once into the barn's deserted innards.

It is said that the reason wooden roofs on stone barns collapse is that after some two centuries of drying, the whole wooden roof shrinks. While stone sides stay put, a vast stretch of wooden roof will actually become inches smaller in a century. The thought of a barn becoming smaller with age seems strange, but such shrinkage is nevertheless plainly measurable.

Like most of the very early American buildings, my barn roof had no rooftree (that board which runs the length of the peak, also known as a *ridgepole* or *ridge rafter*). Each pair of slanting rafters was merely pegged together at the peak and held in place by wide chestnut roof boards. Now, after some hundred winters had imposed their pressing weight, the roofing lay loosely over the rafters like a big soft gray tapestry.

When you tear down an old barn, you begin at the top, and the shingles are always first to go. Harley had explained that to me.

"There's a right way to do things and a wrong way," he said. "Then there's the quick way. That's how city folks like to work, so it costs them most in the long run."

The current method of tearing down barns is by bulldozer and wire cable. But since the old mortised joints are usually stronger than the whole lengths of beam, when a barn is pulled down in this way, good wood splits. The roof then falls like a sodden cape over the whole thing, and demolition becomes harder and takes longer. So I chose the seemingly slower old-time method; I started by removing the roof.

I found that the greenish hue of old roof shingles comes from actual moss, and that rather than causing rot, moss often preserves a roof. It adds to the shingle's ability to "breathe," to swell quickly during a shower, thereby closing each crack or hole. There are old barn roofs through which you can see the stars, yet which won't leak in a hard rainstorm.

Most architectural historians tell us that the fronts of many old buildings were constructed of clapboard, while the backs were shingled. "It was a matter of fashion," they explain. "Shingles were just not fashionable." They forget how weather-minded and wood-wise early builders were—they usually placed the back of a building to the north, where the cold wet winds hit, and for this side they chose cedar shingles simply for greater protection.

Virgin American white cedarwood had a remarkable quality to resist water and damp-rot. During the 1700's, most of the nation's shingle material came from the New Jersey cedar swamps. The demand was so great that by the 1800's these swamplands were depleted of their trees. After that, astonishingly enough, white cedar was *mined* in New Jersey. It was while a stump was being removed from these swamps that several sunken logs were loosened and floated to the surface. The logs had been submerged anywhere from a few centuries to a thousand years!

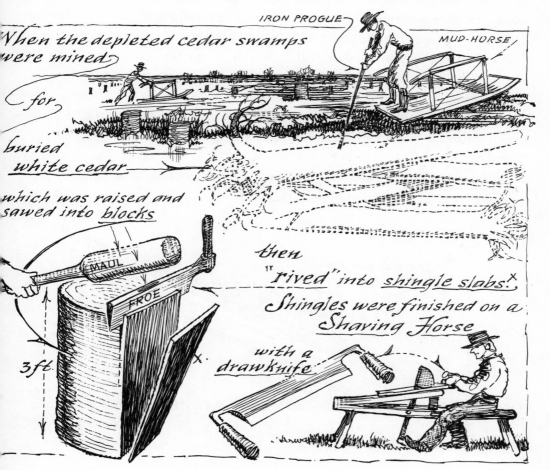

When the depleted cedar swamps were mined

for

buried white cedar

which was raised and sawed into blocks

IRON PROGUE

MUD-HORSE

MAUL

FROE

3 ft.

then "rived" into shingle slabs.

Shingles were finished on a Shaving Horse

with a drawknife

These submerged logs, it was found, were of a superior quality and contained good timber. It was further discovered that a layer of fallen cedar trunks, about twelve feet deep, covered the swamp bottom. When people learned of the remarkable lightness and durability of this material, there was a great demand for it. With the aid of an iron "progue pin," to probe beneath the surface of the water and locate the sunken logs, *cedar mining* prospered until the Civil War.

The roof on Independence Hall in Philadelphia was made of this material, and many of the three-foot shingles on historic American homes are from cedar that had been buried under the water for centuries.

One might not notice it from the ground, but any ancient shingled roof is usually studded with thousands of nails that have pushed outward from the shingles like quills on a porcupine. The reason for this is interesting, for it demonstrates how softwoods tend to breathe with every atmospheric change. Each wetting and drying, heating and cooling, each pressure change of new weather, will bring about some tiny expansion or contraction. At a twice-a-day minimum, in fifty years, this phenomenon will produce about thirty thousand movements, each of which tends to squeeze the old nails out of the softwood. Square nails have more surface area (with that much more friction) and so they do resist more than round nails.

"It's too bad," I remarked, "the way these nails pull out of the shingles. I guess the old-timers didn't figure on that."

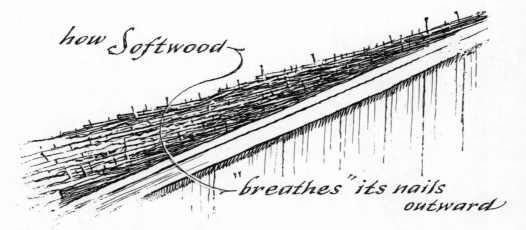

how Softwood

"breathes" its nails outward

242

"We always left them that way on purpose," said Harley. "It kept the snow in place."

"Snow in place? You wanted the snow to *stay* there?"

"Sure," he replied. "To keep the heat in. Most barn heat goes out the roof, doesn't it? Warmest thing we have up here in Warren during February is the snow."

I'm not sure he really meant that, but I do recall being able to pick out all the lived-in homes and barns along the road just by observing the amount of snow on their roofs. An abandoned barn will usually keep its blanket of snow right on into spring. There's an old New England saying—"what with the high cost of heating, the average icicle on a roof costs about five dollars a foot." Indeed, it does cost about that much to melt off roof snow into freezing icicles at the eaves.

Snow, in the early days, was a cherished thing, not the nuisance that we now consider it. Far from being removed from a highway, snow was actually placed on the roads. It was even shoveled onto the old covered bridges. Then it was packed down with snow-rollers to make the only really smooth highways of that time. Sometimes when snow was scarce, it was transported from the forest and spread on the roads. People used to pile cornstalks around the foundation of a house or a barn just to hold the snow there. It kept the winter wind out. They put little spikes and iron eagles with outstretched wings on their roofs, not so much to keep the ice from falling on passers-by as to keep a good blanket of snow there. So I suppose a roughly shingled roof or one with its nails protruding also held the snow in place.

"I'm saving all the wrought nails," I called down to Harley. "Put them in a box. They sell for three cents apiece, you know."

The fact that he didn't reply was no indication of his not having heard. Or that he had no opinion. Why anyone would collect old nails when he could afford good store nails was too upsetting a subject for him to discuss. He once asked me why I like wormy chestnut, yet throw away clothing with moth holes in it. I cause him much wonderment. And as for my making frames for my paintings from "miserable old weathered boards" full of knots and decay—he'll just never understand that.

243

Even to me, for a while, the idea of old worn barn wood for picture framing seemed a bit affected. But the beauty of naturally aged wood has a strong appeal to the human mind. I decided also that its abstract pattern of natural decay is really more pleasing than anything solely ornamental that a frame-maker might concoct. If a frame is part of a painting (and it usually is), choosing the frame should be the important final touch of the painter himself. So my love affair with old wood won out.

Strangely enough, however, wood that is exposed to the weather and the seasons for a long time becomes too "athletic." It seems to get accustomed to the strong breathing caused by atmospheric changes. Barn siding, for example, when removed to the steady dry atmosphere indoors, will exhibit a most remarkable shrinkage. Mitered frame corners will soon pull apart, and wall sheathing will separate a full inch. Because of this, I adopted the foolproof early American "ship-lap" or lapped joint for all my frames, and I still wonder why this simple and strongest of joints is not used more today.

How the SHIP·LAP *frame is made.*

a Mitered joint tends to dry apart, a Ship·lap st

Another old-time feature I have revived is painting on wood. Actually I use a *composition wood*, called Masonite; yet it is very similar to the base used by many early American painters, a flat piece of smooth tight-grained wood. While canvas absorbs dampness from the atmosphere, becoming first limp then taut (causing the crackle that appears in most ancient paintings), hardwood when painted on both sides has a minimum of expansion and contraction.

It would surprise most people to learn how many of our famous early American "canvases" were really paintings done on slabs of wood. Many traveling portrait painters and limners of the 1700's carried stacks of wood panels with them instead of canvas and stretchers, and they were expert at knowing the woods which are least likely to crack, warp, or be affected by moisture. The Peale family of artists, it is said, imported slabs of wood from Europe, much older and dryer than any native American wood.

In 1925, when I met a disgruntled lumber salesman who gave me all his samples of "a new building board," I was the first to try them out as a surface on which to paint pictures. Now, forty years later, about half of all the work of contemporary American artists is done on such composition board. And there's even less warping or shrinking in composition board than there is in plain wood, for there are no pores or grain to harbor dampness.

The surface of the average large antique pine table might change its width by a quarter-inch between midsummer and midwinter! The end clamp-boards, of course, will not change their *length* much, because wood shrinks more *across* the grain than *with* the grain (the difference is more than ten to one). Instead of clamp-boards, *dovetail keys* were sometimes slid into place, strengthening a panel without the use of nails or screws, yet giving the panel leeway to expand or contract.

Bowls, too, unless they are made of root or burl grain, will shrink across the grain with advanced age: the older they get, the more oval they become. The wide floorboards in ancient houses that pull apart and often let you see into the room below are also examples of how woods (like human beings) shrink in old age.

As Harley removed each piece of siding, he leaned it upright against the barn to keep it dry.

"They'll curve up if you lay them flat on the ground," he said.

It is significant that the old barn boards had kept straight for over a

The _shrinking_ of wood when drying, may be seen in a _clamped_* table-top

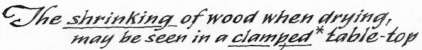

CLAMP·BOARD*

WHICH WILL SHRINK DURING WINTER
AND SWELL DURING THE MOIST SUMMER

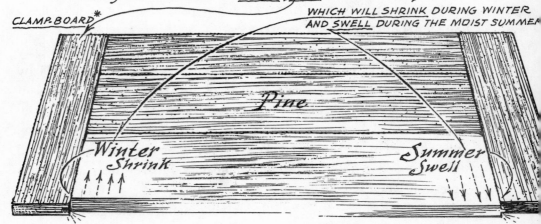

Pine

Winter
Shrink

Summer
Swell

.·or with wooden-pegged furniture after a century of dryi
pegs often protrude ----

PINE

.·or how round wooden bowls become oval with age

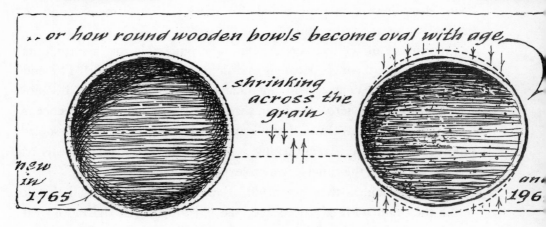

shrinking
across the
grain

new
in
1765

an
196

.·or the wide
spaces between floorboards and in pane.

246

Loosely nailed cellar strips

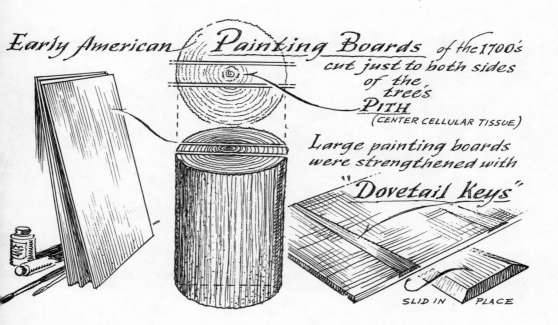

Early American *Painting Boards* of the 1700's
cut just to both sides
of the
tree's
PITH
(CENTER CELLULAR TISSUE)

Large painting boards
were strengthened with

"*Dovetail Keys*"

SLID IN PLACE

century when in place, yet were still prey to distortion the moment they were removed and exposed to uneven drying.

Uneven drying causes warp. That is why I paint both sides of my painting boards, so the entire piece of wood will dry evenly. With one side working against the other, there can be no warp. A board left in the grass will be pushed by the dampness of the ground into a saucerlike shape. Just turn it over and in a day or so the process will recur in the opposite direction. By wetting the top side of a sheet of paper, you can see instantly how this works. I have pictured warp in unseasoned timber with purposely exaggerated drawings, showing that some parts dry and shrink more than others because the grain has forced them to do so.

"Well, there's a scaffold for you!" Harley called out as he hit a last nail five good whacks. The last whack glanced off the nail head and struck the base wood.

"Four times out of five is a good average," I remarked.

"Used to do it six times out of five," he said.

Yankee humor, I thought, but I'll go along with it.

247

the Anatomy of WOOD WARPAGE

Moisture (or lack of it) causes warp

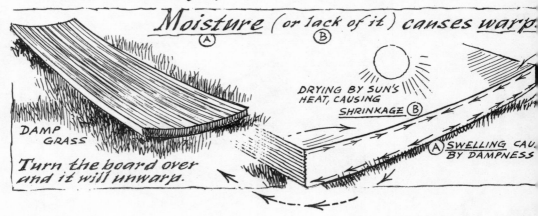

DRYING BY SUN'S HEAT, CAUSING SHRINKAGE Ⓑ

Ⓐ SWELLING CAUS. BY DAMPNESS

DAMP GRASS

Turn the board over and it will unwarp.

... but most warping in today's lumber is from

Seasoning Shrinking

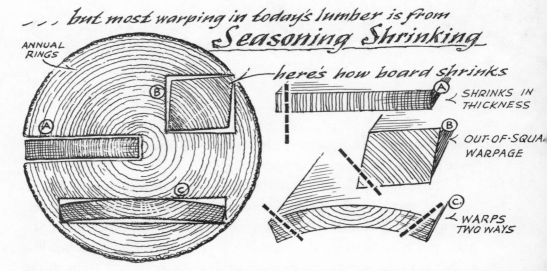

ANNUAL RINGS

here's how board shrinks

Ⓐ SHRINKS IN THICKNESS

Ⓑ OUT-OF-SQUA. WARPAGE

Ⓒ WARPS TWO WAYS

Wetting the concave side

then weighting it, will usually straighten a warped board

HOT WAT.

DAMP UNDERSIDE

Reversing a board is another remedy.

HEART SIDE ALL ONE WAY, CAUSING SCALLOPED CONTOUR

HEART SIDES NOW ALTERNATING MAKES A SMOOTHER SURFACE

248

Uneven drying = uneven shrinkage ∴ warping
Uneven wetting

"So I give up. How did you manage that?"

"Worked overtime," he said.

He attacked another piece of siding with his wrecking bar, making a solid bite, then pushed the board out and away. There was a shrill protest like the trumpeting of a bull elephant, and the nails began to pull out of the ironlike chestnut beams. With one debonair twist of the bar, he freed a fine silver board. It parted company with the barn, balanced on end for a split second, then fell silently into the broom grass beside the barn.

"There's a good oak board for your picture frames," said Harley. "Twenty-one inches wide if it's an inch."

"Looks more like chestnut to me," I said.

Harley climbed down from his perch, lifted the board with his toe, and kicked it over in the grass.

"Seasoned chestnut always looks like oak," he said. "Not many folks can tell the difference. But fresh oak is crisper and the saw marks are always sharper." He pointed to a corrugated pattern in the board. "See here?"

Every groove was a signature of one downstroke of some long-gone, water-wheel-operated saw blade. On every upstroke, a cog had pushed the log an eighth of an inch ahead, leaving a corduroy effect of ridges.

249

"When you see saw-cut marks that crisp," Harley continued, "you can be pretty sure the wood is oak. Looks like it was a big saw blade, too, like the one that was used to mill timber down at New Preston brook. Remember it as a boy. It was there, rusting in the sand, near where we swam, and we used to bang on it at night to make noises like a bell."

"You're quite a detective, Harley," I said, "but I never heard of oak siding on a barn."

He kicked the wood over again and inspected it. "Oh, they had it now and again, but this was a replacement board. Was a floorin' board from the 1700's before it ever reached the barn, though. Second-story floor board, I see. Someone probably put it in to replace a busted pine sidin' board."

"How the devil do you know all that? You're sure guessing a lot!"

Harley showed signs of annoyance at having been doubted. It's not easy for me to recognize annoyance in the average New Englander; it's something you usually have to sense rather than see. I feel that most New Englanders wear a constant look of annoyance. When Harley pushed his hat back on his head with his thumb and sighed at the same time, however, I knew he was annoyed.

"It's floor boardin' all right," he began, "because those holes show where there were plancher nails in them once—those clasp-headed nails they used to make for holding floorboards down. Kept them from popping up. Then there's some lath marks where there was plaster on the underside for a room below; that sure shows it was a second-story floor board, doesn't it? If you look close, you'll see that the lathin' was the kind that's split and opened up like an accordion. They only did that in the 1700's."

Harley was right. An early wooden building usually has more to tell than the average eye sees. And once seen, it is the closest thing to communion with those anonymous pioneers who lived when the American spirit was in its kindling stage. The nails and screws used, the door panels and latches, the laths and the moldings, the way a structure is put together—all these things tend to date any house. The nail holes, the worn stairs and floorings, additions and eliminations made as the years went by,

Dating an old building....

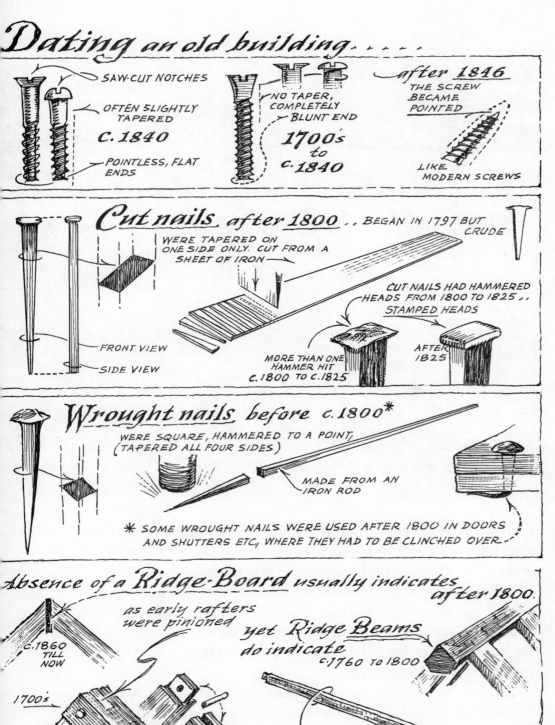

SAW-CUT NOTCHES

OFTEN SLIGHTLY TAPERED

C. 1840

POINTLESS, FLAT ENDS

NO TAPER, COMPLETELY BLUNT END

1700's to C. 1840

after 1846
THE SCREW BECAME POINTED

LIKE MODERN SCREWS

Cut nails after 1800 .. BEGAN IN 1797 BUT CRUDE

WERE TAPERED ON ONE SIDE ONLY. CUT FROM A SHEET OF IRON →

FRONT VIEW

SIDE VIEW

CUT NAILS HAD HAMMERED HEADS FROM 1800 TO 1825 .. **STAMPED HEADS**

MORE THAN ONE HAMMER HIT C.1800 TO C.1825

AFTER 1825

Wrought nails before c.1800*

WERE SQUARE, HAMMERED TO A POINT, (TAPERED ALL FOUR SIDES)

MADE FROM AN IRON ROD

* SOME WROUGHT NAILS WERE USED AFTER 1800 IN DOORS AND SHUTTERS ETC, WHERE THEY HAD TO BE CLINCHED OVER

Absence of a Ridge-Board usually indicates after 1800.

as early rafters were pinioned

yet Ridge Beams do indicate c.1760 TO 1800

C.1860 TILL NOW

1700's

BARN RAFTERS TAPERED USUALLY (BEFORE 1875)

251

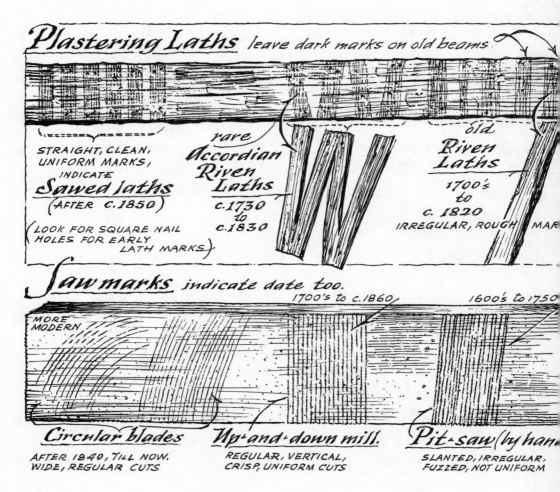

Plastering Laths *leave dark marks on old beams*

STRAIGHT, CLEAN, UNIFORM MARKS, INDICATE
Sawed laths
(AFTER c.1850)

(LOOK FOR SQUARE NAIL HOLES FOR EARLY LATH MARKS)

rare
Accordian Riven Laths
c.1730 to c.1830

old Riven Laths
1700's to c.1820
IRREGULAR, ROUGH MAR

Saw marks *indicate date too.*

1700's to c.1860

1600's to 1750

MORE MODERN

Circular blades
AFTER 1840, TILL NOW. WIDE, REGULAR CUTS

Up-and-down mill.
REGULAR, VERTICAL, CRISP, UNIFORM CUTS

Pit-saw (by han
SLANTED, IRREGULAR, FUZZED, NOT UNIFORM

tell the story of those who lived in it. Most old houses have been so often remodeled, however, that sometimes only the nails and boards and beams of the cellar or the attic can be relied upon to be original.

The antiquarian might argue that his interest in antiques is an appreciation of historic atmosphere, a love of the beauty of pleasing decay. More often, however, his interest in antique art boils down to a reverence for the individuality of the past, what man once stood for, the way he lived and the thoughts he thought.

On my wall I have an early American axe, which is constantly the subject of good-natured joking. A carpenter once said to me, "If you like old tools that much, I'll give you some of my old hammers to hang on your wall." It made a good joke, but it also made me think. His hammer, to me, would be the emblem of a six-hour day, the temporary things we so often build nowadays, and the fact that one modern hammer is just like any other modern hammer. My axe is much more than an ornament with pleasing lines. It is a symbol.

The door from the old barn has become a symbol, too. I saved it and made it into a kitchen-table top. To those who chide me and say they have some good old tables "just the thing to make doors out of," I explain, like a good antiquarian, that I use my barn door as a table just because I like its old wood. But there's much more to it than that. Take those scratches just above where the latch used to be. They indicate almost a century of match-lighting. "It seems odd," I remarked to Harley when we were taking the door down, "that a farmer would light matches on his way into his barn. Barns don't last very long that way."

"That farmer," said Harley, "smoked a pipe. Guess he did just like my dad used to do—never smoked inside the barn, but after the animals were bedded down and the door was locked, *then* he lit his pipe. Those scratches, I'd say, were made on the way out."

I recall that when I was researching the old phrase about "knocking on wood," I learned that the New England farmer used to knock on his barn door "for luck" after closing it up for the night. Perhaps my door, too, has been knocked with thousands of such prayers. I like to think so.

Formerly, when I breakfasted alone, I would read the advertisements on the cornflakes box. Now I look at the scratches on my historiographic table and I enjoy musing about the old barn. There are also scratches below, where the door handle used to be, made by a large dog. I guess the farmer had a little dog, too, for there are scratches lower down. Once I thought they might have been from the same dog, first when he was young and then when he was big; but that wouldn't account for his growing-up time.

Then there's a half-round hole where a mouse used to make his own exit and entrance, and another where a mouse began to gnaw his way through, and then for some reason left off. A melancholy thought. It reminds me of a verse from an old country song:

253

There's an old mouse chewin' on my pantry door,
He must have chewed for a month or more.
When he gets through he'll sure be sore
Fer there ain't a durn thing in there!

Right in the middle of my door-table is the mark of a big square hand-wrought nail where something must have hung, and I like to think it was a Christmas wreath. I recall a mantel in my house where there were some hundred nail holes from Christmas stockings which had been hung there. There were small square holes from eighteenth-century hand-wrought tacks, then the marks of nineteenth-century cut-tacks, and finally the round holes from more recent Christmases.

Actually most early farmers put wreaths not on their house doors, but on their barn doors, because the barn was more symbolic of that holy night. According to an old legend, on Christmas Eve the farm animals are supposed to speak to one another. There is something of Christmas about a barn and its manger.

When I first moved to the village of Warren, I was asked to judge the Christmas decorations on the houses. After touring miles of roads lined with houses decorated by plastic Santas that flashed on and off, and even one neon-lighted Virgin Mary, we came upon a place that truly breathed the spirit of the first Noël. It was a long, dimly lit structure, completely void of cheap ornaments, nestling into a snowy hillside with an almost holy dignity. "That's it!" I said. "First prize!"

"My lands," said my guide, "that isn't anyone's home—that's just an old chicken house."

But it still deserved the prize.

Maybe the nail hole in my door-table wasn't for a wreath. Maybe it was for a "For Sale" sign or even a sheriff's notice, but I enjoy musing over worn old wood and trying to decipher the story it so often has to tell. When Harley eats from my barn door, he seldom neglects to tell me about the new formica table that he got with trading stamps. I know he is obliquely criticizing the holes and marks in my poor table.

Although most early American houses were completely influenced by

254

The Chicken House

Old World architecture, during the 1700's there evolved a series of door designs that might be considered true Americana. The two-board batten door and the same door with continuous battens (lined or double-door) were beautiful in their simplicity and as strong as the virgin American wood from which they were made. Often a door would be made from a single board, and I found one (dated 1742) with a width of thirty-two inches.

In the pioneer days, doors were often symbols. Just as girls filled hope chests, young men planned doors for the houses they would someday build. A house might be built of local pine and chestnut, but the door was considered something special and the wood was often sassafras panels, apple or cherry, or even mahogany brought from the West Indies or Central America. A godly man might prefer a Christian door with stiles (vertical pieces) and rails (horizontal pieces) that formed a Christian cross. A superstitious person might put a Maltese cross in the lower section and thereby make a "witch door" to keep out the evil spirits, or frame the door with ash to make the spell more potent.* Sometimes the inner surface of a door matched the paneling or wainscoting of the room.

---

* *The ash tree was thought to have special magic to ward off sickness and evil spirits. No snake (so the legend goes) would cross a barrier of ash leaves.*

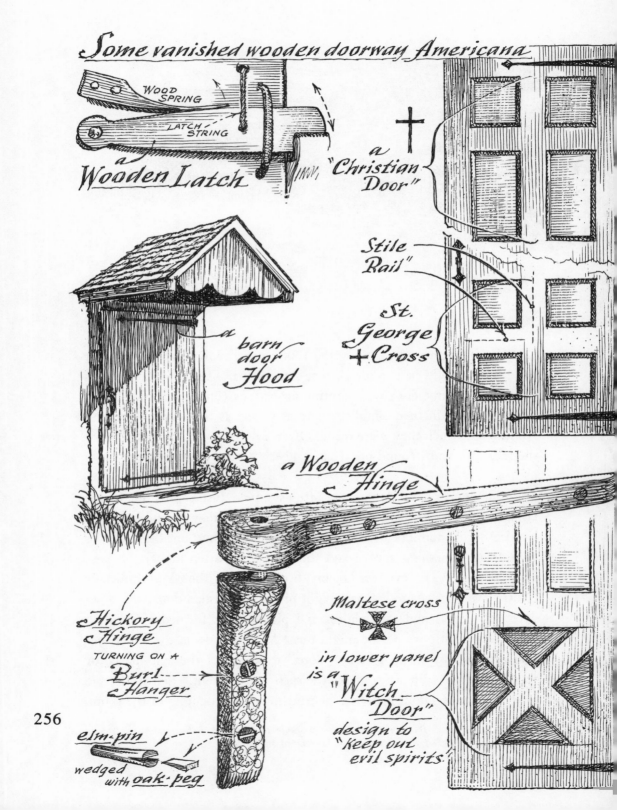

Some vanished wooden doorway Americana

WOOD SPRING

LATCH STRING

a Wooden Latch

a "Christian Door"

Stile Rail"

St. George + Cross

a barn door Hood

a Wooden Hinge

Hickory Hinge
TURNING ON A
Burl Hanger

elm·pin
wedged with oak·peg

Maltese cross

in lower panel is a "Witch Door"
design to "Keep out evil spirits"

256

Batten Barn doors of the 1700's

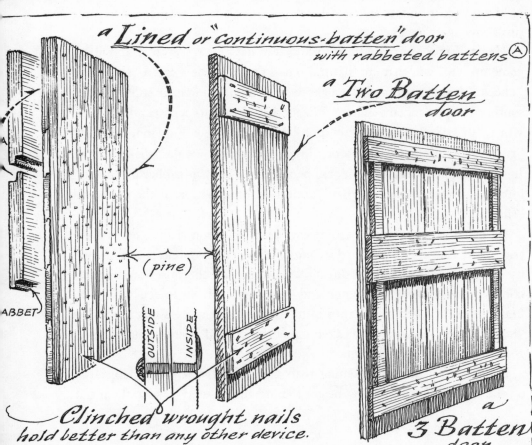

a *Lined* or "*Continuous-batten*" door
with rabbeted battens Ⓐ

a *Two Batten* door

(pine)

OUTSIDE   INSIDE

RABBET

Clinched wrought nails
hold better than any other device.

a
3 Batten door

257

But whatever the design, it was usually the best example of craftsmanship in the whole house.

The stylish sheathed barn door with wooden hinges, wooden locks, and wooden cross-bar for blocking it at night, the door with a closet for guns (or canes), the door set at a slightly leaning-outward angle (so when it opened, it automatically swung all the way back and stayed there)—these, sadly, have become obsolete Americana. The once popular hood that accompanied most barn doors deserves a revival if only for its protection of the entranceway from the weather.

When I began taking my barn down, the only part that I needed was its covering, those boards to make my frames. But when their removal began to expose big chestnut beams underneath, I felt compelled to find some use for them also. Some of the beams had long cracks in them, and I wondered how much this had weakened them.

"Don't worry about it," said Harley. "If it's a heart shake, the beam is just about as strong as ever."

Heart shake? That one took me a few days to research. But what I came up with was that any natural wood crack is known as a "shake" or "check." I always thought a shake was a rough shingle. It still is, in the southern Appalachians where Elizabethan English persists. There the word "shake" also means "to split." Whereas New Englanders would "rive" their shingles with a froe, down south they would "shake" them. In New England and New York, people call a split in timber a "check," but this only originated from a Dutch mispronunciation of the old word "shake," to split.

I learned, too, that there are several kinds of wood shakes, and I have tried to define them in my drawings. These splits or clefts are started by a too rapid loss of sap during seasoning, which causes an unequal contraction between the inner and outer part of the piece of wood. Harley's theory had some truth in it, for the lengthwise splits known as "heart shakes" are not so weakening as the curved slashes that wander, corkscrewlike, around a beam.

Knots are far more weakening than shakes, and when knots appeared on the lower side of a ceiling beam, the old-timers used to slice them out

Sheathed Barn Doors of the 1700's,
(locked from the insides).

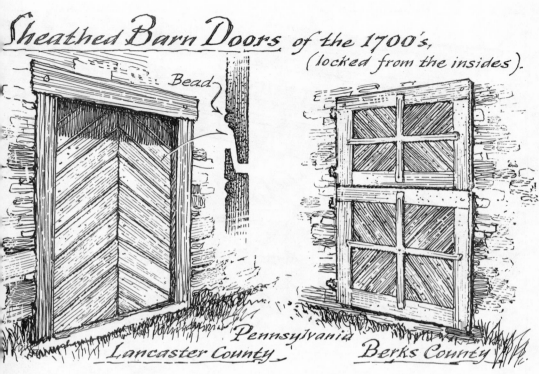

Bead

Pennsylvania

Lancaster County

Berks County

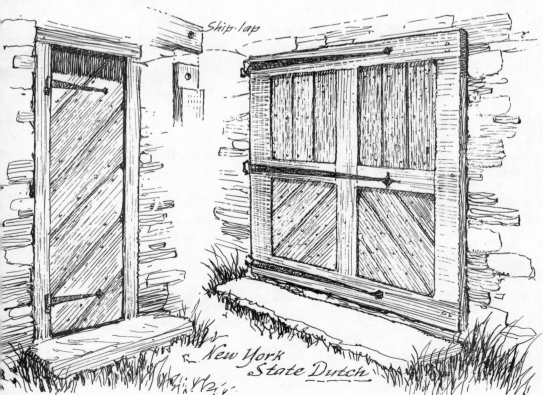

Ship-lap

New York
State Dutch

259

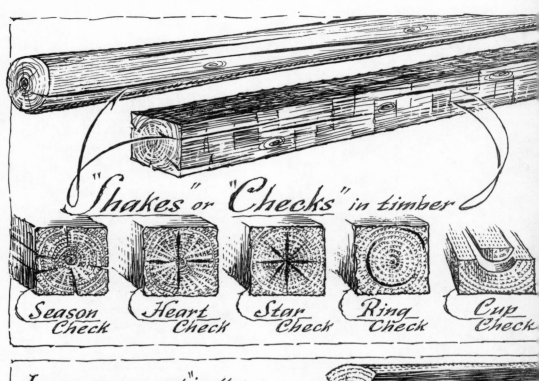

"Shakes" or "Checks" in timber

Season Check **Heart Check** **Star Check** **Ring Check** **Cup Check**

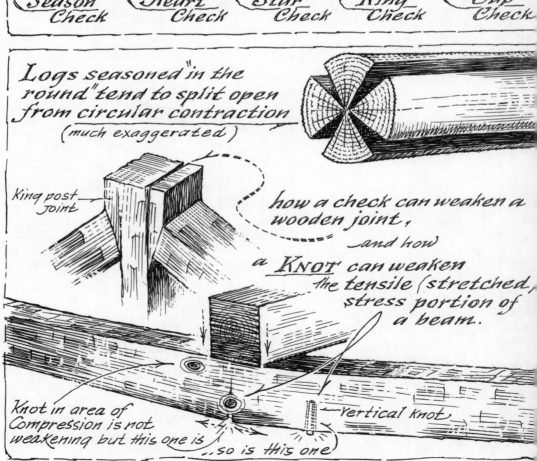

Logs seasoned "in the round" tend to split open from circular contraction *(much exaggerated)*

King post Joint

how a check can weaken a wooden joint,

—and how a **KNOT** can weaken the tensile (stretched) stress portion of a beam.

Knot in area of Compression is not weakening but this one is

—Vertical knot

..so is this one

with an axe on the theory that the loss of wood there would be less weakening than the knot. Often when an old house is being remodeled and the ceiling beams are exposed, these indentations cause some disappointment, for they are usually taken as an indication that some earlier remodeling had been done. Knots on the sides or upper parts of the beams were compressive, and therefore not weakening, so they were never cut out.

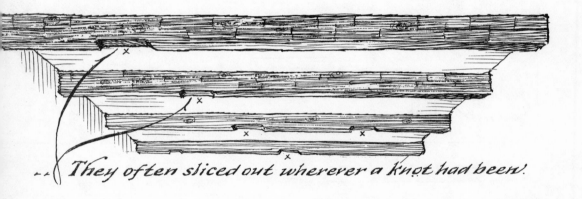

They often sliced out wherever a knot had been!

Builders today wouldn't think of using a ten-inch square beam for framing a small house; in fact, lumber yards don't carry that kind of wood. But the early builder used animal anatomy as his model and he thought of framework as being the bones of his house and the sheathing or clapboards as being its outer skin. Today's house has bones only as strong as its skin. At one time a house's bones were big and much stronger than necessary, but they really furnished the weight to keep the house from blowing away. I have slept in an old barn when a gale was blowing and there was some peculiar comfort and sense of solidity in being aware of the tons of oak and chestnut that made up the framing.

I have heard complaints about the creaking of big house timbers during changes in the weather, but that is something soon accepted by the woodwise. It is as natural a phenomenon as the swaying of a bridge or skyscraper in the wind, and it is something for which a good designer actually allows. To permit this movement, big timbers were pinned with

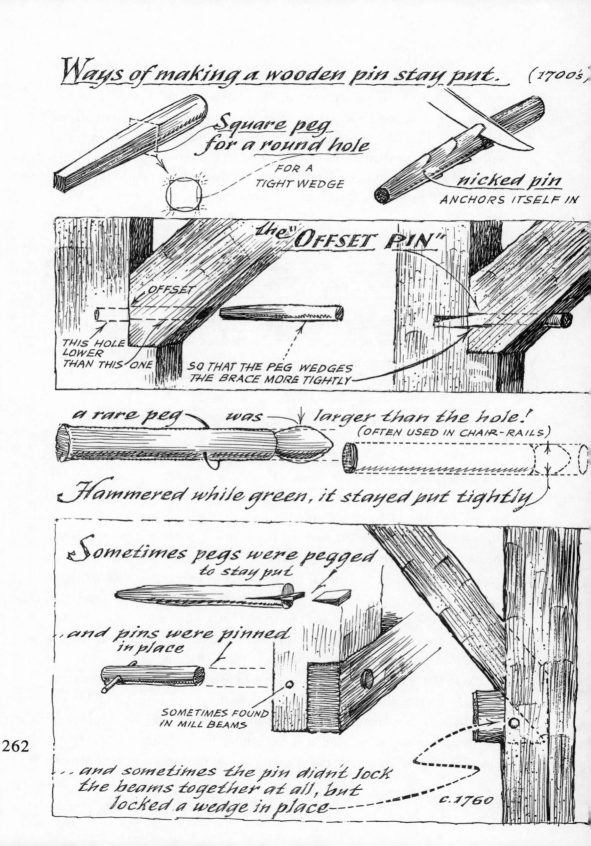

Ways of making a wooden pin stay put. (1700's)

Square peg for a round hole

FOR A TIGHT WEDGE

nicked pin ANCHORS ITSELF IN

the "OFFSET PIN"

OFFSET

THIS HOLE LOWER THAN THIS ONE

SO THAT THE PEG WEDGES THE BRACE MORE TIGHTLY

a rare peg was — **larger than the hole!**
(OFTEN USED IN CHAIR-RAILS)

Hammered while green, it stayed put tightly

Sometimes pegs were pegged to stay put

...and pins were pinned in place

SOMETIMES FOUND IN MILL BEAMS

262

...and sometimes the pin didn't lock the beams together at all, but locked a wedge in place

c. 1760

wood instead of being fastened with iron. The old trunnels (treenails) allowed joints to move with atmospheric changes without being torn apart. Just as the bark on trees tightens when a cold air mass passes through the forest, the great timbers in early structures move on their joints and sometimes make resounding booms through the night.

Early fastening pins or trunnels were just hand-cut pegs, but during the middle 1700's framers used interesting methods for making them secure. Sometimes they were nicked to keep them from working their way out; often the hole in one of the two connecting beams was slightly offset so the trunnel would have to be wedged in tightly. Some framers hammered a square pin of green wood into a round hole. Some didn't pin the beams together at all, but pinned a wedge instead (which left the end of the beam unweakened by any hole).

Pins were usually cut on a shaving horse with a drawknife, but by the 1800's, when many bridges were being built and there was a need for more and larger fasteners, pins were cut on lathes and manufactured by the thousands. They could be ordered by the barrel, and they were sent to the buyer soaked in linseed oil.

It is amazing how often old trunnels become wedded to the joint (it is as if they had been welded there). In disconnecting the rafters of my barn, it was almost impossible to hammer the peak trunnels out. But it was while trying to do so that I came upon something interesting: near the peak of one end-rafter were the remains of what Harley called a

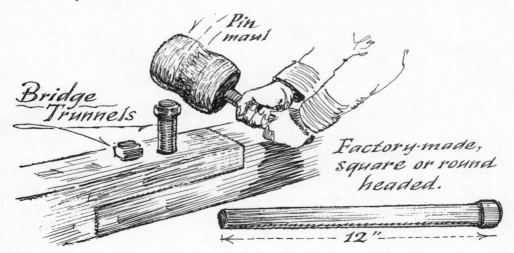

Pin maul

Bridge Trunnels

Factory-made, square or round headed.

12"

"wetting bush," a small sapling that had been nailed there upright by the builder (as is still the custom) when the roof framing was finished.

I knew what Harley meant, for I had encountered the phrase before. The carpenters of a house I once had built asked my wife to please be present the next day when the workmen "wet the bush." Ruth could hardly wait till I returned to ask me what they meant. It took some searching of my memory and some imagination before I realized that they referred to the old New England custom of putting a sapling atop a new house and drinking a toast as a sort of christening ceremony. I am sure they didn't know where it came from, but the phrase "wetting the bush" is as old as the Druids.

Finding the remains of that ceremonial sapling, still held in place by the hand-forged nails, made me all the more reluctant to take the old barn down. The "bush" had certainly brought luck to the building—for about two centuries.

By now, Harley knew my interest in all things made of wood. He didn't ask me if I wanted to keep this or that wooden object, but simply put them in a pile where I might examine them. And before long I had a small collection of harness hooks made from the crotches of tree limbs.

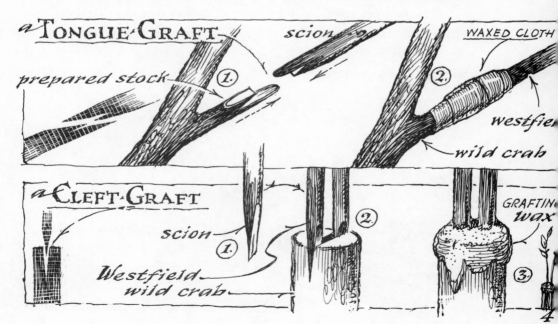

a TONGUE·GRAFT

scion

WAXED CLOTH

prepared stock (1.)

(2.)

westfie

wild crab

a CLEFT·GRAFT

scion

(1.)

Westfield wild crab

(2.)

GRAFTIN wax

(3.)

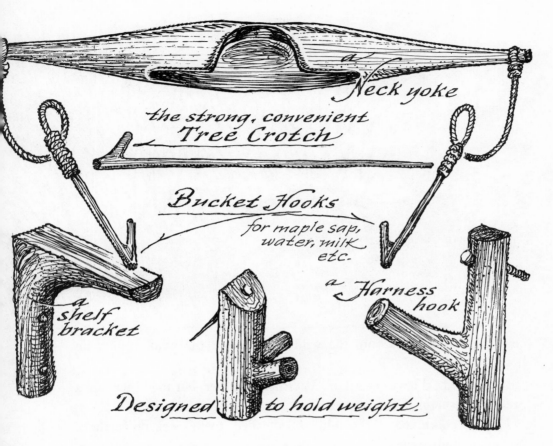

a Neck yoke

the strong, convenient
Tree Crotch

Bucket Hooks

for maple sap,
water, milk
etc.

a Harness
hook

a
shelf
bracket

Designed to hold weight.

"The wood in a tree crotch," Harley explained, "seasons like iron. It makes a good hook. Those harness hooks are all apple crotches. You can still smell the fruitwood if you rub it."

"I thought they seldom cut down good apple trees in the old days."

"You're right, they didn't. But like as not those harness hooks were made from apple prunings. About this time of year my father used to take me up on that hill yonder with a load of Westfield prunings* to graft onto wild crabs."

"Wild crabs?"

Harley sighed at my ignorance. "Crabs are just wild apple trees. They don't bear fruit worth a hang, but they're strong. An orchard seedling wouldn't last through a New England winter, but a forest crab will stand up to weather like any strong tree. We used to tongue-graft and

265

* Some country people call a scion for grafting a "pruning."

1865   1965

cleft-graft Westfields onto the wild crabs. Now the whole mountain has good apples."

I confessed I'd never heard of "Westfields" either, but then there are a great many things I've never heard of.

Harley continued, "The old folks called them Seek-no-furthers. Never did know why."

"Sounds like something they made up themselves," I said.

"No, it's an old English name. Fellow from Westfield, Massachusetts, is supposed to have planted the first one on top of Dudleytown Mountain back in the 1700's. I saw it about fifty years ago and they say it's still there."

"I know that apple trees can last for a hundred years, but I didn't think they could live for two centuries."

"Oh, in a way it's not the same tree," said Harley. "It just kept growing and falling down and growing up again. Some day I'll look for it. If it's still there, I'll show it to you."

That night I thought about Harley's story of the Seek-no-further apple tree that "kept falling and growing up again." It seemed more interesting than working on the barn. And so before noon of the next day, we were shoulder-deep in thickets of a forest slope searching for the old tree.

"There she is!" Harley said suddenly. "She's done it again! That's the old tree I carved my initials on when I was about ten years old."

He sliced away some forest brush so I could get a better look. Resting on a bed of leaves and young shoots was the hulk of an old apple tree well over three feet in diameter. It had fallen from old age, yet some of the branches which were still living when the old tree fell had struck into the ground and miraculously taken root to become offspring of the parent tree. As the fallen trunk decayed, new apple saplings had rooted all around it, giving the appearance of a family gathered around a dead giant on his bier. The old tree had dug its branches like fingers into the earth, a strange and striking sequence of resurrection.

This process had perhaps occurred over and over, each fallen tree plunging downslope. The hulk we now beheld was probably about sixty feet from the original tree. I traced the path of resurrections uphill to a piling of stones such as might have been grouped along a rail fence. Here, I thought, the first Seek-no-further apple tree might have grown. I wondered what the countryside had looked like then.

... there I imagined grew the first "Seek-no-further" apple tree.

267

1865

The heft and feel of a well-worn handle,
The sight of shavings that curl from a blade;
The logs in the woodpile, the sentiment of huge
                    beams in an old-fashioned house;
The smell of fresh cut timber and the pungent
                    fragrance of burning leaves;
The crackle of kindling and the hiss of burning logs.
Abundant to all the needs of man, how poor the world
                    would be
Without wood.

269

Everard Hinrichs

The Cleared Land

Until the 1860's the farmer was hailed as the most noble and independent man in American society, but suddenly he became a national comic figure named Reuben or Silas, with funny boots, chin whiskers, and hayseeds in his ears. He and his ways were old-fashioned, and "old-fashioned" had become a shameful word. *The Country Gentleman* of 1865 ran a column called, "Why Do Young Men Leave the Farm?" When the boys came home from the war, it was usually just to pick up their clothes and head for a job in the city.

During the period of the Civil War, the upheaval of American society resulted in much ugliness and some deterioration of taste. Before that time, agriculture and the preservation of tradition were a cherished part of the good life, but from then on the philosophy of "change for the sake of change" became a dominant force in American thinking.

Hardly were the battles over when the iron factories, which had been making the hardware of war, began seeking inventors and inviting them to set their sights on peacetime production. For a while there were born countless intricate machines devised to do any job faster and poorer. By

1865 there were four hundred and fifty-two all-metal apple-parers invented, yet the old-timers preferred the paring knife. William Morris recognized his age, remarking that the great achievement of those post-bellum days was "the making of machines which were the wonders of invention, skill, and patience, used for the production of measureless quantities of worthless makeshifts."

Anything which hitherto had been made of wood was quickly duplicated and mass-produced in iron. And to replace the beauty of handmade design, ornaments were added. A locomotive stack might be fluted and flowered; a steam engine's walking-beam might become a replica of an Ionic column. Carpenter's tools, house architecture, and even farm machinery got the treatment. It was an era of doodads and decoration. The American reverence for wood had become old-fashioned and obsolete almost overnight, and the individual makers of wooden things became rare artisans.

There rose a quest for new ways to use wood, even to the point of wasting it. The corduroy roads of the past (where logs had been laid out in wet places) were revived in the form of sawed planks, and plans were made for all main highways to be "plankroads." Even the city streets used wooden blocks. Sawmills became so busy and so wasteful that navigation was often stopped by the sawdust and chips which were emptied into the rivers. Often such blockage had to be burned, and "river fires" that burned for weeks added hazard to blockage. One average-size sawmill at Orono, Maine, was required by fire-prevention law to burn 36 thousand cords of scrap wood a year.

The English criticized us, saying that the Americans "seem to hate trees and cannot wait to cut them down." Indeed, we seemed to have gone out of our way to use wood, solely because it was so plentiful. British locomotives were designed to run on coke in the 1850's, while the American railroads were using hardwood fuel.*

* In 1865 the amount of wood used for fuel in America was possibly at its height. Steamboats and locomotives were still using wood, and it is difficult to estimate the amount used yearly. But the Boston and Worcester Railroad used 8,000 cords and the Western Railroad (between Worcester and Albany) used 18,000 cords. All of the railroads in Massachusetts used 53,710 cords. The wood by this time was mainly pine, and the price per cord averaged $3.25.

a log jam in a "river of wood". c. 1865

Looking north from Cornwall over Connecticut's Berkshires, one sees an unending series of rolling hills. From the Revolution to the Civil War this land had given most of its tree growth to feed the iron furnaces. Every thirty-five years, which is sufficient time for hardwood trees to grow into useful timber, the hills were harvested. In the Berkshires, people called it being "coaled." The furnaces there were making about three million dollars' worth of iron each year and over half of that was paid for wood consumed as iron-making charcoal. But money value of those days is a poor basis for comparing quantity now, so instead try to imagine a square of forest four miles long on each boundary. That much had to be stripped for one year's production of Berkshire iron. "Stripped" is no exaggeration, for should you have happened to view that countryside from any elevated point, you could have counted the big trees on the fingers of your hands. The big trees appeared two at a time, placed as "husband and wife trees" when a house was built. They were usually on

273

Husband·and·wife·trees.

the east side of the house or at each side of the entrance; you could pick out the farmhouses on any New England landscape by these double clumps of green.

Hidden in the ravines and river valleys, however, there were still groves of tall virgin pine. They stretched skyward above the sea of forest shade in their effort to reach sunlight, their trunks mastlike before they burst into foliage, often as high as seventy-five feet. Some still bore the scars of the "King's Broad Arrow" that had marked them a century before as property of the British Navy. They were left standing only because charcoal made from them was unsuitable for the making of iron. The pitch in pine could explode into flame and destroy a week's work of charcoal making. So the "cathedrals," as people used to call pine groves, continued to flourish while the surrounding hills were being coaled off.

Pine charcoal was considered by some people to be a superior grade for a few special uses (indeed the United States mint in Philadelphia used it), but the iron makers insisted on hardwood charcoal. When you realize what specialists early Americans were and how knowledgeable they were in the characteristics of each kind of wood, it is understandable that pine should be considered inferior as charcoal. (A chair might contain fifteen kinds of wood, each serving a specific purpose, one wood often reacting against another to keep the joints tight. Even a fishing rod of three pieces was made of different woods—ash for the first joint, hickory for the second, and bamboo for the tip.)

274

Pine wood was used for kindling: except in an emergency, few would consider using it as fuel. It burned too quickly, it scattered sparks, and it made a very hard and inflammable kind of chimney soot. Even its ashes, which ordinarily would be used for making soap, were inferior to those of hardwoods.

Wood needed to throw out a given amount of heat.

Hickory   *White Oak*   *Hard Maple*   *Soft Maple*   *White Pine*

The early pitch pine of New England was called candlewood, and it was actually sold for that purpose, particularly for lighting one's way from the house to outbuildings or for carrying a flame from one fireplace to another. Even now when you find a bundle of candlewood tucked away in some attic or over an ancient barn beam, there will be enough pitch in the slivers to make them ignite at the touch of a lighted match. Yet pine's softwood classification kept it out of the early American woodpile.

Candlewood
the New England torch

275

It was in the late 1800's that the American farmer lost his special regard for wood as a fuel, even to the extent of forsaking the many pleasures of the hearth. By 1900 the farm fireplace had been walled up and the kitchen stove had taken its place. Wood was still burned, but it was shoved into the stove without ceremony; though you face a fireplace and enjoy the flames, when you shut the fire up in a black iron box, you tend to turn your back on it. It is strange that most of the walled-up fireplaces still contain their andirons—perhaps because they, too, were unwanted symbols of the obsolete and old-fashioned.*

Possible evolution of the Andiron.

"The "Log Cradle"
Before 1700

The "Fire Dog"

TEETH TO HOLD
LOGS IN PLACE

c. 1720

End-iron with

a "Cob Iron"
c. 1650

Andiron c. 1750

* Andirons were really a British device, never a product of early American design, for the colonists of the 1600's made simple "fire dogs" for holding logs, using a "lug-pole" (a heavy green stick) for holding pots by a chain. In the 1700's, when spits became popular, end-irons were added to the fire dogs for holding the spits.

The farm woodlot began to disappear by the late 1800's. At one time it was the farmer's main cash crop; his corn and grain and vegetables were mostly for his own family's use, but spending money came from the wood for splints, barrel hoops, shingles, charcoal and the countless other things that were harvested from woodlots. By 1865 most cultivated hardwood groves were gone, and in the Berkshires as far as the eye could see, there was only a rolling patchwork of farm plots held together with a thin black stitching of stone fences. Even as stone fences grew, the wood rails that usually lay on top of them were being sold to the charcoal-makers; the man whose land was enclosed with whole timber was considered well-off indeed. In the South, where stones were less abundant, there were farmers who had abandoned their land and buildings for no other reason than a lack of new fence material.

In Connecticut, when snake-rail fences began to rot and no fresh replacements were available, farmers piled stones around to keep them upright, so that in time there grew a sort of "snake-stone" formation. Years later when the rails disintegrated and disappeared and new forest growth came, a riddle arose. Why should anyone choose to build a zig-zag stone fence? And without realizing that the forest was once cleared fields, there are those today who wonder at stone fences built directly through dense woods.

Most history books comment upon wire fencing as comparatively recent Americana, giving such dates as 1873 for the invention of barbed wire and 1883 for woven wire. Yet Benjamin Franklin is said to have experimented with wire for enclosing cattle, and a lengthy "Account of Wire Fencing" was read at the Philadelphia Agricultural Society on January 2, 1816. By then, there were several Pennsylvania farms using wire fences.

The 1816 account spoke of "living trees connected with rails of wire," and true to the early American philosophy of looking far ahead, it compared the cost of wire fencing with wood fencing over a period of fifty years. It came to the conclusion that there was a cash saving of $1,329 per hundred acres enclosed. The plan, however, was indeed unique for it enabled the fence to *earn money!* Why plant dead posts in

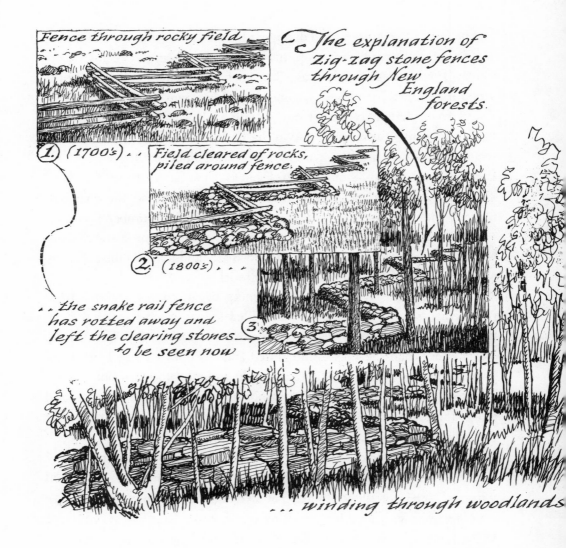

Fence through rocky field

The explanation of Zig-zag stone fences through New England forests.

1. (1700's)...

Field cleared of rocks, piled around fence.

2. (1800's)...

...the snake rail fence has rotted away and left the clearing stones to be seen now

3.

... winding through woodlands

the ground and wait for them to rot? Why not plant live trees instead and let them bear fruit and nuts and firewood which would then give profit to the farmer? Using a hundred acres as an example, the Society suggested the following plan of live tree posts and showed what they might earn a farmer within fifty years (allowing no harvest for the first ten years of growth):

278

244 apple trees producing $1 per year	$	244
30 cherry trees " 50¢ per year		15
20 pear trees " 50¢ per year		10
10 plum trees "		3
10 shellbark trees "		10
50 chestnut trees "		12
5 butternut trees "		20
5 English walnuts "		5
20 walnut trees "		5
250 buttonwood trees (24 cords firewood taken from tops)		72
	$	396

multiplied by 40 years' harvests $15,840
deduct the cost of wire rails 1,751
to the credit of live tree posts and wire fence in 50 years $14,089

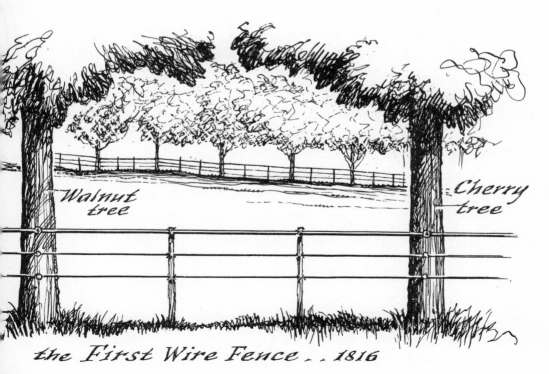

Walnut tree

Cherry tree

the First Wire Fence .. 1816

"Besides this great earning," the account goes on, "the soil around the fence will benefit by shade and the falling of leaves and twigs. Whoever might wish to see a wire fence of this plan may observe its benefits at R. Watkin's Tavern, at the Falls of Schuylkill." The report is signed, "Hon. Richard Peters, pres. of Agrict. Society, January the second, 1816."

But America was a country of wooden wealth, and wire fences seemed sacrilegious to the average farmer; it took another century for the wire fence to become generally popular, and then only because there was no wood left for making wooden fences.

After the Civil War, the U.S. Army made inventory of the nation's seven million miles of wood fences, because they were considered to be of importance in the field of battle. This might sound strange, yet the word *fence* was originally short for *defense*, and the use of a fence to hold in cattle was something quite American and recent. General James Brisbin, who took over the job, estimated there was "over two *billion* [a word seldom used in those days] dollars worth of wood fencing in America," and the cost of repairing it came to about one hundred million dollars a year. At the then current average of three hundred dollars a mile, our wood fences had added up to something like the national debt.

It can be understood why farmers were very particular in their choice of fencing material. To replace a rotted fence around a five hundred acre farm might be a full year's work. If locust, cedar, chestnut, walnut, or white oak (fencing was chosen in that order) was not available nearby, a man might haul proper fencing by ox-cart from a considerable distance. So it was that Jeremy Wolcott contemplated such a journey. His land at Cornwall had been fenced with oak some twenty years before by his father, and the town fence-viewer expressed wonderment at oak lasting that long. Some of it was too far gone for selling to the charcoal man even as scrap.

"The idea of journeying to New Haven and back with loads of wood," said Jeremy's wife, "sounds ridiculous to me. Hauling chestnut rails to sell is bad enough, but hauling back locust posts that you've bought . . . that seems like such a waste of time. Besides, I'll miss you."

"Jonathan will take good care of you, Sarah, and it will take his mind from all the war he's seen. There's nothing like splitting rails to rest a man's mind and give him healthful exercise. By the time I've returned he'll have enough new rails split to start the new fence."

"Won't they have to season?"

"Chestnut rails can season right in the fence if we hang them right. It's the posts that must be seasoned. The Long Island posts have been seasoned for two years; with a little charring they should last as long as we do. Connecticut needs posts as much as Long Island needs rails."

"It sounds like 'The Boston Post Riders' to me," said Sarah.

"The Boston Post Riders" was a well-known story of early times, for when the road was opened, two mail riders started out from opposite ends, riding at full tilt to save time. They met midway, exchanged sacks, and sped back to their respective towns. It seemed like a timesaver until a small boy asked, "Why don't you just pass each other and keep going? You're not saving any time."

"Well, it may sound like 'The Boston Post Riders' to you," said Jeremy, "but it makes sense to me."

The story of Long Island's locust trees is of historic interest. The scraggly locust that looks like a dying tree even at its best, during the summer, is perhaps the only remaining sign of early Long Island farm days. Native to North America, the locust was brought from the Appalachians to Great Britain in the middle 1600's. There it was rejected as wood that splits easily, warps badly, and works with much difficulty. The English, however, adopted it as hedge or fence material because of its thorns. But by the time of the Revolution, after some of the hedges had been left to grow into trees, it was found that full-grown locust trees harbor borers and other insects and "that damned American locust tree" was blamed for all sorts of plagues and banned. Oddly enough at the same time, America was blaming English barberry for a plague of wheat rust, accusing the British of planting barberry wild in order to ruin our wheat crops. A law was passed that barberry could be destroyed even if it meant trespassing to do so.

But Long Island had learned much about locust from the British and began planting it first as low hedging and then left it to grow as fence-

Black Locust . . . (common or yellow locust)

LEAVES PODS

Long Island Americana

post material. So well did Long Island become known for its locust trees that it soon suffered a shortage of all other timber. For a while Long Island was "swapping wood," with a regular shipping lane across Long Island Sound, locust going to the Connecticut shore, chestnut and pine coming back to the Island.

The honey locust, so called because its pods contain over twenty-five percent sugar, became an important cattle food on Long Island. Some farmers crushed the pods into a sweet meal and used that instead of sugar in their cooking. But during the timber shortage of the late 1800's, the Island's supply of locust ran out and only those locusts used as hedging or fencing remained. Now one may still see some of these, dying in their old age, fifty feet higher than the hedge of which they once were part, solitary symbols of an era.

Jeremy Wolcott did haul his rails to the shore, and his son did remain behind to get the last of the chestnut (lest the charcoal men got there first). The charcoal burners always were a strange breed, living a lonely

282

life in the forest, almost like wild beasts. And when hardwood became scarce (and later when coal was used for the job of making iron) the charcoal makers' life and habits fell into a deplorable decline. Not only shunned, they were often feared.

At its best, the job of making charcoal was not for any normal human being. The time required for charring a small mound varied from one to two weeks, but with mounds of wood thirty feet or more round, a month was average. During all that time, through every kind of weather, the maker of charcoal lived with his mound, sleeping only in dozes for fear a flame might start and explode into a full fire which would demolish the mound. There was no time for washing; there was seldom more shelter than a bark lean-to. And there were so many things to watch for in a "live mound" that the man became almost part of it.

At first lighting, a black smoke poured from holes in the middle of the mound; this was quickly smothered until a blue haze arose. This was kept

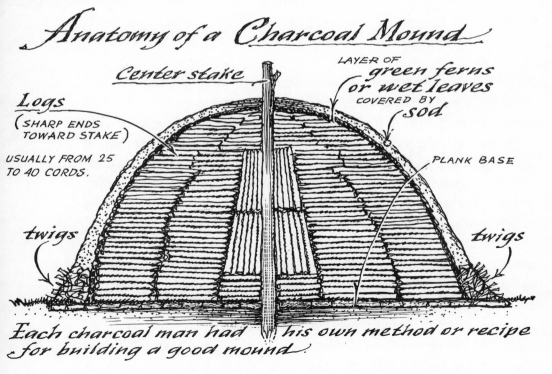

Anatomy of a Charcoal Mound

Center stake

LAYER OF green ferns or wet leaves COVERED BY sod

Logs
(SHARP ENDS TOWARD STAKE)

USUALLY FROM 25 TO 40 CORDS.

PLANK BASE

twigs   twigs

Each charcoal man had his own method or recipe for building a good mound.

283

The blackest job in America

alive by constantly smothering any flames with moist charcoal powder. Then there was a "sweating period" when the mound emitted a yellowish smoke; at that point, moist charcoal or mud was quickly applied until the smoke turned gray. Until the heat subsided, the mound never stopped "working" and neither did the man. By the end of each charring, his body had become completely black outside and exhausted inside. Knowing how and when to walk on the mound was an art in itself, and many a man fell through into the furnacelike heat.

Charcoal during the 1800's was used for many things other than making iron. People cleaned their teeth with it. Although the first results may look ghastly, there is actually nothing more beneficial for teeth than charcoal powder. Swallow some of it? Also good; there is nothing better for upset stomach. It even sweetens the breath. If you want to purify water or remove an offensive odor from anything, use charcoal. Sailors used to throw burnt muffins into their water supply when it became stale or smelly; meat packers used to pack their meats in charcoal. Ice was stored in charcoal, gunpowder was made with it; printer's ink, black paint, medicines, even highways were made from it. In 1865 someone dreamed up this idea, thinking that since charcoal is the longest lasting of materials, a road made of it would be very durable. Timber was piled along the middle of the road and burned right there; then the charred material was raked out and tamped down.

It is interesting to note that early iron is better in many ways than modern iron because of the use of charcoal, which is carbon without imperfections. Some of the tools made from Berkshire iron resist rust and hold an edge better than today's Pennsylvania iron, which is made in a furnace fueled by coal.

Country people made their own charcoal in either cross-laid or tepee-arranged wooden sticks. With wet leaves and sod as covering, and a small hole for draft (and for watching the progress of charring), it took three days and nights for a mound to char completely. When finished, the pile of charcoal simply collapsed within the mound; then the sod covering was removed. This was the only coal known in the early days, and it was needed for all blacksmith work. Charcoal was sifted in a spleen sieve; the fine powder and "charcoal-meal" were saved for cleaning teeth or for the

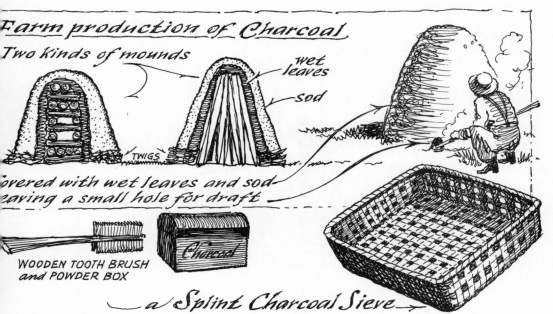

Farm production of Charcoal
Two kinds of mounds

wet leaves

sod

TWIGS

Covered with wet leaves and sod leaving a small hole for draft

WOODEN TOOTH BRUSH and POWDER BOX

Charcoal

a Splint Charcoal Sieve

285

medicine cabinet. In the cities the charcoal vendor sold from his cart at forty cents a barrel (the price at about 1865) and his well-known chant was:

Charcoal by the bushel,
Charcoal by the peck,
Charcoal by the frying pan
Or anyway you lek!

It was an era of charcoal and a time of disappearing trees.

In Cornwall, Connecticut, and wherever iron was made in the Berkshires, you may still see where the burning mounds were: the hardwood is coming back in those hills, except for the chestnut, which reaches about ten feet before it browns and succumbs to the blight of 1904. There are still hulks of chestnut tree trunks stretched across the forest floor or caught in their fall by surrounding limbs. Some are still sound enough to dull the edge of a handsaw. And each spring there are new shoots that rise from stumps cut a century ago by the long-gone charcoal men.

Chestnut . . .

. . . 1904 . . . . still trying to come back

Jonathan Wolcott's work of splitting rails was not made easier by his father's journey to the coast. Ordinarily logs were snaked out of the forest as soon as they were felled, but these logs had been barked and left in place to season, which meant that they had to be split on location in the woodlot. It was the New England custom, for the sake of safety, never to work alone a distance from the house. And the almanac suggested splitting rails later on, during the wane of the moon. Like most people of that time, Jonathan knew that when the almanac spoke of moon phases nothing mystical was intended. It was just a way of identifying time (as our present-day calendars do) by moon positions, and at the same time indicating the periods of the greatest amount of moonlight for jobs that usually continued after darkness. Jonathan had to make use of the waxing Gibbous moon, working until it was almost overhead before he started for home.

Farmers sometimes used bark for tanning hides, but home tanning was difficult and messy work, so most farmers took the hides to town for tanning. Tree bark was either left to rot in the woods or sold to the tanneries. But the Wolcott bark was given to the charcoal men, who in these lean times were glad to have anything that might earn them a dollar.

Jonathan seldom saw them, for they picked up the scraps either early in the morning or late in the evening; the bark would disappear and there would be telltale footprints all about, showing that the Raggies had been there. Perhaps the name Raggy started from the charcoal men who lived around Mount Riga; one seldom knew their names and when one asked, it was often an unpronounceable European name, so they were just called "Rigys" in those days. But when wood became scarce and coal was introduced into iron-making, the Rigys became very poor and ragged. Then the name Raggie seemed to fit even better.

The dull thud of Jonathan's maul could be heard each time he struck the glut to split a log, and the Raggies knew exactly when he started and stopped working. An experienced woodsman could even tell what kind of tree was being worked on and what kind of axe or wedge was being used. The sound of an axe cutting into soft pine is very different

287

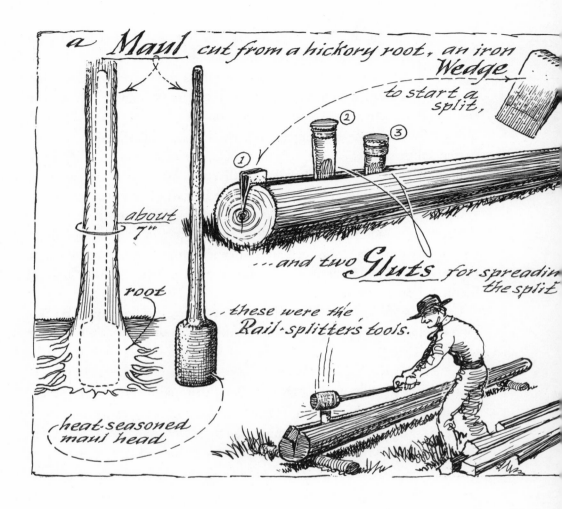

a **Maul** cut from a hickory root, an iron **Wedge** to start a split,

① ② ③

...and two **Gluts** for spreading the split

...these were the Rail-splitter's tools.

about 7"

root

heat-seasoned maul head

from the sharp ping of hardwood being cut; even the sharpness of a blade produces a certain sound to the ear of an expert, and Jonathan had often heard his father say, "Your axe sounds dull, son. Give it a sharpening when you get home."

So one day when Jonathan found some basswood trees in the Wolcott woodlots and felled a few, he was not surprised that the Raggies knew what he was about. The whack of an axe into the softer pulp of linden (or basswood as it was known) had aroused their curiosity. Four Raggies approached him.

288

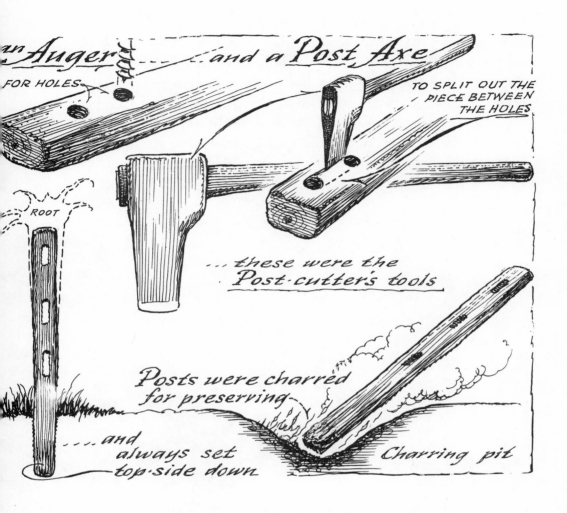

...an Auger... and a *Post Axe*

FOR HOLES

TO SPLIT OUT THE
PIECE BETWEEN
THE HOLES

ROOT

*...these were the
Post·cutter's tools*

*Posts were charred
for preserving*

*....and
always set
top·side down*

Charring pit

"Greetings!" said Jonathan, holding a box of snuff in his extended hand.

All four nodded and each took a pinch of snuff, inhaling it in very fine European manner. The American woodsman had learned to wad a pinch of snuff into a ball and place it under his upper lip. These men, thought Jonathan, cannot speak English. But one of them stepped forward and tried his limited vocabulary. He held out a small wooden berry box.

"We need berry-wood for boxes. We will give you berries."

Jonathan knew what he meant. He knew how the Raggies had been

289

living almost exclusively on the berries that grew on the coaled hills. He also knew that the berries could be made into a liquid for which the Raggies had become famous. It was called "rattlesnake medicine," and it helped them to forget bad times. But during the summer they peddled berries in basswood boxes which were made in the nearby village of Milton. They wanted basswood to bring to the box-maker, who would reimburse them for the raw material by giving them a few finished boxes.

Jonathan understood. He held out his hand with five fingers spread.

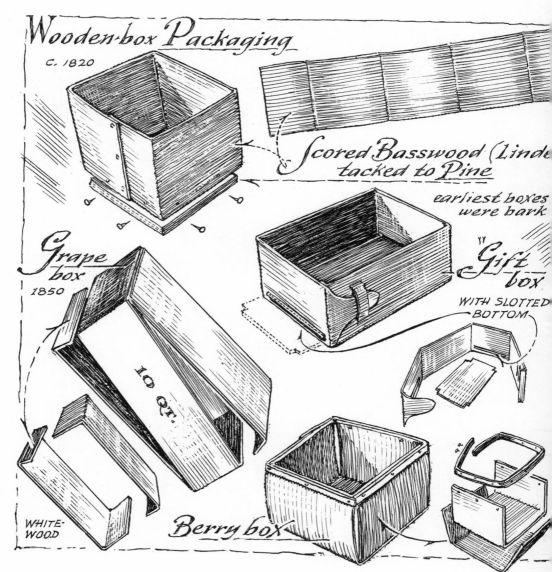

Wooden-box Packaging
c. 1820

Scored Basswood (Linde tacked to Pine
earliest boxes were bark

Gift box
WITH SLOTTED BOTTOM

Grape box
1850

10 QT.

WHITE-WOOD

Berry box

"Five basswood trees," he said. "You take them. No berries. I'm giving you a gift."

With much bowing and many gestures of gratitude, the four men departed.

By the time of the Civil War, boxes were machine-made, and America had started its amazing career of packaging. Paper cartons and paper bags came later, the first patent being for a cone-shaped paper bag in 1867. There are illustrations of Abraham Lincoln waiting on customers with a

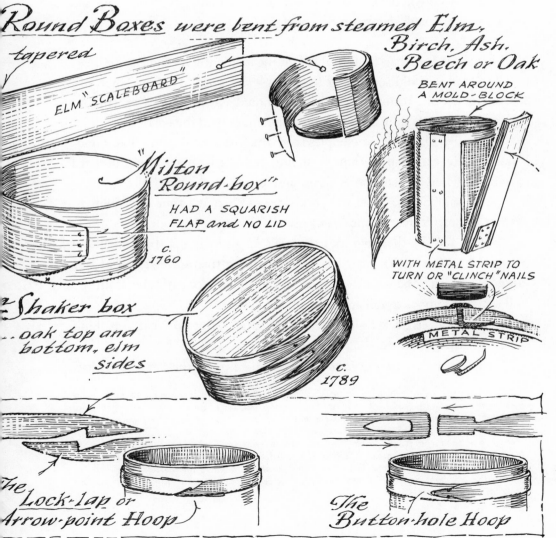

Round Boxes were bent from steamed Elm, Birch, Ash, Beech or Oak

tapered

ELM "SCALEBOARD"

BENT AROUND
A MOLD-BLOCK

"Milton
Round-box"

HAD A SQUARISH
FLAP and NO LID

c.
1760

WITH METAL STRIP TO
TURN OR "CLINCH" NAILS

METAL STRIP

Shaker box

...oak top and
bottom, elm
sides

c.
1789

The
Lock-lap or
Arrow-point Hoop

The
Button-hole Hoop

291

square type of paper bag, but these really didn't appear until after 1872. Before that, you went to a store with your own basket or jug or cloth bag; the idea of a wooden package designed to be sold along with the food it contained was something uniquely American.

The first wooden boxes were from Maine; they were made of birch bark and used for holding berries. Basswood and tulip (whitewood) strips were later made into thin "scaleboards" and bent into all sorts of clever shapes, forming boxes with lids and even some made in one piece. Basswood was the favorite box material because when it dried it was very light and could therefore be weighed along with the food it contained without appreciably increasing the weight.*

That night Jonathan told Sarah about the incident with the Raggies.

"I'm glad you did something for them," she said. "They are such unfortunate people. I am sorry we haven't more basswood to give them, but the way things are now, the wood is worth more than the berries."

"They live on berries and apples from the forest crabs and what woodchucks they can trap. I think I should tell them to take our orchard gleanings when we harvest. At least they can have the windfalls."

"Yes," said Sarah, "that's a good idea. When it's time for them to gather apples, let them come to our orchard."

"But so few of the Raggies can speak English; it will be difficult to explain it to them. We can't have them helping themselves to all of our apples—let's give them all the apples from just one tree. Maybe from the old one that's about to fall apart. It still bears well."

"That's our old Seek-no-further!" said Sarah. "But do what you think best, Jonathan."

"I shall make a sign—'*Gift to the Raggies.*' I guess they can read that.

---

* *The Shakers, who specialized in making things of wood, made round and oval boxes that seem to outlast metal. There are still herb, pill, and spice boxes stronger now (through seasoning) than they were a century ago; their metal counterparts have become rusted and been discarded. The Shakers used elm, maple, and oak in their boxes, but considered basswood too fragile. The "fingers" or lap ends of Shaker boxes usually turn to the right because of a religious belief in the word "right" which made the Shakers shun anything going toward the left. It was contrary to order to kneel on the left knee first, to put on the left boot first, or to step first with the left foot. Their furniture was a masterpiece of "right angles."*

Then I'll just print '*Seek-no-further*.' Maybe they will know what that means, too."

"It's a funny name!" said Sarah. "I wish *I* knew what it meant."

We do therefore ... dedicate and solemnly devote this tree to be a Tree of Liberty. May all our councils and deliberations under its branches be guided by wisdom and directed to the support and maintenance of that liberty which our renowned forefathers sought out and found under trees and in the wilderness.

from a Dedication to a Tree of Liberty
Providence, Rhode Island.

The Warehouse

In October of 1765, a group of American merchants met under a "Liberty Tree" and agreed that certain articles should not be brought into this country from England. There were many such trees, placed as monuments to spirit and patriotism, and designated as sites for meetings and the signing of charters. As John Adams commented in his diary, "In the course of this year, there have been innumerable monuments erected in the several colonies and provinces." What better monument to America, as an emblem of its God-given independence, than a tree? It was at this meeting in 1765 that the word "independence" took on a special and widespread meaning.

"With our land's wealth," said one Boston merchant, "we can all afford to be independent. There is probably nothing a man needs that we cannot make or grow in America. Look about you! Except for a piece of silk here and there, the clothes on our backs and every stick in our houses

297

is American. We can be, indeed we *are*, the most independent people on earth!"

Those days, when the nation was struggling to be born, were perhaps our most poignant times, for it was an era when each man was forced to live with piercing intensity and perception. Two centuries later, when an American turns on the water and the lights in his apartment, he has little awareness of where these things come from; the greatest pity, however, is that he says, "Who cares where it comes from, as long as it keeps on coming?"

In 1765 everything a man owned was made more valuable by the fact that he had made it himself or knew exactly from where it had come. This is not so remarkable as it sounds; it is less strange that the eighteenth-century man should have a richer and keener enjoyment of life through knowledge than that the twentieth-century man should lead an arid and empty existence in the midst of wealth and extraordinary material benefits.

That century of magnificent awareness preceding the Civil War was the age of wood. Wood was not accepted simply as the material for building a new nation—it was an inspiration. Gentle to the touch, exquisite to contemplate, tractable in creative hands, stronger by weight than iron, wood was, as William Penn had said, "a substance with a soul." It spanned rivers for man; it built his home and heated it in the winter; man walked on wood, slept in it, sat on wooden chairs at wooden tables, drank and ate the fruits of trees from wooden cups and dishes. From cradle of wood to coffin of wood, the life of man was encircled by it.

One of the remarkable things about wood is its self-expression. Whether as the handle of a tool, as a dead stump, or alive in a forest where every branch is a record of the winds that blew, it is always telling something about itself. This is why man has an affinity with wood not only as a mere material, but also as a kindred spirit to live with and to know. The children of a century ago were expert at knowing trees and their characteristics; they grew up thinking of trees as having human qualities and, almost Druidlike, they tried to acquire the qualities of trees. A man might be as "strong as an oak," or "bend like a willow"; if he had

298

World of Wooden Things

tankard

sap funnel

Noggin

cup

dipper

—burl

Apple butter scoop

meat pounder

plate

pie crimper

piggin

Rundlet

Eel trap

Sap Spoon

Churn

Fork

Stirrer

Oven Peel

Grain Shovel

299

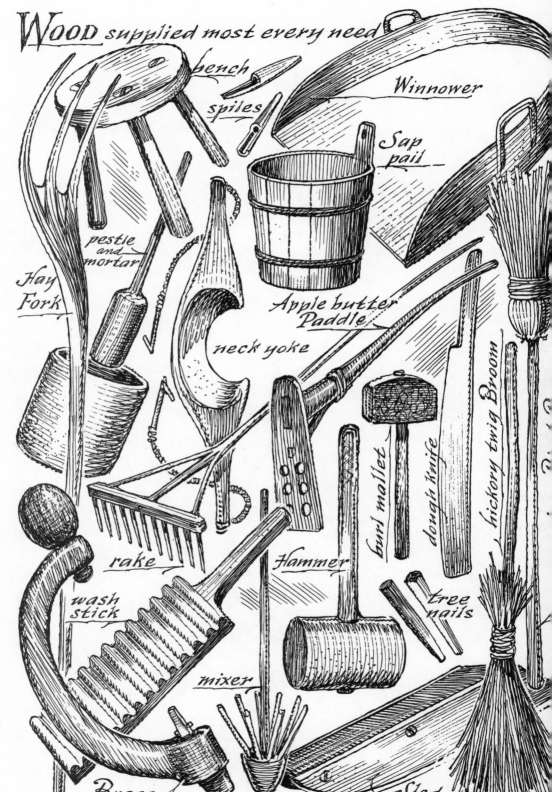

WOOD supplied most every need

bench

spiles

Winnower

Sap pail

pestle and mortar

Hay Fork

Apple butter Paddle

neck yoke

rake

Hammer

burl mallet

dough knife

hickory twig Broom

wash stick

tree nails

mixer

Brace

Sled

300

proper "timber," he'd become all the stronger from the winds of adversity.

The woodshed was an important part of the early American school, and so were the "horn books" or slabs of wood that held lesson cards in place. Even the classroom "slate" was wooden at first, made from a wide pine board painted a dull black. Even now, we still call it a "black*board*," although it is made of slate or plastic.

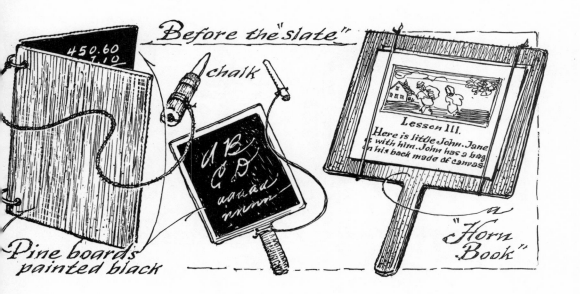

So it can be seen that in the pioneer days, everyone accepted wood in a way that we do not today. We can see why the early American's attitude toward the forest was reverent, and why when the colonies sought an emblem of independence for their flags, it was a tree. When they sought a symbol for the first coinage, the Massachusetts Bay Colony also chose the tree; the Pine Tree shilling along with the Willow Tree and Oak Tree coins seemed perfectly to symbolize America. Their designer, Joseph Jenks, said "What better thing than a tree, to portray the wealth of our country?"

In 1765 Benjamin Dean considered himself a rich man, although he had little money. He had bought half of his father's mill and some of the

301

"Bunker Hill Flag"

"Continental Flag"

AN APPEAL TO HEAVEN

Washington's Cruisers

LIBERTY TREE

AN APPEAL TO GOD

"Liberty Tree Flag"

Vermont Flag

DONT TREAD ON ME

Massachusetts (navy)

..these were once "American Flags!"

MASATHVSETS

and this our first coin

New England Symbol.

Cornwall acreage that went with it: the Connecticut countryside had offered him everything that a pioneer American could wish for. His father, Reuben Dean, had, in his own words, "knocked down three score of trees and piled them into a serviceable house." And when that was done, he'd made use of the stream nearby and had gone about building the machinery for grinding. The first mill wheel was a small one with only enough power for grinding bark and herbs for the making of dyes and medicines. The recipes of "Doctor Reuben" had come from such sources as the Scatacook Indians, and his warehouse was no more than the surrounding forests. Chestnut-oak made a dark yellowish tan that most Cornwall women used for dying their woolens. Birch bark made an oil for perfume, and it also produced a lovely yellow dye; butternut made a deep brown. Tulip tree bark made a rich golden color, and Norway maple made a rosy tan. The ink used at Cornwall school came from pitch-pine lampblack and butternut juice. A good furniture stain was made from red oak bark, and if you wanted to make your own paint, you could get the best linseed oil base when Doc Reuben ground flax seed.

But he earned the name of "doctor" by his medicinal concoctions. He ground native holly bark for the relief of the ague. Fever bush or fever root were also cures. There was swamp laurel for diarrhea, slippery elm for a sore throat, black elder for skin infections, bayberry for dysentery, and ground aspen bark made a good substitute for quinine. The fine tan-colored "sawdust" left by the lyctus beetle (powder-post beetle) was collected and used as a baby powder. When spring came and tonics were in order, people asked for the essences and bark powders for sassafras and spice teas, birch beer, root beer, maple beer, and spruce beer. Doctor Reuben Dean's warehouse had an almost inexhaustible supply of remedies, and his mill was seldom silent.

Son Benjamin, however, had other interests. He had always enjoyed the sight of a blade passing through good wood; his nose was delighted by the tang of fresh sawdust and his ears tingled at the whine and clatter of sawmill machinery. His father had been content to copy the water wheels he'd seen and he'd never studied the mechanics of water power or the mathematical equations of power application. These were things for a younger mind. Hence, when Benjamin took over, his mind raced with the expectation of a bigger and better mill that would saw heavy timber, perhaps having gang saws so that a number of floor boards could be cut at the same time. He even knew what he intended to do with the sawdust and chips. He'd seen the new icehouses people were building, with

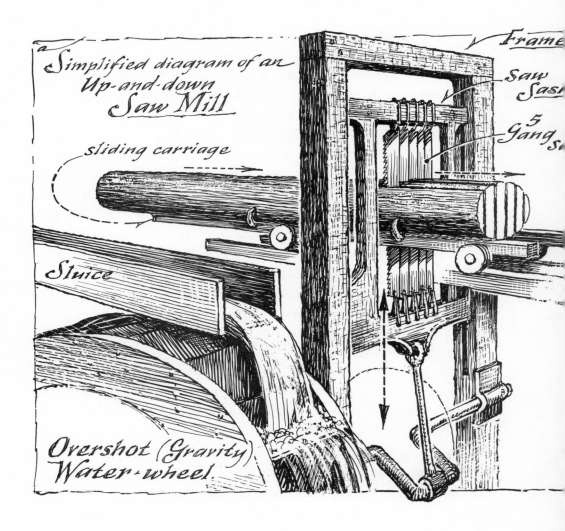

Simplified diagram of an Up-and-down Saw Mill

sliding carriage

Sluice

Overshot (Gravity) Water-wheel.

Frame

Saw Sash

5 Gang S

charcoal-filled walls to preserve the ice; he felt certain that sawdust would work even better.

People were riving panel boards and wall sheathing by hand, so sawn boards should sell quickly, particularly those the width of the Cornwall pines—perhaps twenty to thirty inches. English homes had been traditionally walled with oak, but the colonial American home was usually wainscoted with pine. Not only was there an abundance of pine in America, but the wood had a soft and glowing patina and lavish widths of clear grain.

304

Wainscot has since become a misused word, for most people pronounce it "wains-coat" and they believe it refers to a wall-lining of wood at chair-rail height. Actually, it is a word taken from "wagenscot" (wagon-panel) and it is still to be pronounced the old way (like "wainskut"). Some ridicule this Maine pronunciation, not realizing that the pronunciation is correct. Wainscoting means any wooden wall-lining, whether it be sheathing or paneling, horizontal or vertical, floor-to-ceiling or chair-rail height.

A panel in the true sense of the word should look like the underside of a shallow bread pan. In fact, that is where the word came from. Nowadays we speak of "pine-wall paneling" in describing tongue and groove

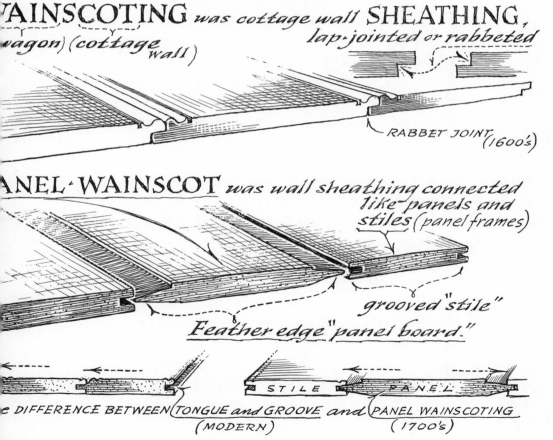

WAINSCOTING *was cottage wall* SHEATHING, *lap-jointed or rabbeted*

(wagon) (cottage wall)

RABBET JOINT *(1600's)*

PANEL·WAINSCOT *was wall sheathing connected like panels and stiles (panel frames)*

grooved "stile"

Feather edge "panel board."

STILE · PANEL

The DIFFERENCE BETWEEN TONGUE *and* GROOVE *and* PANEL WAINSCOTING
(MODERN) *(1700's)*

305

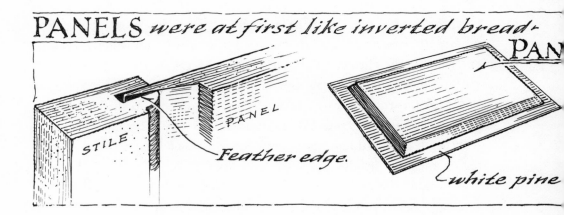

PANELS *were at first like inverted bread-* PAN

STILE

PANEL

Feather edge.

white pine

sheathing (or wainscoting). We also speak of "pumpkin pine" and some believe this is a kind of tree: pumpkin pine is merely ancient white pine. When new, it is tan-white, but softening and drying for over a century, it mellows into its pumpkinlike condition.*

Benjamin Dean's mill began to take form, and his household on nearby Dudleytown Hill saw him only at dinner and bedtime.

"As soon as we can," he told his wife, "I think we should sell this place and move into the valley near the mill."

"You can't work at the mill," said Ruth, "and still make the trip uphill each night. So move we shall, but I shall miss my orchard. It is just ready for its first good harvest."

"We shall have two orchards," said Benjamin. "The valley soil is thick with peat from prehistoric forests, and that will manure our orchard; it will grow the best eating apples."

"Then we shall leave the hilltop orchard for cider. It's taken hold now and needs just an occasional pruning."

And so it was. By the time the hilltop orchard had reached its peak, the Deans had moved into the valley next to the mill, and a new eating-apple orchard had been set out.

Planning an orchard in the 1700's was extremely exacting work, for apples were no occasional food. They were America's national food, and

* *Well-seasoned white pine was also known in New England as "apple pine."*

cider was the national drink. The first colonists had been instructed to drink as little water as possible. They had obeyed this dictum so well that even small children were brought up on teas and beers, and cider was served at every meal. In fact, there was apple at the table in some form all year round. So an apple orchard was planned to supply fresh eating apples and proper cooking apples for each season. Only the most poorly planned orchard would be in full bloom, with all the trees bearing at the same time. By proper planning and hastening or retarding ripening, an orchard might start its harvest period in summer and finish after the snow had arrived.

Scratching the bark of a fruit tree at certain times will hasten its bloom, and it was even a custom to shoot buckshot at an apple tree to help it bear in an "off year." Beating a tree's bark will bruise the layer just beneath it and check the descent of sap, forcing an early bearing. People used to beat fruit and nut trees with softwood clubs, and an old rhyme mentions this:

A woman, a watchdog, and a walnut tree,
The more you beat them the better they be.

There were tricks, too, in preserving eating apples. It started at picking time, when two men harvested each tree, using heavy gloves. No hand should touch the apple, and no two apples should rub against each other. The apple should be lifted upward to snap the stem off; if it were pulled, the stem would be ripped out of the apple and decay would start at once. Two apples at a time were handed down to a gloved packer who laid the apples carefully in straw (on a sled), and then covered them with a black cloth. A wheelbarrow or wagon jiggled too much, so a sled was used, and the apples were skidded over hay to the packing cellar. Sometimes they were packed in barrels; in that case the barrel was lifted by two men and walked to a sled. The man who was caught rolling a barrel of apples lost his job at once. "Watch a man gather apples," said one old almanac, "and you will see either a careful man or a careless man."

There were about two thousand well-known apples, and each one was

307

Picking Bag c.1790

Apple picker's "chair."

Picking Ladder

scissors c.1860

SPLINT BASKET

apple sled

Shaker device

OPEN END

x sharp blades

to be picked at a specific time for a specific purpose. The maturity of an apple was indicated by the condition of the seed, so one apple was opened and used as a test. Winter apples were picked when mature, yet not ripe; late winter apples were picked before the first good frost, but when they were just hard enough to withstand thumb pressure.

Eating apples were often placed on their sides in baked sawdust, or in well-dried timothy chaff. Noah Webster recommended packing apples in heat-dried sand. Most people hung their special apples "by their tails" (stems), and some packed them in grain. It was the custom when shipping apples overseas to ship grain at the same time; in this way apples

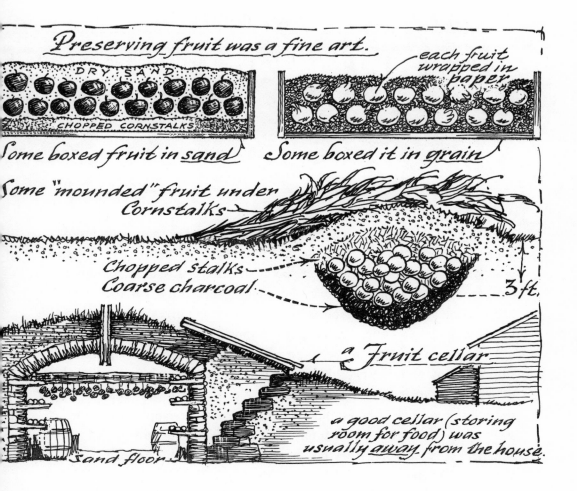

Preserving fruit was a fine art.

DRY SAND
CHOPPED CORNSTALKS

Some boxed fruit in sand

each fruit wrapped in paper

Some boxed it in grain

Some "mounded" fruit under Cornstalks

Chopped stalks
Coarse charcoal

3 ft.

a Fruit cellar

a good cellar (storing room for food) was usually away from the house.

Sand floor

could be packed in with the grain. Marble shelves were popular in the Vermont and Connecticut apple cellars, as they kept the apples cold and dry. Some had windmills that operated fans to keep the air moving (thus retarding spoilage), but every housewife knew enough to fan the air each time she went to the storage room. There are reports of apples correctly packed or hung in the "correct atmosphere" that have kept for more than two years.

Perhaps no tree has given America more of itself than the apple tree. Besides its vinegars and medicines, we might recall apple duff, apple brandy, applejack, apple dowdy, also crowdy and dowler (pies), apple waffle, apple butter, apple cake, applesauce, apple leather (broiled and

... By their tails.

dried apples), apple slump, candy apple, and numerous other examples of apple Americana. Its wood was used for machinery, particularly for cogs, wheels, and shuttles; whenever a spoon or stirrer was used for apple butter or sauce, applewood was the choice. Jonathan Chapman, who became known as Johnny Appleseed, said, "Nothing gives more yet asks less in return, than a tree; particularly the apple."

Whenever you walk in the forest and you come upon an apple tree, stop and look about. Very likely you will see several others, too. And perhaps some ancient, stunted lilac bushes. Nearby there will probably be the ruins of an ancient house foundation, a cellar where apples were once stored, kept throughout the winter, fresh for the table before the heat of summer. It is still like that on deserted Dudleytown Mountain near Cornwall. There, in about 1910 when the blight had already turned the first chestnut leaves brown, the last of the Dudleytown houses fell into its own cellar. People began talking about the "curse of Dudleytown" and history books told about this "deserted ghost town," with its eerie place names—Dark Entry Road and Owlsboro Lane.

Actually, there is no mystery about the place; its disappearance as a village was just part of a cycle. When people first moved there in the early 1700's, they settled on the high areas for their own protection. The lowlands were wet, covered with moss, and did not present inviting sites for homes. But within a half century, when the valleys were hunted and harvested and mills (which had to be near water) were established, the hilltop settlements were abandoned. Further, the hilltops have much less topsoil on them, and so they were "farmed out" quickly.

Remnants of the Dean hilltop orchard can still be found in the third growth of forest. If you stand where the Dean house was, you may be standing eight or ten feet above the old excavation floor, for the forest has a habit of building up a compost to cover old wounds. Near the site of the old house there is a pile of stones, which marks the end of a long-gone rail fence; there an old apple tree hulk remains rotting on the ground. But if you walk along its body, you will come to a live shoot, fed in some mysterious way by the fallen parent. The tree was upright when Benjamin Dean left for Ohio in 1810. Ruth remembered it well, for she took some of it with her—the only part of Cornwall which they didn't leave behind them.

She had bent a branch of the tree downward one midsummer, and after slicing through the tender bark so that some day it might root, she had inserted the branch into and through a pot of earth. For two seasons

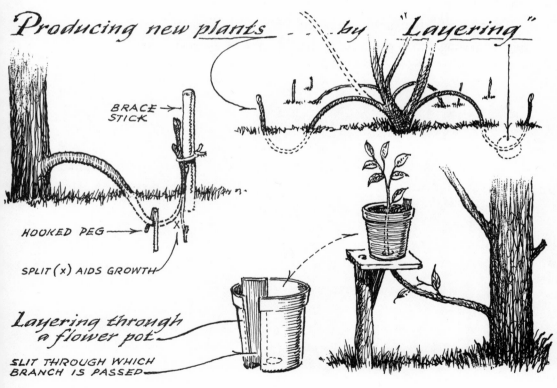

Producing new plants — by "Layering"

BRACE STICK

HOOKED PEG

SPLIT (X) AIDS GROWTH

Layering through a flower pot

SLIT THROUGH WHICH BRANCH IS PASSED

she had nursed the "layering pot," keeping it wrapped with cloths and watering it daily, until roots had emerged from the cut portion within the pot. When separated from the parent plant, it was put, pot and all, beneath the big tree, and Ruth had called it "mother watching over her baby." Benjamin enjoyed the spectacle, but when the time came to unearth the pot and transport it to Ohio, he rebelled.

"Why in the world," Benjamin had said, "do you want to carry that heavy box with you? Such a tiny tree will likely die on the long trip. Anyway, there are plenty of apple trees in Ohio."

"I know that," Ruth replied, "but women are sentimental and men forgive them. It's not such a heavy box, and I shall take care of watering and shading it till we get to Ohio. If the tree lives, it will be worth all the trouble. It will be taking some of our old place with us. It was our favorite tree—it came from England and it can make another historic trip."

"Very well," Benjamin consented. "It's a silly idea, and a silly name, too. Traveling across the country with a baby 'Seek-no-further'!"

1665

In 1665 Harvard College graduated an American Indian named Cheeshahteaumuck.

314

The New World

For so young a nation, it is strange that the beginnings of America should be so shrouded in mythical legend. Any schoolboy will tell you that Betsy Ross designed the Stars and Stripes and that the Pilgrims were the first settlers to step on the shores of New England (on Plymouth Rock, in fact).

Actually, when the Pilgrims sailed for our shores they had an extraordinarily good map of New England and more travel literature than one might expect. The map they used was made a half-dozen years before, and it showed such names as Boston, Hull, Dartmouth, Cambridge, Norwich, Southampton, Ipswich, Oxford, and Sandwich. Oh, yes—there was also a place named *Plimouth!*

Of course there were other maps of the New England territory, for by 1620 there were many fishing stations in Maine. That year a Maine gristmill had sent a shipload of grain to England, and three years before, Pocahontas had died in London. This rather explodes the schoolboy picture of the New England coast as an unexplored land of savage Indians.

Among the Indians that the Pilgrims met were those who spoke English. "Welcome! Welcome, Englishmen!" said Samoset. "But wait—I shall get Squanto who was educated in London. I am sure he will speak better English than I."

When the new Verrazano Bridge, connecting Brooklyn and Staten Island, was built, there were very few schoolboys who had ever heard the name. Yet a century before the Plymouth Plantation was established, a gentleman named Verrazano described the New England coast: "We found another land high ful of thicke woods," he wrote. "The trees were of firres, cipresses and such like are wont to grow in cold Countreys." He suffered from poor publicity, it seems, for his accounts are seldom mentioned; Cartier did a little better. As he went up the New England coast, he wrote about the "pleasant countrey full of all sorts of goodly trees, Ceders, Firres, Ashes, Boxe and Willowes." Captain John Smith is well known for his romantic exploits, but his impressions of the New World had more talk about wood in them than anything else. "The treasures of this land," he wrote, "have never been opened, nor her originalls wasted, consumed or abused . . . overgrown with all sorts of excellent woodes for the building of houses, boats, barks or shippes." It is interesting that unlike European maps, all the early maps of America have trees drawn upon them. And with the slightest research, it is easy to see that the New World was not one of "freedom" so much as it was a gigantic warehouse of wood.

In the spring of 1665 a ship lay in Bristol Harbor, ready for journeying to the New World. Its hold was full of cargo for the people of Massachusetts. But by making the most of their new-found wealth, the colonists had become largely self-sufficient in four decades, and British merchants were hard pressed to find goods to entice the American taste. Glass, nail-rods, silks, teas, and spices took up very little room and weight, so English bricks were added to ballast the ship in case of a rough sea. The colonists were making good brick already and had little need of bricks from Britain, but as they were sold at a loss on this side of the ocean, they were always welcome. No need for ballast on the way back, for chestnut and oak and hickory have good weight.

The ship was not a new one; it had made the crossing almost a hundred times, mostly as a sassafras carrier. It was one of a fleet of its kind—the *Susan Constant*, the *Discoverer*, and the *Treasurer* (which had carried Sir Thomas Dale and Pocahontas from America to England).

Sassafras is a tree very closely associated with America, although few are now aware of its history. As the early American wonder drug, it was our first money crop and object-in-trade of the first American cartel. In 1622 the Jamestown Colony was committed by the Crown to produce thirty tons of sassafras, with a penalty of ten pounds of tobacco on each man who did not produce one hundred pounds of it.

Sassafras was supposed to cure almost any ailment; used as a tea or a tonic it became the favorite drink of England. And when rumor started that sassafras retarded old age, the sassafras trade reached its peak.

No cure-all has had better publicity than sassafras. Its popularity began

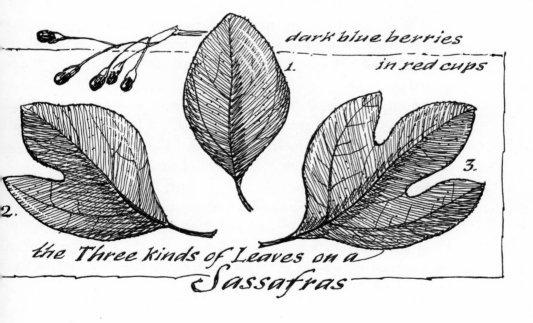

dark blue berries
in red cups
1.
2.
3.
the Three kinds of Leaves on a
Sassafras

with the writings of Doctor Nicolas Monardes in 1569. "It healeth opila-tions," he wrote, "it comforteth the liver and stomach and doth disopi-late; to give appetite to eat; in the headache, in griefes of the stomach; it causeth to cast out gravel and stones; it removeth the impediments that cause barrenness and maketh women to conceave; in the toothache; in the evil of the poxe and eville of the joints." Then an incident occurred in Roanoke that really captured the public imagination: it concerned a group of Virginians who had traveled far beyond the camp where their food was stored and were, therefore, reduced to eating their dogs, cooked in a soup of sassafras. When their dogs were all eaten, the Virginians lived on sassafras soup alone, which was reported to give them a strange new vitality.

When Sir Francis Drake visited Roanoke in 1586 and brought some of the half-starved colonists back with him, he also brought back a load of sassafras, livened by the tale of the "wondrous root which kept the starving alive and in fair goode spirit."

The smell and taste of sassafras is unlike any other spice, and legend has it that the odor alone will keep away sickness and evil, as well as vermin. Spoons were often made of sassafras wood, cradles were inlaid with it, noggins of sassafras added extra flavor to a drink, and Bible boxes were made of the wood to keep away evil spirits. It was said that a ship with sufficient sassafras wood in her hull would never be wrecked. Indeed, the ship at Bristol had fared well; the pungent odor of sassafras still per-meated her holds.

The ship's master, Robert Carter, was dining at the estate of Ralph Austin, "an extraordinary practicer in ye art of planting." The dinner had been a bon voyage meeting, for Robert Carter was to leave on the next tide. The time for fruit and brandy had come.

"I envy you your journey," said the host, "and drink Godspeed to you. You will reach America at Goose Summer, and the harvesting will be at its peak; it will be an exciting and colorful spectacle."

"In America they call it Indian Summer," said Carter, "and indeed there is color such as we never see in England. They say the first frost sets the leaves afire, and from then on a man can look at the hills and tell by the colors what kinds of trees are there. The browns and tans are hickory, the yellows are tulip and beech and ironwood; the black gum and oak and maple turn flaming red, while the purples are the leaves of white and mountain ash."

"They say that the orange colors are so bright they hurt your eyes."

"Yes, they do—those are the leaves of sassafras and sugar maple."

"And when you arrive in America," said Ralph Austin, "I hope that you will remember to gather what information you can about the orchards there. The plague of ice that struck us here in England last year must surely have killed many orchard trees; only the most hardy can have survived. I shall want grafts and layers of them for England. And you must keep accounts for me, telling me of all the astounding trees of the New World."

"I shall do this indeed," said Robert, "but I am of the opinion that many of the American trees would not survive the temperate mildness of the air of Britain—they seem to need the intense atmospheric changes of America. Birch, for example, has been known to grow in England for centuries, yet nothing like the American birch has ever been seen here. The Indians choose one large birch tree and make two cuts down its trunk on opposite sides; then they make two encircling cuts at top and bottom. In the spring when the bark is peeling, the Indians lift away these two curled pieces of bark and sew them together to make a boat which they call a 'canoo.' "

"Remarkable!" said Ralph Austin. "And what do they use for sewing?"

"Again a tree! They use the roots of the white spruce, and to make the boat watertight they heat the wood of balsam fir until its resin oozes out and they mix it with the pitch of pine. But the biggest 'canoos' are the ones made of solid wood. There is tale of one made from a hollowed sycamore that is sixty-five feet long and carries nine thousand pounds. In America the old sycamore usually has a hollow trunk, and great barrels are made with the slightest effort. Even well-linings are made from these hollow

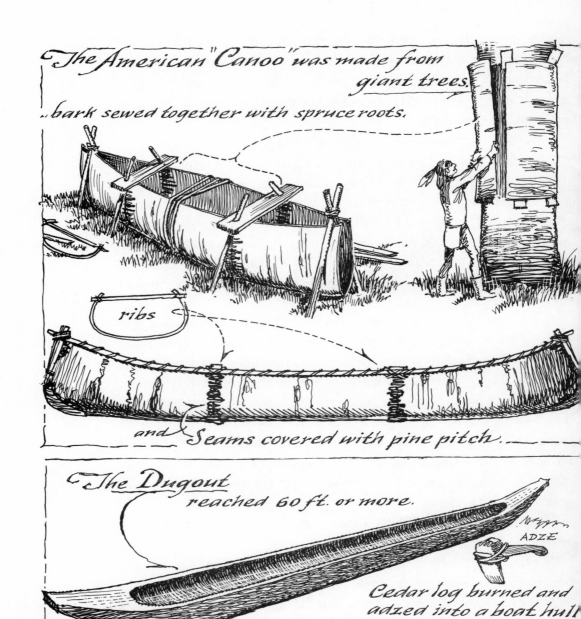

The American "Canoo" was made from giant trees.

...bark sewed together with spruce roots.

ribs

and Seams covered with pine pitch.

The Dugout reached 60 ft. or more.

ADZE

Cedar log burned and adzed into a boat hull

320 sycamore trunks, and sometimes they are used as storage bins, as big around as an armspread and a perch in height."

"This very year," he continued, "a mast was felled in Maine which

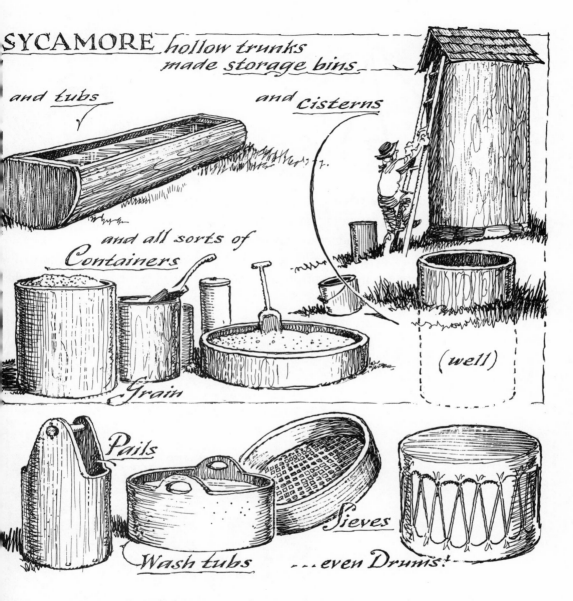

SYCAMORE *hollow trunks made storage bins*

and tubs ... *and cisterns*

and all sorts of Containers

Grain

(well)

Pails

Wash tubs ...*even Drums!*

Sieves

proved too big for any of our mast ships.* Even after it was hewn and shaped, it had a useable length of one hundred and thirty feet and

* There were special ships for carrying mast material for the British Navy. They were bargelike and had long, uninterrupted floors that could hold hundred-foot lengths. The masts were slid through a door in the stern, and the largest mast ship could hold fifty masts. Pine trees more than two foot in diameter (three feet from the ground) were reserved for masts for the Royal Navy, and the "Broad Arrow Mark" was placed on tree trunks by Royal Tree Viewers, marking them as British property.

321

weighed over twenty-five tons. Why, there are pines in Massachusetts that have no extending limbs until a hundred feet from the ground!"

"But these wonders are not what I can write about in these times," said Austin. "England is badly in need of timber because of the waste of its resources; we must implant the value of the growing tree and inspire the

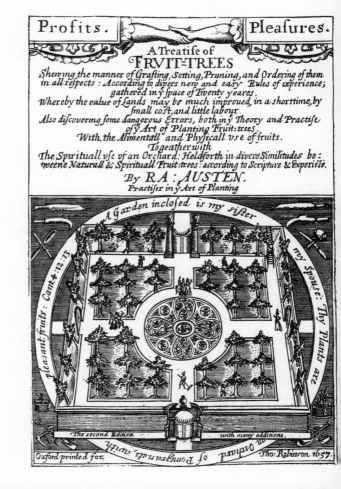

322

The Spirituall use of an
Orchard, or Garden of

FRUIT-TREES.

Set forth in divers *Similitudes* betweene
Naturall and *Spirituall* fruit-trees, in their
Natures, and ordering, according to
Scripture and Experience.

The second Impreſſion; with the Addition of many *Similitudes*.
By *R A: A U S T E N*, Author of the firſt part.

Hoſ: 12.10. *I have uſed* Similitudes *by the Miniſtrie of the Prophets.*
Jer: 17.8. *He ſhall be as a Tree planted by the waters, and that ſpread-
eth out her Roots by the River, and ſhall not ſee when heat cometh, but
her leaſe ſhall be greene, and ſhall not be carefull in the year of drought,
neither ſhall ceaſe from yeilding fruit.*
Rom: 11.23. *And they alſo, if they abide not ſtill in unbeleiſe, ſhall be
grafted in, for God is able to graft them in againe.*
Joh: 15.1, 2. *I am the true Vine, and my Father is the husbandman.
Every branch that beareth fruit he purgeth it, that it may bring forth
more fruit.*
Cant. 2.3. *Like the Apple-tree among the Trees of the forreſt, ſo is my
beloved among the ſonnes. I ſate downe under his ſhadow with great
delight, and his fruit was ſweet to my taſt.*

O X F O R D,
Printed by HEN: HALL, Printer to the UNIVERSITY,
for THO: ROBINSON. M.DC.LVII.

farmer in a Godly way, so that he will plant and know the benefits of propagating timber trees and orchards."

"I have read your writings, good Ralph," said Robert, "and I can perhaps even quote you. 'The world is a great library, and fruit trees are some of the books wherein we may read and see plainly the attributes of God.' Perhaps America will need such a philosophy, too, before it wastes its trees, thinking of them as just so much material wealth. I shall take your book with me and show it to those who will read its wisdom."

Agriculture and husbandry during the 1600's and 1700's were not a business, but a way of life. This explains why writings about agriculture were so filled with Biblical quotations and moral philosophy. Austin, in speaking of pruning, for example, tells how fruit trees that spread widely and grow low near the ground bear more and larger fruit than high trees, and the fruit is easier to reach. This might be forgotten by the reader, except for the typical religious application as he writes, ". . . and humble Christians, too, bring forth more and fairer fruit than lofty persons, while their acts are easier to reach."

A servant entered with a tray of nuts and fruits, and Austin passed them to his guest.

"England's orchards of forest trees are most depleted. Some of the boat builders are using fruitwoods, as are the joiners. Nothing is wasted now, but it is almost too late. The ship *Mayflower* is now the beams and rafters of a barn in Buckingham. Whatever new wood we need for our navy will come from the New World."

Robert Carter broke an apple in two, admired its meat, and sprinkled it with cinnamon spice. "It is time for me to leave," he said. "I should like to take one of these fine apples with me and plant the seed in America."

"What a fine idea! But the seed would not propagate that same apple, and a graft might not last the voyage. But wait! I shall get you a layering plant, and you shall be the first to bring my prize across the ocean. I have worked a long time to create this variety; I have not named it yet. I would be pleased for you to name it. Perhaps the 'Westfield,' after your farm in Massachusetts? Perhaps it might be named after your ship! What is the name of your ship?"

"It is called the *Seek-no-further*."

a compact description for recognizing a few of the typical American Trees

On the following pages—not alphabetically listed or at all complete—are illustrated a random selection of trees that might be seen in a stroll through the countryside. Points of recognition—leaf shapes, cones, coloring, size—as the author knows them, are shown in the sketches and explained in the text, thus identifying the woods pictured in the color insert at the beginning of the book.

Just as it is possible to recognize certain people in a crowd by the way they stand or act, it is also possible to identify a tree—even at some distance—by its size, color, or shape. Some trees grow in small groups within the forest, while others mass together and crowd out everything that is unlike themselves. There are stunted trees that grow in poor soil, and there are towering beauties that mark places of rich soil. The aspen leaf quivers in the wind, the oak leaf whips about, and the beech and maple leaves turn over. Each kind of tree has its own movement or manner of growing that is just as interesting to note as the scientific properties given in a precise tree guidebook.

Grotesque, stately, vaselike, prim, solemn, rugged—these are the words a woodsman uses in describing trees, though he probably does not know their scientific names. It is the woodsman's point of view that is employed in the text and represented in the illustrations on the pages that follow.

325

SYCAMORE (Buttonball and/or Buttonwood)—is easily recognized by its bark whic resembles "old scraped-off wall paper." The trunks of mature sycamores ar often hollow; their limbs are remarkably light in color, ranging from cream t gray, pale green, and tan. The fruit is a ball of seeds.

TULIP TREE (yellow poplar or whitewood)—an outstanding tree in the forest, it ha a magnificent straight trunk and neatly furrowed gray bark. It is not really poplar, though many country people call it "popple." Its flower is like a tulip its fruit a cone of many winged seeds.

CHESTNUT—has disappeared from the American forest except as a small tree tha rises from old blighted stumps to a height of about ten feet before it, in turn succumbs to the blight. The leaves are very long, prominently veined, and sharp-toothed.

AMERICAN ELM—flares up and outward in a vaselike fashion. Its wood, difficult t split, was used for ship blocks, wheel hubs, and yokes; its bark was used fo cord and for chair bottoms. The SLIPPERY elm leaf is larger than that of the American elm, but has smaller teeth, and is rough all over the bottom. Thi tree is not as tall and is less vaselike in appearance than the American or white elm.

AMERICAN ASH—has leaves set opposite each other on the twigs. Recognizing the different varieties of ash trees is difficult for there are red, white, blue, green, black, and yellow ashes. Shown opposite are the two most valuable kinds— American (or white) ash and black ash. All of the ash trees have a single winged seed. Ash *bends* with supreme strength, but since it *splits* with pre- cision, splints for baskets, chairs, and hoops were made from the black variety. Blue ash produced a dye from its inner bark, and its wood made superior pitchfork handles. White ash was second in value to oak, being the best material for tool handles, oars, and for any implement where elasticity and strength were required.

SYCAMORE

has limbs like a Javanese dancer's arms and *Bark like torn wall paper*

BUTTON·BALL FRUIT

TULIP TREE

NO POINT AT END OF LEAF

MOST LIKELY TULIPS

fruit
CLOSED   OPEN

flower

CHESTNUT

STILL TRYING TO GROW!

American ELM *can be recognized by its shape*

"ONE SIDED" LEAF

Slippery Elm leaf is bigger

thin waferlike seeds

WHITE or AMERICAN ELM

American ASH (white ash)

LEAF HAS FAIRLY LONG STEM: OTHER ASHES HAVE LESS OR NO STEM

BARK ASH GRAY

Black Ash

WHITE ASH SEED

BARK FURROWS SELDOM CROSS

seed   wing

327

BLACK CHERRY—a valuable timber tree, is prized by cabinetmakers. Because it can be polished to a deep and glowing red, many of the finest early table tops and interior panels were made of cherry wood. Varying from shrubs ten feet tall to trees one hundred feet high, black cherry is often plagued by rot, tent caterpillars, and other insects. The young tree has beautiful, reddish, smooth bark with conspicuous horizontal marks. As the tree ages, the bark becomes black (like pine) and, starting at the bottom, cracks off in thin brittle scales. Pin cherry and sweet cherry are small trees. Choke cherry is even smaller—really only a shrub—and bears an unpalatable dark red berry.

AMERICAN HOLLY—is the best known of about fifteen varieties of holly. It reaches about twenty to fifty feet in height, with nearly horizontal limbs and an ash-gray bark, somewhat like beech. Its wood is compact with a satiny texture, and is used for wood engraving, inlay work, screws, and tool handles.

WALNUT—a most valuable hardwood, has leaves that are fine-toothed, pointed, smooth above and hairy beneath. There are from fifteen to twenty-three leaves on a black walnut branch and from eleven to nineteen leaves on a white walnut (butternut) branch. Black walnut has a darker bark and its round nut grows in a thick green husk. The butternut spreads more and has lighter, grayer bark and slightly broader, more hairy leaves. Husks from both of these walnuts produce a fine yellow dye. Black walnut was used in making water wheels and as charcoal for gunpowder. Sugar was produced from the sap of the butternut.

LIVE OAK—symbol of the Southland, this tree spreads tremendously. Its leaves are somewhat like those of the laurel and willow oak, but are more elliptical, blunt-tipped, and leathery, and are green throughout the year. The wood of the oak is valued for hardness, strength, and durability.

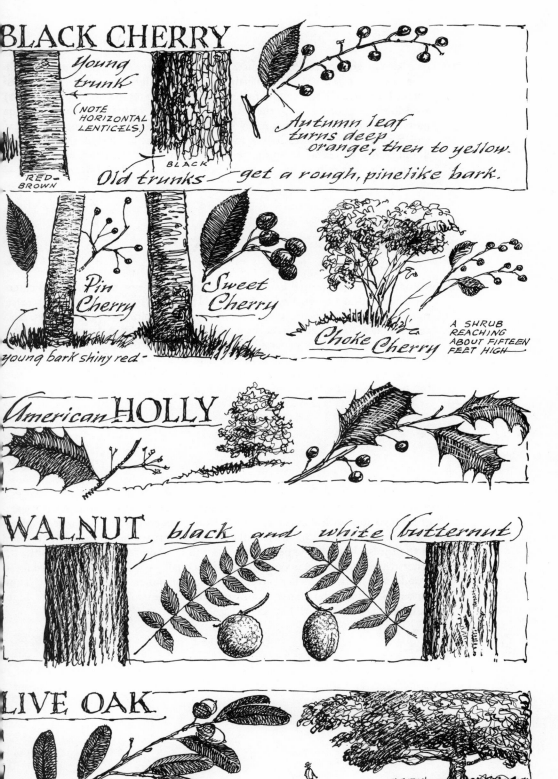

BLACK CHERRY

Young trunk

(NOTE HORIZONTAL LENTICELS)

RED-BROWN

BLACK

Old trunks get a rough, pinelike bark.

Autumn leaf turns deep orange, then to yellow.

Pin Cherry

young bark shiny red —

Sweet Cherry

Choke Cherry

A SHRUB REACHING ABOUT FIFTEEN FEET HIGH

American HOLLY

WALNUT *black and white (butternut)*

LIVE OAK

329

HICKORY—can be recognized by the three large top leaves on its compound branch. The SHAGBARK variety has brittle bark, a straight, narrow trunk, and vertical fissures. The fruits of the PIGNUT and MOCKERNUT (not shown) resemble each other, and the bark of each is somewhat similar to the pattern of walnut bark. Hickory wood is an excellent fuel that burns brightly, and during Colonial days it was used in most hearths for both warmth and illumination. In tensile strength, hickory is on a par with wrought iron. In autumn, the tree's dress turns to many beautiful shades of yellow.

BIRCHES—are readily identified by the tissue-paper quality of their bark and caterpillarlike catkin flower. CANOE (paper) birch grows to one hundred feet or more and has oval leaves. WHITE (gray) birch usually grows in thickets and reaches only about thirty feet in height. BLACK birch has aromatic twigs, and a tighter, blackish, less papery bark that is inclined to crack in a downward direction. It is often mistaken for black cherry. YELLOW birch grows as tall as one hundred feet and has bark that peels into yellow-silver strips. RED birch, found near streams, has a loosely peeling, shaggy, reddish bark.

AMERICAN BEECH—a stately tree, has shiny, velvet-smooth gray bark. Its nuts are great favorites with animals and birds. The foliage has an iron-rust color in the autumn. HORNBEAM, a shrublike tree that grows under the larger trees in the forest, has what appear to be "muscles" along its black-gray trunk. Its other name, IRONWOOD, is descriptive of its quality—it is one of the strongest woods and hence excellent for levers and handles. HOP HORNBEAM (not shown) is a taller relation that grows from fifteen to twenty-five feet high and, like the elm, its bark has vertical scales.

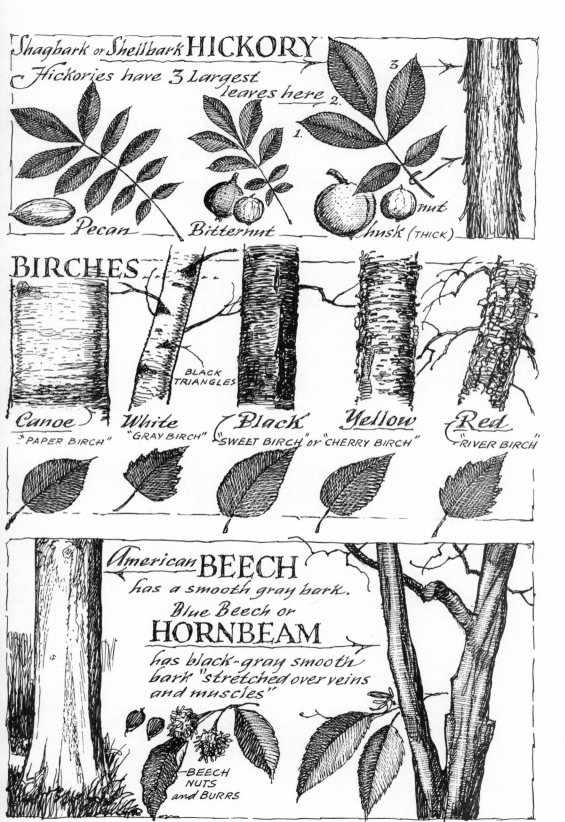

Shagbark or Shellbark HICKORY

Hickories have 3 Largest leaves here

3
2.
1.

Pecan

Bitternut

husk (THICK)

nut

BIRCHES

BLACK TRIANGLES

Canoe
"PAPER BIRCH"

White
"GRAY BIRCH"

Black
"SWEET BIRCH" or "CHERRY BIRCH"

Yellow

Red
"RIVER BIRCH"

American BEECH
has a smooth gray bark.

Blue Beech or
HORNBEAM
has black-gray smooth bark "stretched over veins and muscles"

BEECH NUTS and BURRS

331

MAPLE—all varieties bear two buds, directly opposite each other on a twig. From these twin buds come twin branches and twin leaves. The leaves and twigs are adjacent, but usually extend away from each other. Properly called samara, the fruit of the maple, because of the way it hangs in clusters, is also referred to as "keys" or key fruit. In autumn, the maple trees put on a brilliant show of colors, making recognition easy—even at a distance. Bird's-eye and curly maple are not distinct varieties, but rather are common maple with grain irregularities that give them these names.

SUGAR MAPLE (also known as Rock Maple and Hard Maple)—has bark that becomes —with age—deeply furrowed, gray, scaly, and brittle. Its leaf is about as long as it is wide; its limbs grow upward and outward. NORWAY maple has a leaf similar to the sugar maple, but it is wider than it is long. This, and also a milky juice that can be seen when the leaf stem is broken, distinguish it from sugar maple.

MOUNTAIN MAPLE (Dwarf Maple)—is shrublike with small-toothed leaves and gray bark. STRIPED maple (Moosewood) is another midget-sized maple. Its trunk is a dark green, striped with white; its leaf is large and round-bottomed.

SILVER MAPLE (White Maple)—this large tree is distinguished by its deeply cut leaves. Its keys are very long, with one wing of this fruit often shorter than the other. The leaves of the silver maple turn a dull yellow in the fall season. SYCAMORE maple is also called "False Sycamore" in the United States; in Europe it is known only as the sycamore. It, too, has key fruit that clings to the twigs throughout winter, and its buds remain green. The bark breaks off in small squares, making its trunk resemble that of the American sycamore and thus accounting for the name.

RED MAPLE—has some red color through all seasons of the year. In spring, the buds are red; in summer, the keys ripen to a deep shade of red and the leafstalks and veins remain red; and this maple is the first tree to turn red in the autumn. The ASH-LEAF maple (box elder) is an exceptional maple with compound leaves. It is valuable as a shade tree because of the rapid rate at which it grows.

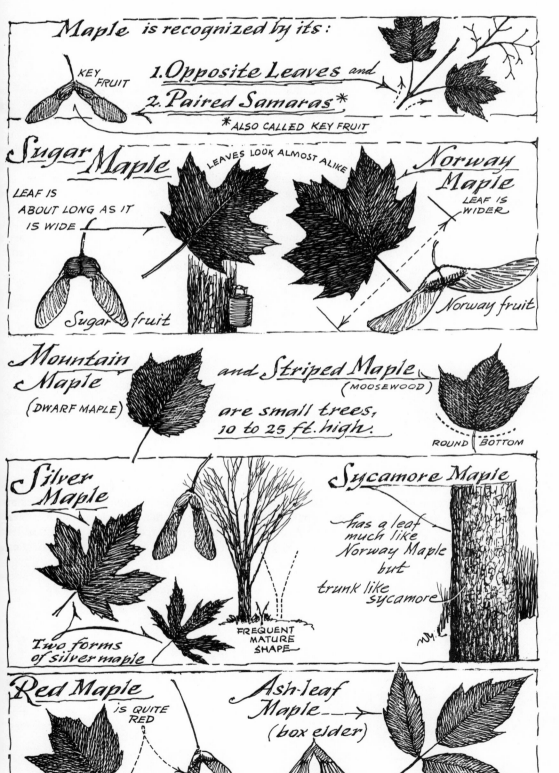

Maple is recognized by its:

KEY FRUIT

1. Opposite Leaves and
2. Paired Samaras *

* ALSO CALLED KEY FRUIT

Sugar Maple

LEAVES LOOK ALMOST ALIKE

Norway Maple

LEAF IS ABOUT LONG AS IT IS WIDE

LEAF IS WIDER

Sugar fruit

Norway fruit

Mountain Maple

(DWARF MAPLE)

and Striped Maple

(MOOSEWOOD)

are small trees, 10 to 25 ft. high.

ROUND BOTTOM

Silver Maple

Two forms of silver maple

FREQUENT MATURE SHAPE

Sycamore Maple

has a leaf much like Norway Maple but trunk like sycamore

Red Maple

IS QUITE RED

Ash-leaf Maple

(box elder)

333

PINE—is a softwood that is used in modern building more than any other wood. Some species are even used for flooring. This tree was of enormous wealth to the early Americans, for it provided them with fuel, turpentine, resin, tar, paints, lampblack, tanbark, and pitch. Pines grow to great heights and some in New England have reached more than two hundred and forty feet. There is no true flower; rather, the seeds develop in cone-shaped clusters. The many varieties of pine can be identified by close observation of this cone, along with the length and number of needles in a cluster. On the page opposite are a few of the more common American varieties of the nearly five hundred species of pine. WHITE pine is the most used and can be recognized by its five-needle cluster. PITCH pine has three-needle clusters. SHORTLEAF pine has sometimes two- and sometimes three-needle clusters, cinnamon-colored bark, and valuable yellow wood. (There is also a LONGLEAF pine, which has needles up to ten inches long and is a prominent source of turpentine.)

SPRUCE—the cones of this tree hang down, while the cones of the FIR grow in an upright position. Spruce needles are four-sided and pointed; fir needles are flat with rounded tips. HEMLOCK needles are flat, and dark above, silvery below. This tree bears sprucelike cones, and has a reddish bark that is excellent for use in tanning leather. Hemlock wood is too brittle for carpentry work and too resinous for fuel.

334

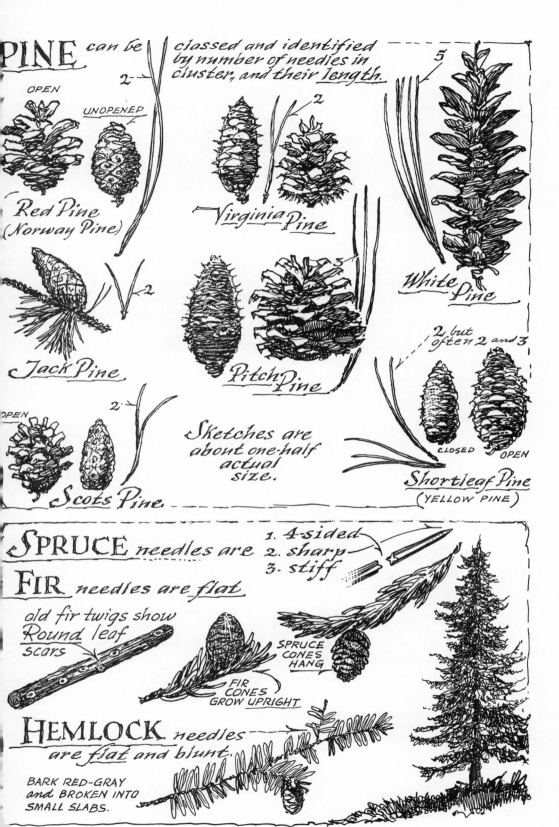

PINE *can be* classed and identified *by number of needles in cluster, and their* _length_.

2

OPEN

UNOPENED

Red Pine
(Norway Pine)

2

Virginia Pine

5

White Pine

2

Jack Pine

3

Pitch Pine

2, but often 2 and 3

CLOSED   OPEN

Shortleaf Pine
(YELLOW PINE)

OPEN

2

Scots Pine

Sketches are about one-half actual size.

SPRUCE *needles are*   1. *4-sided*   2. *sharp*   3. *stiff*

FIR *needles are flat*

old fir twigs show **Round** *leaf* **scars**

SPRUCE CONES HANG

FIR CONES GROW UPRIGHT

HEMLOCK *needles are flat and blunt.*

BARK RED-GRAY *and* BROKEN INTO SMALL SLABS.

335

OAKS—the acorn is the distinguishing feature of the nearly three hundred kinds of oak trees. Another item that helps in recognition is its leaf, which is strong and has a leathery appearance. Though by then it will be dry and shriveled, it will often stay on the tree through the winter. The bark of the WHITE variety is, as its name implies, pale in color, and it flakes off in vertical strips. The BLACK variety's darker bark breaks off in irregular chunks. White oak leaves have rounded lobes; the leaves of the black are sharp-toothed and pointed.

PIN OAK has branches that grow close together, often near the ground. The leaves are slender and have sharp points. The twigs are rubbery and strong.

SCARLET OAK displays magnificent, most brilliant colors in the autumn. Its leaf is like the pin oak's, but it is fuller; its acorn is large.

BLACK OAK has rough bark that is black nearest the ground. When a cut is made in the outer bark, a yellow-orange inner bark is seen. This inner bark, which produces a dye, is the black oak's identifying mark. Its acorn is small and orange-yellow inside.

RED OAK has smooth areas between the furrows in its bark. The acorns are large and set in a shallow cup.

WHITE OAK was the American colonists' favorite oak. It is broad and majestic in shape, with gray, scaly bark, and limbs that reach out in a horizontal direction.

BUR OAK (also called Mossy-cup and Overcup) has wood that is tough, close-grained, and durable. Its acorns are enclosed in very large, fringed (burred) cups.

CHESTNUT OAK was once called rock oak, and it is found on rocky hills. The bark is not as rough as that of most oaks, and its leaves are similar to those of the chestnut, though they are shorter and without the chestnut's sharp-pointed teeth. The acorns are large and sweet.

SWAMP WHITE OAK has a wedge-shaped leaf and light gray-green bark. This tree's wood is the one most preferred by boat builders.

BLACK JACK OAK is a small tree that is found in our southern and south-central States. Its black bark breaks into squarish plates.

WILLOW OAK is an eastern oak. It has smooth leaves and its light-brown wood is soft, but strong and heavy.

BEAR OAK (Scrub Oak or Dwarf Oak) now rare, once covered much of the poorer New England soil.

WATER OAK is found in the south and southeastern United States. Its obovate leaves are blue-green, and its wood is hard and coarse-grained.

SHINGLE OAK has shining laurel-like leaves. Its wood is used for shingles in our western States.

336

OAKS are generally grouped as:

WHITE (PALE BARK, ROUNDED LEAVES) and BLACK (POINTED LEAVES)

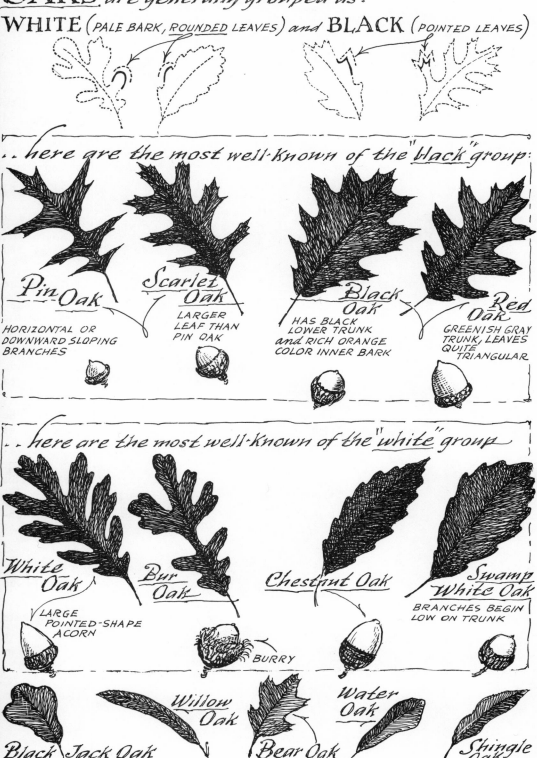

.. here are the most well-known of the "black" group:

Pin Oak — HORIZONTAL OR DOWNWARD SLOPING BRANCHES

Scarlet Oak — LARGER LEAF THAN PIN OAK

Black Oak — HAS BLACK LOWER TRUNK and RICH ORANGE COLOR INNER BARK

Red Oak — GREENISH GRAY TRUNK, LEAVES QUITE TRIANGULAR

.. here are the most well-known of the "white" group

White Oak — LARGE POINTED-SHAPE ACORN

Bur Oak — BURRY

Chestnut Oak

Swamp White Oak — BRANCHES BEGIN LOW ON TRUNK

Black Jack Oak

Willow Oak

Bear Oak

Water Oak

Shingle Oak

337